Philippa Poole (née Curlewis) was born in Sydney and educated at Wenona Girls' School, North Sydney. She trained as a preschool teacher and graduated from the Sydney Kindergarten Training College at Waverley. She worked as a teacher in the inner city areas and was Director of Peter Pan Kindergarten for several years prior to her marriage in 1957 to Adrian Poole. Her home is at Dellawong in Wellington, New South Wales, and she has four children, Peter, Belinda, Susan and David.

Philippa and her grandmother enjoyed a close association for many years, and the interest shown by people of all ages in the life of Ethel Turner, led her to giving informal talks to local country organizations, historical societies and groups of school children. The talks later developed into a broader request and so prompted her to gather together the contents of this book.

Ethel Turner, aged about 16, taken whilst still at school. It was about this time that she started her entries in the diaries that were to record the daily events of her life for the next 63 years.

The Diaries
of
ETHEL TURNER

Compiled
by
Philippa Poole

COLLINS
Australia

ACKNOWLEDGEMENTS

My sincere thanks go to my parents for all the assistance, encouragement and enthusiasm that they have given so generously during the past months — also I am indebted to my husband and children for their infinite patience while I undertook the task.

Thanks to Miss Suzanne Mourot and the staff of the Mitchell Library; Miss Margaret Taylor, assistant archivist of the Fisher Library, University of Sydney; Miss Shackley, head-mistress of Sydney Girls High School; National Library, Canberra; Mr R. B. Sturrock; Capt. W. F. Cook M.V.O.; Mr Peter Lindsay; the Warden of St Paul's College, Rev A. P. B. Bennie; *The Bulletin, The Sun, Sydney Morning Herald, Daily Telegraph;* Ann Twells for her meticulous design; and the editorial staff of my publishing firm, in particular Peita Royle who has been so helpful throughout.

© Philippa Poole, 1979

First published by Ure Smith, Sydney, a division of Paul Hamlyn Pty Ltd, 1979
First published by Collins Pty Ltd, Sydney, Australia, 1987

Printed by Kyodo Printing Co. Ltd. Singapore

National Library of Australia
Cataloguing-in-Publication data

Turner, Ethel, 1872-1958.
The Diaries of Ethel Turner

Includes index.
ISBN 0 00 217808 7.

1. Turner, Ethel, 1872-1958 – Diaries. 2. Women
authors, Australian – Diaries. I. Poole, Philippa. II.
Turner, Ethel, 1872-1958. Diaries of Ethel Turner. III.
Title. IV. Title: Diaries of Ethel Turner.

A828'.203

Contents

Foreword	7
Before You Fairly Start	9
I'll be a Millionairess Soon	13
So Small and Still and White	29
The Course of True Love Never Did . . .	41
He Would Far Rather Bury Me	71
A Red Letter Day	91
Fame Seems Coming to Me	103
We are Going to be Very Poor	123
And the Morning and the Evening Were the First Day	139
Dreamed Sweet Dreams	157
That Strange Little Urgent Cry	171
Flying Down the Tram Line Tracks	181
The Land is Ours	195
There are Too Many 'Departments' in Life	211
Ports and Happy Havens	229
Oh, Boys in Brown	241
Catching Sunbeams	255
When the Sun Went Down	267
And Last	269
Appendices 1-8	270
Index	286

To my Father and Mother —
who have always been an inspiration to me.

Foreword

The decision to publish my mother's diaries was made after great deliberation and discussion with my family, as they were not written with any idea that they might some day be open to general viewing. During the last twenty years since my mother's death I have received hundreds of letters asking me for information about her early life — some came from aspiring authors and biographers, some from university students, and others interested in her life's work. In answering these requests I found myself searching through papers, articles, verses, voluminous correspondence and repeatedly turning to her diaries for the information that they needed.

All these things finally decided me. I felt that words from my mother's own hand, written at the time when she was young, could best describe life prior to and at the turn of the century.

My daughter, by infinitely patient and time-consuming research extending over a long period has by explanatory notes to the diaries, answered nearly all the questions that were asked. She has rediscovered many photographs, articles and manuscripts that for years have remained hidden and forgotten. These give an illuminating insight into the character of Ethel Turner.

Our family hope that this book may, in some small way, add to our Australian history.

Adrian Curlewis

Sarah Jane Shaw, Ethel's mother, in her early 20s.

Before You Fairly Start

These words written by Ethel Turner over 80 years ago, at the very beginning of the book *Seven Little Australians*, gave her readers a word of warning about what they were to expect. Therefore it seems a suitable way to begin this introduction, so that 'before you fairly start' these extracts from her diaries, I should tell you how this has all come about and why it is that these personal diaries are now being released for publication.

Ethel Turner had, and in fact still has, a wide circle of valued friends, some known to her during her lifetime, but many of them still living today and, unbelievably, ranging in age from three years old to ninety-three.

The 1973 A.B.C. television production of *Seven Little Australians* re-awakened a remarkable interest in the life of the authoress. Quite unexpectedly early in 1974 I was asked by a member of the Lemington branch of the Country Women's Association whether I would come and talk about my memories of Ethel Turner, and tell a little about her life. I duly arrived at the village hall, a sleepy little building standing alone in the middle of an autumn sun-drenched paddock with cattle silently grazing nearby. Intruding on this peaceful scene, to my astonishment, I found over one hundred CWA members had gathered to hear what I had to tell them.

So started a series of talks, and it was with a great sense of pride and humility that I met so many of my grandmother's friends and admirers. During the talks I would occasionally read several extracts from her diaries, and it was only then that I realised that people in the present-day world of television, radio, automation, mechanisation and the increased pace of life, long for an opportunity to turn back the hands of time and re-live the saner, more leisurely and gracious age of yesteryear.

I was surprised also in speaking to groups of young school children, breast-fed on the sometimes frightening or futuristic programmes on television, that they also were fascinated to hear about someone who lived so many, many years ago and yet had thoughts and experiences so like their own.

On a number of occasions, at the conclusion of the talks, people would suggest that perhaps I could write her biography. This seemed quite beyond my capabilities, as I can vividly recall that the writing of essays, stories and poems were always a most arduous task during my school days. I didn't ever have the disappointment of a rejection of a story from the school magazine, (as did Ethel Turner before starting her own, the *Iris*) for the simple reason that it never crossed my mind that I should submit one. Therefore it seems a strange task to have fallen to me, when I know that each sentence I write will be re-written many times before passed by my own critical assessment.

In due course several other people suggested that if I couldn't write her biography, perhaps I might consider taking extracts from the diaries and compiling them into book form. This, I thought, had vague possibilities.

A brief and delightful meeting with a well-known and much loved figure in the A.B.C.* resulted in immediate action, and with her constructive and sound advice I was inspired to attempt it. Added to this I had the encouragement, the personal involvement and the unending enthusiasm of my father. Together we have enjoyed countless hours reconstructing this enormous and fascinating jig-saw, so that to the best of our knowledge, all details of the book are historically accurate.

A question I have often been asked is 'Did you know your grandmother well?' A year ago I would have answered, 'Yes, very well indeed.' I realise now that I only knew her as a playmate — someone to spend delightful hours with browsing through books, making puppets or match-box furniture for the dolls' house, doing oil painting together or becoming absorbed with a cupboard of tiny items collected from her overseas trip.

Now I know her so much more intimately and understand her more fully. I often wondered why, each time she would read me the beginning of a writing album that she kept about her first child, she would hurriedly replace it in the bottom of the drawer and with deep emotion would say, 'We will look at it some other time my darling.'

If Ethel Turner kept diaries whilst still at school they have been lost, but from 1889 to 1952 they are intact and complete. Reading them we accompany her through many stages — her entry into the Sydney literary and social scene, a long and turbulent engagement period, her marriage and domesticity, motherhood, an overseas trip, war years and through to the loss of her beloved daughter Jean in 1930. With this tragedy her heart was broken.

The thread that binds this story together is her true love of writing and the great gift that she had of expressing her thoughts. For those of you who loved Ethel Turner I am writing this collection, as I want you to share with me her joys and sorrows, her ambitions and disappointments and through them understand her more completely.

It will be apparent that not every day has been recorded. This is because my grandmother occasionally neglected to fill in certain dates, and some entries are unimportant when looking at the final picture. However the reader may be assured that the entries are faithfully recorded and that censoring occurred only on two or three occasions when it was considered a possibility that the words could be libellous or offensive to the descendants of people referred to.

Ethel Sibyl Burwell was born in Doncaster, Yorkshire, England. Her mother, Sarah Jane Shaw was married three times. Her first husband, George Watnell Burwell, was descended from a well-known Scottish family; he was well read, an excellent linguist and a merchant by trade. They had two daughters, Lilian born in 1870, and Ethel born on 24th January 1872. When Ethel was only two years old George

---

*This was Miss Barbara Vernon whom I met only twice before her untimely death early 1978.

Burwell died when he suddenly became ill, whilst on a business trip to Paris. A year or so later Sarah Jane married for the second time. This time to Henry Turner, a man nearly 20 years older than she was and who already had a family of six children (it is thought all sons). Both Lilian and Ethel took the name of Turner. Sarah Jane and Henry had one daughter, Jeannie Rose born in 1876 and the Turner family at this time were living in the Attleborough Quarry House near Nuneaton.

As children, living in the cold climate of northern England, they spent a great deal of time indoors reading, unlike Australian children who are used to freedom and sunshine from a very early age, and spend most of their time outdoors. Lilian and Ethel were inseparable all through their childhood and in fact throughout their lives, and the common bond that linked them so closely was their love of books. As children they had an insatiable appetite for reading and this resulted in the girls living in a land of make-believe and fantasy. Their dolls were not waxen or lifeless creatures but living things, and through them they re-enacted the exciting and daring adventures that they devoured each time a new book was taken down from the well-stocked shelves. Rose was quite different from her sisters and enjoyed more boyish pursuits — therefore she was frequently excluded from the constant game of 'pretending' that consumed her half-sisters.

Henry Turner died after a cruelly long illness leaving the family poor, overwhelmed with troubles and debts, and the young widow with the responsibility of a family of nine on her shoulders. Knowing that this was beyond her capabilities she decided to take her own three small daughters to a land where the sun was always shining, a land that offered great opportunities for those who could face the challenge. She also feared that if Lilian, who was very delicate, stayed in England, she would not survive the bitter winters. So with great courage Sarah Jane, Lilian, Ethel and Rose sailed for Australia just after Christmas 1879. Their arrival in this new country was a bitter disappointment and a disillusionment to them all. Sarah Jane had hoped to find a position as a governess, but prospects looked gloomy for a well-educated lady to find a suitable position. She finally found employment as a supervisor in a large Sydney department store and, at the time, they were living in Stanley Street in the heart of Sydney.

On 31 December 1880 Sarah Jane married for the third time. Charles Cope was a clerk in the Sales Division of the Department of Lands and the marriage took place at St Peter's Church of England, Woolloomooloo (now Darlinghurst). A son Rex was born to this marriage the following year, 1881.

Three Little Maids written by Ethel Turner in 1900 has been acknowledged by her as a true and authentic account of her early life. However with true literary licence she occasionally veers away from the historically accurate, but at least one can catch a glimpse of those early days. (Strangely enough none of the three girls were ever known by their descendents to talk about their life in England or the voyage on board ship, and it is supposed that their memories of those days were not happy ones.)

Sarah Jane Cope had artistic ability and excelled at painting, wood carving, leather and copperwork.

Ethel showed, from a very early age, a competitive spirit in the literary field, and the first entry in a small red note book entitled *Pen Money*, records that £2 2 0 was won for an 'Essay on Ventilation' in the under 12 section of *Juvenilia*.

She attended Sydney Girls High School from 1883 to 1888 and was one of the original 37 pupils. The school was situated then in Elizabeth Street on the site of the present David Jones department store. In the archives at the school, in large bound volumes it records that Ethel Turner passed her Junior with the following results: A standard in English History, Latin, Geography and Geology, B standard in French, Arithmetic and English. At the same time she did examinations in Algebra, Euclid, German, European History, Greek, Plane Geometry and Perspective, Bible History, Music and Painting, but no results were available for these subjects.

At that time, the editor of the school magazine, the *Gazette*, was Louise Mack and after submitting an entry to the paper Ethel wrote in an article years later,

'The editor of the school paper proper evidently considered the aspiring contributions I used to drop into her box as beneath contempt, so in a wrathful moment I rallied my particular friends around me and started a rival paper'. This was the beginning of the *Iris*, whose motto was 'Dum vivo, canto' which, when interpreted means 'While I live, I sing'. (Several contributions have been recorded in Appendix I to give a sample of the type of material in it).

'It – it is a poem, isn't it, mother?'
Three Little Maids

1889
I'll be a Millionairess Soon

Ethel, now aged 17, has gained great experience from editing her school newspaper, and hoping for a more ambitious enterprise, she and her sister Lilian launch a new monthly publication called the *Parthenon*. This magazine was deemed to have considerable literary merit and many references are made to it during the next three years. The content was unusual and varied, and covered subjects such as book reviews, social chit chat, contributions of poems and stories from its readers, and a wide spectrum of many other diverse subjects. In an opening address to their readers, the sisters say:

> Into the untried waters of this fair, unruffled year we launch our little bark, our virgin bark, with youth certainly at the helm, but something beside pleasure at the prow.
> Will you receive it in all good faith, oh, older wiser sailors . . . will you forgive the faults in its build, the errors in its navigation, and take it as it is, a little bark filled with the thoughts and fancies of girls, and ballasted by those of wiser heads.
> This, our 'Parthenon', is not in both senses of the word a maiden effort. 'Of the virgins' it certainly is, as the old Greek word suggests, but we have guided a small rudder before, the rudder of a little bark with '*Iris*' for its name, and hope soon to guide this one better, as every day leaves us older and, we will suppose, wiser.

Little did the young editors realise that an error in the navigation would occur so soon after the launching.

With school days behind her and a new life opening up ahead, the diaries continue the story.

3rd April
Practised 1 hour, sang 20 minutes. Cleared out boxes and drawers, cartloads of rubbish and old letters, etc. Addressed Parthenon *wrappers and then in afternoon went to town — Lil bought a new dress, I am penniless. At night tried to write a poem and failed, so instead read and idled.*

6th April:
Went to Newington Sports. Took cab to the grounds. The Sports were very poor. I walked with Mr Curlewis a little and after with Mr Curnow. We left Annie*, then Lil* and I hurried off and caught the 5 o'clock train to Picton to stay with the Daintreys.

---

*Annie — Annie Christian   Lil — Ethel's elder sister

10th April:

Mr Daintrey took us all in a buggy to Douglas Park for a picnic. It was a fearfully long drive but very pleasant there, we went mushroom hunting. Afternoon we went to the Show. It is the first country show I have been to. We had tea on the grounds with the Abbotsford Antills and a lot more people.

24th May:

Mr Cope* took Lil and me to the opening of the Darlinghurst Skating Rink. It was too crowded to skate but we got our season ticket.

6th June:

To-night Lily and I went up to the Christian's and wrote the invitations for our Parthenon Dance and we posted them coming home — we have asked about seventy-five people and have ordered the lemonade, programmes and pencils, etc.

18th June:

Busy all day decorating the rooms, waxing the floors, setting the supper tables, making claret cup, etc. We went home to dress at 6 — Lil wore a crepe dress, Annie blue liberty and I my pink and silver dress. I enjoyed the night immensely.

10th July:

Went house-hunting with Mother — Woollahra, Double Bay and Darling Point. Walked quite 10 miles with usual result — loss of time and temper. Went to Annie's for dinner and evening. Mr Lawes and Mr Curlewis came up — the latter would not be so bad if he was not conceited — he talks rather well which is more than most boys do.

20th July:

We went to the Darlinghurst rink this afternoon — I skated with C. Osborne, M. Backhouse, and D. Benjamin — no one else there. We got invitations for Felix dance for 7th August. Wrote for Parthenon *at night. I liked Maurice this afternoon very much and promised to keep him a dance or two.*

24th July:

Mother and I went to town to Anthony Horderns. I bought a pair of dancing shoes, a fan, a diary and some skates for a prize for Parthenon *competition. Went to Fresh Food and Ice for lunch —*

25th July:

Made the drawing room pretty, wrote Aunt Elgitha; corrected proofs, etc. In afternoon Nina Church came up to see us — she is growing really lovely but she is frightfully conceited and drawls dreadfully. Went to dancing lessons, had 2nd and 3rd figures of the Minuet and the Quadrille, Polka and Lancers. Did Parthenon *work till 12 o'clock. Kate left, I am so sorry. I never liked a servant so well.*

---

*Mr Charles Cope — Ethel's step-father.

26 July:
The five of us went to distribute the toys at Prince Alfred Hospital and the Deaf and Dumb Institute. What a lot of dreadful things there are in the world, and how free from them we all are — we oughtn't to be discontented so often.

2nd August:
Had a grand clearing out of boxes and drawers and the result is an abnormal state of tidiness exists in my bedroom. Sewed pearl beads on my evening dress, trimmed some pretty underclothing and stitched ribbons on my long gloves. Mr McKinney* and his little girl came; he said he was sure she had been very careless and took a list of words to see if they were invented. Rex ** was very ill in the night, we were up with him for a long time. Went to Felix dance at night and came home after the twelfth dance. Lily wore her pink silk, I my white liberty and jonquils, Annie white liberty and hyacinths.

9th August:
This morning I made myself a black lace hat. Idled in afternoon. At night went to Articled Clerks dance and wore my white liberty again, this time with crimson flowers and snowdrops. M. Backhouse asked me for a dance and then did not account for it. I shall never notice him again. He was a bit intoxicated last night I think, it is a pity, he might be such a very nice boy. I'm awfully sorry for him.

10th August:
Lil, Annie and I slept till 9 am, talked and idled about all the morning. Went to Darlinghurst Rink and I got a spill, the first I've had this year. To-night I tried over a lot of songs, I do wish I could sing.

14th August:
We all went to Bondi for a picnic. It was a lovely day but Lil and I had so much writing to do we really ought not to have gone. A second letter came from Mr McKinney requesting us to apologise and pay costs one guinea. Of course we refused to do either so I suppose they will take proceedings.

17th August:
Went to University Sports in the afternoon saw and walked with Mr Belbridge, Drummond and Read — saw M. Backhouse and cut him, ditto K. McCrea.

---

*Mr McKinney: Irate father of E.M. who had submitted a list of 687 words containing letters from the word 'Regulation'. The editors of the *Parthenon*, Lilian and Ethel published a statement that she must have invented the words to find such a lot.

**Rex: Ethel's step-brother born in 1881 to Sarah Jane and Charles Cope.

19th August:

Lil and I went to town, we are thoroughly tired of the work of the Parthenon *and quite ready to give it up. I should not at all mind being a governess on a station though I should not like it in Sydney. A third lawyer's letter on the McKinney case came, so we went to Mr William Cope* and asked him to defend our case — he is very nice indeed and said he will see to everything. We would rather the case went on; it would be so good for the* Parthenon. *Mother and I went to the editor of* The Bulletin *to see if he would take the* Parthenon *and retain us as writers. He is to let us know. At night wrote the Children's Page and several things till 11 o'clock.*

26th August:

Wrote hard all the morning at an article for the Parthenon, *idled this afternoon. It strikes me I idle a great deal of time away — I really ought to practise and do lessons. To-night Cope Lethbridge** and Sid Mack*** came and we went to the hall for a rehearsal. Afterwards the boys came home for supper and stayed some time. I think Cope is one of the nicest boys I know.*

27th August:

This morning I wrote a little and read Faithful and Unfaithful. *Did some cooking as it was too wet for tennis. Our new servant Phyllis came, thank goodness. To-night after a lot of fuss we got Mr Cope to take us to see* Pepita, *it was simply splendid. I never laughed so heartily in my life.*

30th August:

Practised a little and did my accounts. Charlie Button came and bought us two lovely bunches of flowers, roses and camellias. I arranged them all and went to Sydney to see solicitors Cope and King as we have had another letter re our libel case. I am afraid we shall be obliged to register the paper. Lil bought the score of Pepita, *I of* Monte Christo. *At night tried over new music, then read a little French History and went to bed early.*

2nd September:

Copied out E. McKinney's words and went to Dr Rutledge's, he put us in a cab and took us first to the University, then to Professor Scotts. P. Scott said as far as he was concerned many of the words were absurd and he's going to write. He was very nice. Then we went to Cope and King. Mr William Cope came in and although I hated him at first he has such good true eyes that I felt I could trust him with anything and someway I could not help liking him exceedingly.

---

*Mr William Cope: a solicitor and brother of Charles Cope.

**R. Copeland Lethbridge, later Manager Perpetual Trustee Co. 1926.

***Later Sidney Mack Q.C. Brother of Louie and Amy Mack.

Circular Quay, Sydney, circa 1880, would have looked like this when Sarah Jane Turner arrived with her three daughters from England.

This early tram is seen in Military Road, Mosman. The driver and the conductor are in the foreground and it is interesting to note that the driver had no protection at all from the weather.
By kind permission of Mr R. B. Sturrock.

Ethel's class, 1888, her final year at Sydney Girls High School. Front row sitting: *the Misses F. Johnson, Ethel Turner, Louise Mack, and Ethel Maynard.* Second row sitting: *the Misses Elmina Sutherland, Marion Bolton, Henrietta Orr, Lily Jones, Dora Elphinstone.* Back row: *the Misses Maud McPhee, Ruth Bowmaker, Lily Grace, Evelyn Green, and Florence Delohery.*

Sydney Girls High School. This etching by Sir Lionel Lindsay shows the school when it was in Elizabeth Street, on the site of the present David Jones department store.
By kind permission of Mr Peter Lindsay.

3rd September:

Went for a run in the park before breakfast with Rose.* Helped the dressmaker with the Hospital Bazaar dresses. Read and tried to start a new tale but failed dismally. I can't get a single idea for one. To-night Cope Lethbridge came up alone and stayed all evening chatting in his free boyish fashion. He is just the kind of boy I should like for a brother.

4th September:

Tried again to write a tale and again could not get in the vein. H. Curlewis wrote a very 'cranky' letter, — I suppose he has found out Socrates in Stray Shots *is his beloved self and it has made him feel amiable to me. I don't know why he should like me, I always snub him unmercifully.*

5th September:

Lil and I went to town and bought collars at Farmers. Saw F. Parker and Maurice Backhouse and cut the latter again, — I'm afraid he'll never get over it. At night Lil, Annie and I went to Theatricals at Victoria Barracks — we went with Colonel Spalding's party — saw Arthur Barry who looked as grumpy as usual.

12th September:

Went to Hospital Bazaar early this morning and worked hard till 1 o'clock. Flew home, put on uniform, blue serge dress, white apron, cap, etc. and went back. Lord Carrington** opened the Exhibition and came and talked to Mother for some time. Business was not very brisk this afternoon. At night it was a little better, then the band played and we had sets of lancers. It looked very nice all the nurses dancing.

27th September:

Went with solicitor to the Supreme Court, it was all so strange; we had the paper registered. Then Lil and I went to see Mr William Cope and he said the same as he always does. I don't like him much now. Then Lil, Mother and I went shopping to David Jones. Bought Rex two suits, etc. a lovely little drawing-room chair, new door mats, stair cloth, liberty silk, etc. etc. At night I corrected proofs and did Parthenon *work. Lottie our new servant came, she is a bright English girl.*

4th October:

Lil and I did some shopping at Farmers, I bought a brown parasol for myself and a red one for Rosie. Then we went to Lavender Bay and I had a bathe and Lil watched me but did not get in. I read this afternoon and sent the rest of the Parthenons. *Played a practical joke on Mr Cope by sending him a letter containing a formal proposal for 'my own hand'.*

---

*Rose: Ethel's younger sister, four years her junior.

**Lord Carrington: Governor of N.S.W.

5th October:
Tidied my bedroom, put flowers in the drawing room, etc. Mr Cope came home at 10.30 am, funny about the letter — he thought it was real, I never saw him in such a state. I am sorry now I did it but it was only a joke. He declares he would rather bury me than see me married. It is extremely hot, I read life of Handel, Goethe, etc. this afternoon — did Geography, Latin and French at night.

7th October:
Eleanor Addison came and stayed an hour or two, she is our new secretary and we were initiating her. Idled all night and drew up a programme of future lessons to do with Lil. We both have a happy knack of 'making little lists' like the Mikado. *I think we would like to take pupils to make a little more money each, just three or four. A bad boating accident on the harbour, six or eight drowned.*

16 October:
Went to Church of England Depot to buy Sunday school prizes. We were there such a long time, from 11.15 am to 3.30 pm. We bought 68 books and spent £5 11 8 with discount off. Then I went down to Bondi for Rex's picnic — he got 16 beautiful presents, the best one was from Dr Barry, a splendidly fitted-up paint box, far too good for a child.

24 October:
Went to Sunday School picnic by 9.30 am boat, I did not like to go in the tram with all the children. Spent quite a nice day at Chowder, I took my class up the rocks for their dinner, and stood with Arthur Barry watching the races. They made me go in the teacher's race and I came in second, about 1 foot behind the winner. I liked Arthur Barry to-day. To-night Mr Cope, Lil and I went to hear Snazelle. He is very good. Nellie and Marcia were sitting just behind us. Marcia looked at me and bowed most sweetly, I looked her full in the face.

25th October:
Decided to have the play on October 30th, wrote out programmes, etc. Tonight Cope Lethbridge and Fred Belbridge came up for rehearsal, the latter was very nice and took the part willingly. After all was over we came home for supper and a chat. I quite liked F. Belbridge, I generally hate him.

27th October:
Church this morning. Sunday School — prize-giving day and flower service. Read Coming Thro' the Rye.

29th October:
Got a letter from Press Association asking me to call. I went and the editor Mr Astley was very nice — he said he liked my style of writing and offered me the position of fashion writer and warehouse noter (about £60 a year). I refused for I should not like to go to the places taking notes. He told me to write him a specimen leader — Women's College Bill.

30th October:
Busy cooking and preparing all day. The play went off splendidly — Sleeping Beauty, Uncle Tom's Cabin, *etc.* Waxworks *with A. Barry as showman very good. Baby Show noisy but fun. Everyone said we acted splendidly, but there was a very poor attendance, the girls did not sell their tickets.*

4th November:
Started to make a new dress, a pale blue zephyr, I'm going to save expense of dressmaker because I want my money for singing lessons. Had eight replies to my advertisement, I shall learn from Madame Vera, she is an Italian and a member of Schubert Society. At night played accompaniment for Mr Cope, read parts of Hamlet, *did a little theory and a little German.*

8th November:
Had my first singing lesson, scales and notes. Mother and Mr Cope went for a little picnic to themselves to Watsons Bay. I had a frightful headache after my lesson. In afternoon idled and read. At night young Charlie Button came up and bought with him a boy Alex Smith, who it seems was exceedingly anxious to be introduced to us. They were here an unconceivably long time.

15th November:
Singing lesson at 9 am. Had a letter from Gordon and Gotch saying they had been served with a writ *for us, we shall have to go to court. Bought Baccherini's Minuet in A and went to Edwards Dunlop for Review Books. At night practised a little and wrote a ballade about Xmas bells.*

16 November:
Letter from Mr Astley asking me to go down to see him; he says if I will practise leader writing under his correction, I shall write leaders for him. Read to Rex at night, he has such a bad cough.

18th November:
Lil and I went to Sydney to Palings and School of Arts. Then to Free Library and looked out the words *in Webster, unluckily most of them are given, though they are obsolete. I am afraid we are rather in a 'hole'.*

23rd November:
Practised quarter of an hour. Went to Sydney to buy a flower for my new hat and strawberries for dinner. Mother and Mr Cope had a fearful row. He smashed her gold bangle to atoms to aggravate her and there was a terrible piece of work. Heigho — I wonder do all married people have rows. I wouldn't be married for anything. Mother and Rex have gone to Barry's for the night. Rex has whooping cough.

27th November:
Lord Mayor's Ball. Annie and I went to town to buy flowers, we got maiden hair and roses. We went to the ball with the Caro's in a brougham. I wore my white silk with pink roses and maiden hair, did my hair very high and wore an aigrette in it. I didn't like the ball — I never liked any dance less and I thought I was going to enjoy it so much. I danced four times with H. Curlewis — also I liked fairly C. Lawes, W. Maitland*, Mr Nelson, C. Osborne. Mr William Cope, our solicitor was there and looked so nice, he bowed and we bowed and a'that. The Thompsons were there and none of the boys asked us to dance 'cause it seems we've cut them, altogether accidentally as we've nothing to cut them for. Maurice Backhouse was there and put on such a peculiar look each time I saw him. Mrs Roberts introduced me to Miss Harris. She looked so terrified when she had to dance with Lord Carrington.

29th November:
Mr Davis, editor of Hermes *called and I was alone. He says he and Mr Brennan, the other editor, like the parody I wrote for* Hermes *and are going to put it in. In afternoon Mother, Annie and I went to Government House Reception. Lady Carrington had such a funny dress on, a dark silk with pale blue net-like sleeves.*

4th December:
Lil and I went to Bronte for a bathe. I think I shall take some lessons, I can't swim well and can't dive properly. In afternoon did some cooking. Mother went to a meeting to Naval Home Bazaar and had a long talk with Lady Scott, who she says is very nice and unaffected.

7th December:
There was a good review of the Parthenon *in the* Herald *to-day. The parody I wrote for* Hermes, *'Altar of Examdomania' was put in this number. Lil and I went to town, did a little shopping. I went to Mr Astley, he is to give me a lot of writing to do. He has engaged me for certain to write the Ladies letter, at a guinea a letter, I am to write some political leaders too, and an Australian story. I'll be a Millionairess soon.*

9th December:
Mother and Lil went to town. M. paid Penfold for me the old Iris** *debt, he said we had behaved very handsomely and honourably to him. In afternoon I read some Review books. After tea Mother and I went house hunting. At 10 Rex was taken very ill, we had to send for Dr Quaife, Mr Cope was so horrid and scolded poor little Rex. He is* intensely *selfish. I did not undress all night, but Rex got very quickly better.*

---

*Later Sir Herbert Maitland (a leading Sydney surgeon) and best man at Curlewis–Turner wedding.

**Iris: this was the rival school newspaper edited by Ethel and Lilian while they were still attending Sydney Girls High School.

13 December:
Mother and I went to town to Edwards Dunlop to buy prizes; 2 years prizes were for B. Watkin, a handsome gold mounted glove case in red plush with companion; for B. Summerbelle, a nice floral album. Then to Mr Maclardy at Daily Telegraph *and he has agreed to take the advertisements, subscribers, everything of* Parthenon *for 6 months, we are to do the whole of the writing and have half share of profits.*

16th December:
Practised one and a half hours. Sang half an hour. Tried to write but could not get 'in the vein'. Mother and Mr Cope's birthday. Mr C. gave her a lovely French bonnet, all lilies of the valley and rosebuds, and seven pairs of kid gloves. M. gave him a boudoir photograph of herself, Lil and I gave him a photo of our dog Rover and Rex, and Mother a parasol.

17th December:
Got a letter from Mr Astley, he sent back my leader with a number of notes in the margin — he said it 'showed good capacity for high class leader work'. He didn't use it because it was on the fiscal policy but he asked me to write one for Xmas. I wrote at it all the morning and then Bobbie *in the afternoon. Copied out leader and* Bobbie *at night till very late.*

18th December:
Went to Cope and King and saw our barrister Mr G. W. Reid* — the brief is an immense one, about twenty huge closely written sheets. He asked us a good many questions. Then shopping, I bought a song, my first, Only a Year Ago *by Claribel. Afternoon we went house hunting to Glebe. Mother and Mr Cope are still rowing about moving. He is awfully selfish about it.*

25th December:
Went to church, all the six of us. It was beautifully decorated, it is the first year I have not helped decorate. Everyone wished everyone a Merry Xmas outside the church. In afternoon I read All Sorts and Conditions of Men *and munched almonds, raisins, figs and biscuits.*

31st December:
Rose and I went to see a house at Newtown, it is such a nice one. It is in a terrace and the two terraces stand in a big piece of ground with good carriage drive and tennis courts and a lovely ball room. The house has drawing room, dining conservatory and six bedrooms, finished beautifully with tiled hearths, electric bells, etc. etc. In afternoon Mother, Mr Cope, Lil and I went out to see it, they like it very much.

---

* Later Sir George Reid, High Commissioner for Australia in London.

Her involvement with the *Parthenon* monthly magazine was very time-consuming. If she didn't receive sufficient contributions from the readers, she would have no hesitation in writing articles herself and signing them with a variety of fictional names' The impending law suit doesn't seem to daunt her unduly, in fact she sees it as a good form of advertisement for the paper.

'You're trespassing – this is the first-class deck.'
Three Little Maids

Left: *Lilian Turner, aged 20,* Right, *Ethel Turner, aged 18. Throughout their lives the two sisters shared an absorbing love of literature.*

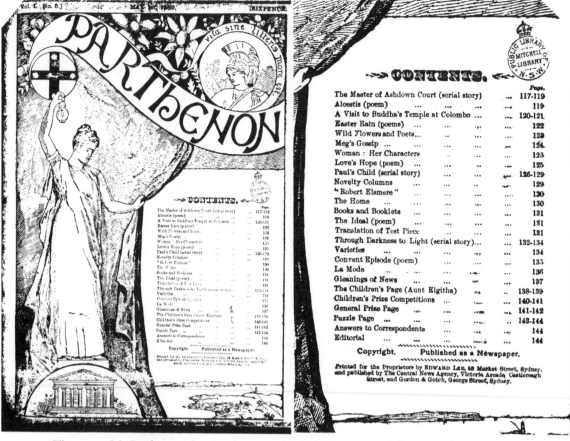

The cover of the Parthenon, *showing the unusual and varied contents of the magazine. The Latin motto* vita sine letteris mors est *translated means 'life without literature is death'.*
By kind permission of the Mitchell Library.

The Bulletin *newspaper office was situated in lower Pitt Street near Circular Quay. Many of Ethel's earlier stories appeared in* The Bulletin.
By kind permission of the Mitchell Library.

THE PARTHENON.

Vol. I., No. 1.   Sydney, 1st January, 1889.   Price 6d.

The Year.

IN TRANSITU, 1888–1889.

Age has not chill'd thee, disease has not smitten,
Ice has not fetter'd thee, frost has not bitten,
All in thy summer-glow, all in thy prime,
Cometh the warning decreed thee by Time.
Yet, 'tis but a warning : The page of our story,
Tho' turn'd by his hand, is not clos'd to thy glory ;
The blank sheet lies open, and lo ! even now
A new name and number he sets on thy brow.
While the chimes of the midnight thy transit are pealing,
His index the Mandate of Mercy is sealing,
Which bids thee again on thy circuit to start,
Progressive in spirit, but faithful at heart.

MRS. BARTON.

Ourselves.

SLOWLY and sadly the midnight bells have rung out the old year, slowly and sadly it has departed, gone to join the thousands of years that hands, now mouldering dust, have rung out, and to whose music ears, long deaf to the ebb and flow of life's ceaseless ocean, have listened. It has gone, the sweet, the sad old year, gone to form one more link in the chain of the grand, silent eternity, and sorrowfully a voice whispers to our hearts, " Never more, ah, never more."

And what has it been to us, this year that is fled ?

Happy and blessed ?—Thank God for it, and make sadder lives happier.

Sad and dark ?—Look upwards ; a Hand that cannot err has drawn that cloud over your life, that cloud which still is silver lined.

Spotless ?—Ah, no,—no,—soiled and stained in the " smoke and stir of this dim spot which men call earth," shall we wish it back ?—no, let it go,—go with our tears and sighs, our past follies and sins. See, spotless and white as snow stands the New Year, joyfully, gladly let us welcome it, and strive to keep it pure.

Standing on what too long we bore,
With shoulders bent and downcast eyes,
We may discern, unseen before,
A path to higher destinies.

Nor deem the irrevocable past
As wholly wasted, wholly vain,
If standing on its wreck at last,
To something nobler we attain,

A happy new year, a blessed, thrice blessed new year, we wish you all.

Into the untried waters of this fair, unruffled year we launch our little bark, our virgin bark, with youth certainly at the helm, but something beside pleasure at the prow.

Will you receive it in all good faith, oh, older, wiser sailors,—will you forgive the faults in its build, the errors in its navigation, and take it as it is, a little bark filled with the thoughts and fancies of girls, and ballasted by those of wiser heads.

This, our " Parthenon," is not in both senses of the word a *maiden* effort. " Of the virgins " it certainly is, as the old Greek word suggests, but we have guided a small rudder before, the rudder of a little bark with " Iris " for its name, and hope soon to guide this one better, as every day leaves us older and, we will suppose, wiser.

We anticipate many rebuffs, such as magazines here too often meet with. There are very, very few Australian magazines devoted to literature only, they might easily be counted on the fingers of one hand, and yet they are very little encouraged. People prefer to import magazines from England and America, magazines that are certainly of exceedingly high literary merit, but yet which once had to be started, and which once needed encouragement. Needed ! —yes, and received it well.

We are a young country ; shall it be again said of us that we care only for racing, for amassing money, to the neglect of more gentle, refining pursuits,—a state of things which will most assuredly " grow with our growth and strengthen with our strength."

Too often has it been said that high literature and high education is a mistake in Australia, that Australians cannot appreciate such things, and still worse, make no effort to appreciate them.

We will say no more on the subject, except to express a hope that in the bright glowing future that is opening to Australia, literature will play a very prominent part, and that our motto, " Advance Australia," will come to be used, not only with regard to the money market, but in a higher and wider sense.

Again, dear reader, we wish you a happy, prosperous New Year. Will you wish us the same, and say " God speed " to our little bark ?

The editorial welcome in the first issue of the Parthenon.
By kind permission of the Mitchell Library.

Pitt Street in the 1890s. The popular meeting place for young people was a restaurant called Fresh Food and Ice and was situated in Pitt Street between Market and King Streets.
By kind permission of the Mitchell Library.

Ethel Turner 1890. Early this year Ethel and her sister were ordered to pay legal costs in a libel suit brought against them by Mr Hugh McKinney on behalf of his daughter who had entered a competition in the Parthenon.

The District Court, Queens Square where the libel action McKinney v Gordon and Gotch was held.

By kind permission of Capt. W. F. Cook, M.V.O.

Government House in the 1890s. Ethel first attended a reception here when Lord Carrington was Governor of N.S.W.

By kind permission of the Mitchell Library.

1890

So Small and Still and White

Ethel is starting to feel the power of her pen and recognises that she has a talent for writing. She is excited by it and shows her ambition when she says 'I'll be a Millionairess soon' — this is her first indication that it could be a source of income which could lead to independence. She is obviously affected by a fairly unstable relationship between her parents and she wonders whether it is usual behaviour in other homes. It must make her dubious about wanting to be married herself.

Moving house was a fairly regular occurrence during her early life and the family now move to the Avenue at Newtown.

16th January:
Lil and I went to town to Cope and King. Mr Gibson is our barrister now and the case will come off immediately.

19th January:
Church. Sunday School in afternoon, gave all my girls a little keepsake each, they all seemed sorry I was going and I know I am awfully sorry to leave them all. Church at night, Mr Otley preached a splendid, helpful sermon and afterwards we all went into the Parsonage for an hour.

22nd January:
Packing all day. Case did not come off thank goodness. Mother, Rex and I went to new house, it is all so beautifully fresh and well fitted. I put my bedroom in order, decorated the walls with new pictures, stacked Parthenons *in a cellar, unpacked books, etc.*

24 January:
My birthday, Mr Cope gave me a nice pair of gloves and Rose a dear little butterfly handkerchief. Case came on, all morning we were waiting about Sydney killing time and at 2.30 pm we went to District Court with Mr Cornish. The upshot of the matter was we lost the case, Fitzhardinge the judge seemed prejudiced against our side the moment the other barrister spoke. The Judge gave a farthing damages against us and both of our costs to pay. I don't know how we shall pay them.

25th January:
All the papers were full of the libel case, the S M Herald *had a column in the law report, a leader and a piece in News of the Day. It is an awful shame that we have lost it, the child undoubtedly cheated. Cope and King sent us two letters, they are not satisfied with the verdict and want to see us.*

From *Sydney Morning Herald:* News of the Day, 25 January, 1890:

> A libel action of a somewhat peculiar nature was heard yesterday in
> the District Court before Judge Fitzhardinge. It was brought by Mr
> Hugh McKinney against Messrs Gordon and Gotch, for an alleged
> libel published in reference to plaintiff's daughter in a periodical
> known as the *Parthenon* which is managed by lady editors and
> secretaries. It appears that the proprietors of the paper started a
> competition among girls under the age of 17 in order to see who could
> furnish the largest number of words derived from the letters com-
> posing the word 'regulation'. Miss McKinney competed, and after
> close study of various standard dictionaries, she forwarded such an
> astounding list numerically (937 words), to the lady editors that they
> seriously questioned the authority or existence of some hundreds. For
> greater security they forwarded a list of the doubtful words to
> Professor Scott who designated them as mostly obsolete and upon this
> a paragraph was published in the *Parthenon* on 1st August informing
> Miss McKinney that she was disqualified and expressing regret that
> she had 'used quantities of words that she must have herself invented
> to make up a large score'. But the sting of the libel was contained in
> the following somewhat ambiguous paragraph:— 'A word here and
> there wrong we can account for as slips, but when given in large
> numbers to make a big total we can only think they are done with
> deliberate intention'. Plaintiff complained that the insinuation was
> that his daughter had made out the list with deliberate intention of
> deceiving, whereas the words had been collected in a perfectly bona-
> fide manner. Only nominal damages were asked for, and his Honour
> therefore gave a verdict for the plaintiff in the sum of one farthing,
> with costs on the lower scale.

On the same day the Leader in the *Sydney Morning Herald* after summing up the case
added 'but the important feature of the whole affair is that the publishers of the paper
Messrs Gordon and Gotch, have, by a curious legal technicality, been rendered liable for the
costs of the case. It was obviously impossible for them to know all the contents of the paper,
or to control the utterances of its anonymous editors, seeing that they merely acted as agents
for its sale. But still they are none the less legally liable, and the result of this case will
doubtless act as a wholesome caution to publishers who unthinkingly make themselves
responsible for the contents of papers of this kind.'
    There was also a detailed report of the case in the Law Section of the *SMH* under
McKinney v. Gordon and another, and an article in the *Evening News.*

26 January:
*Rose and I went to church, for the first time to St Stephens. We sat in Mr Brock's pew.
The church is pretty but I don't like the minister, he read his sermon which was on
Socialism and only repeated badly what has been often said — there was no depth like
there is in Dr Barry's sermons.*

30th January:
Tried all morning to get into a writing humour and I couldn't; the muse came on however in the afternoon and I wrote hard and fast then and all evening at a new tale A Daughter of Ireland. That wretched unfair Herald *has not printed a word of the letters in our defence that I know have been sent.*

4th February:
Had my music and singing lessons. Did housework, etc. in morning, read a little French. Rose and I played tennis in the afternoon and I beat her 6–2. At night Lil and I sat writing an article for the Parthenon on the Libel Action (see Appendix II) till after 12 pm.

26th February:
Wrote and finished a chapter of Bobbie. *Only Rose and I and the servant at home — it is lovely.*

21st March:
Mother stayed in bed with a bad headache. Lil and I went to town, Mr Curlewis was in the tram and came over to us. He told me he was going to send tickets for University Commemoration, and also for a Social there. At night I pondered over my accounts. I don't know what to do for winter and evening dresses, I'm bankrupt and no prospect of pay.

22nd March:
In afternoon idled and talked. Night talked to Rose, she was in a terrible row for being rude to Mother. I think I understand her a little better and must let her come more with me.

3rd April:
We were just going to dress for evening at Mrs Henry's when Mr Cope said 'I won't allow you to go, I express a wish'. He always says that. There's such a row. He tries to tyrannise far too much and we are too big for it.

11th April:
Remade with Mother my last winter's green dress skirt. In afternoon Lil, Mother and I went to Government House Reception. Lady Carrington had on a white silk, the Countess of Hopetoun a spotted dress with pink ribbons.

14th April:
Did a little cooking and a good deal of talking and then to the University Commem at 11. Mr Curlewis was with us a good deal of the time, he looks very nice in his BA gown. Lord and Lady Carrington, and Earl and Countess of Hopetoun, etc. were there. The students were awfully wild and had a good deal of fun.

22nd April:
Mr Cope is far from well and did not go to the office. Dr Edwards came and he said it is typhoid fever. We are all nearly beside ourselves — it is the second time he has had it.

25th April:

I put silk facings on my black jacket and altogether made it look nice. Mr Curlewis called for us to go to the University Boat Race, Rose and I. I had my white muslin and a black lace hat. It was exceedingly nice, I hardly ever enjoyed myself more. We came home with Mr Windeyer and Mr Lopez who were going back to St Paul's College and they asked us to come to tennis and afternoon tea at the College.

22nd May:

In afternoon Lil, Rose and I went to junction to meet Mrs Church and Nina for the tennis. Mr Curlewis came to call for us, like his impertinence — we were vexed. I'm getting so tired of him. I was introduced to heaps of others and at night talked, played and sang.

23rd May:

This morning at 9 am, Mother, Mr Cope and Rex went off to catch the mountain train — they are going to stay at Springwood for a time. Lil, Rose and I are consequently alone. In the night, at least about 10.30 pm we thought we heard someone walking overhead. Mary was out and we began to scream and hammer on the wall. Rose nearly went mad with fright. Mr Weiss and Mr Litchfield came in with guns. I think they were laughing at us for they could not find anyone.

24th May:

Nothing in particular and a good many things in general in the morning. In afternoon Miss Weiss and I, and a young King's School boy called Waddy went first to University football and then to Newington, came home with Mr Sands and Blunt. Night the Weisses came in and we spent a jolly evening singing and playing games and had supper in our sitting room.

26th May:

Public Holiday. Afternoon the Lorelli tennis club played against the Avenue. Mr Brock made us bet, we backed the Lorelli's, gloves against ties, he was so confident of winning. The Lorelli's won! We are to get a pair of splendid gloves each. We had afternoon tea outside, such fun. I played a game of chess with Mr Litchfield and lost. Night we went in to Weiss'; played, sang and had games till late. Mr Blunt and Lily were together — as usual.

2nd June:

(Mr Blunt asked Lily to marry him.) I am almost afraid to write it, there will be such a storm when they come home. Dear old Lil, she is in love, and he — he fairly worships her.

3rd June:

Walking Party. Cooked all morning and packed in afternoon. At 5.30 pm we started from home and all met down at the Mosman's Bay ferry. It was the most glorious moonlight night imaginable. We crossed to Mosman's, went part of the way, had supper *walked to Middle Head, then back to the boat which we just missed and had to wait till 11.40 pm. All trams had stopped, some got cabs, but the rest had to walk — we walked right to Newtown from the Quay. I was tired. I walked chiefly with H.C.* and F. Currie.*

6th June:
Lil and I went to town, bought a black *dress each. We both had a whim to wear black, bought also gloves and stockings. At night Mr Curlewis came and brought up some writings for the* Parthenon, *(see Appendix III) also two books.*

9th June:
Made my black skirt, it really looks very nice, it is my first attempt quite alone, it's not quite finished, pocket, hooks, etc. I'm quite proud of it. At night I played chess with Mr Cope, and Lily took the opportunity to tell Mother that she is engaged to Mr Blunt.

10th June:
Potted ferns and pottered about talking to the travellers all morning, Mother looks well and Mr Cope and Rex look splendid. In afternoon Mother told Mr Cope that a young gentleman was coming to ask him might he pay his addresses to Lil. She might just as well have fired a bombshell in our midst. There is a storm in the camp. At night the Parthenons *came, we played and sang a little and started a chapter of* Bobbie.

26th June:
It teemed with rain all day. Tidied sitting room, hemmed a sheet, started a chemise and did various domestic matters. At night Mrs Wolstenholme came and talked a lot of palaver in which the aim I found was she wanted her neice Maud Fox to be Nydia in the Greek play instead of me. I wasn't going to let her see I cared so I said she could have the part and welcome. At night Mr Litchfield and Mr Blunt came and we played bagatelle and other games.

3rd July:
In morning did Children's Page. Afternoon went up to the Curnow's. Night went to the Women's College Tableaux at the School of Arts. They went off very well, after I had done my parts, Mr Harry Russell took me upstairs to see the rest, I sat with Mr Curlewis. We had great fun going home, Mr Lloyd, Davis, Curnow, Curlewis, Russell, Walker, Wolstenholme B.A.'s, Miss Baly, Blanche Curnow, Ada and I went to Clifton for supper and had an exceedingly jolly evening. Mr Curlewis brought Ada and me home at 2.45 am. W. Curnow is very nice, I quite like him now, he has given us such a long article for the Parthenon.

---

* H.C.: Herbert Curlewis, sometimes referred to as H.R., Mr C., H.R.C. or just simply C. or H.

8th July:

Sewed my new scarlet evening dress skirt, I shall have to remake it though, it hangs badly. Mr Blunt and Lil were talking all morning. I don't like him, none of us do but of course Lil. Mr Cope was horrid to him.

18th July:

Morning went in to Weiss, and did one hundred of the programmes for Parthenon *dance — tied pencils and silk on. They are so pretty. In afternoon Lily, Rose and I went to St Paul's College and we were given tea and shown all over the College and also the men's rooms. It was very jolly. Mr Lopez says a lot of the College men are coming to our dance.*

23rd July:

Parthenon Dance: Went up the line to Searls for flowers. We all were awfully busy all day getting ready, the supper table really looked extremely pretty. It was a lovely dance, I hardly ever enjoyed anything more. I wore my eau-de-nil. Nina Church looked lovely. There were some very nice people there. I danced with Mr Mulliver, Bode, Walker, Hinder, Lopez, O'Bohrsman, Doak, C. Hunt, Curlewis, Mulliver, Mack, Bohrsman, Hinder, Litchfield, Curnow, Curlewis, Taylor, Spencer, Blunt, Schatz, Cohen, Alexander. C. begged a rose from me and I gave it.

28th July:

Ada and I went to town, we are going to have another dance to pay off balance, everyone liked this one so, bought the cards, etc. Changed Parthenon *money into notes ready for Cope and King. Posted our law expenses at last, thank goodness.*

8th August:

We had a letter from Cope and King and they returned seven guineas of the amount, refusing to take it all, it is really a godsend.

9th August:

Sewed in morning. In afternoon, Lil, Blanche, Ada and I played tennis. At night we went to the University Dramatic Society. Rose and I wore red, Lil white. Mr W. Curnow went with us and a lot of others. Curlewis sat by me but I would not speak. I walked home with W.Curnow: through the Avenue with Curlewis. I am afraid I said awfully unkind things, I was in such a temper.

13th August:

Brush Farm. In morning we played quoits and had Marie Birkeffotoff's journal read aloud. It is simply delicious, I never read such a book. Then we went buttercup and fern hunting and walked miles, had afternoon tea at the sweetest, cleanest little cottage at Concord and went back. Got a letter from Lil with one enclosed from Mr Curlewis — ten closely written pages of explanation, etc. he wrote on Sunday.

14th August:
Went hunting for maiden hair, made up flowers and came home. I have seldom spent four such happy days. Lil said Mr Curlewis came up on Tuesday and told her a good deal — he says he can never forgive me for the indignity I have put upon him in doubting his word.

15th August:
St Paul's College Ball. It was a lovely ball though I think I enjoyed our own more. I danced every dance, my partners were Doak, Mack (2), Conlon (3), Hunt Macdermott, Lopez, Hyde, Bode, Uther, Coyle, H. Ealles, H. Russell (3), W. Windeyer, Campbell (2), D. Thomas, Belbridge, Lloyd and Waldrow. Mrs Cooper left early, I was to have gone home with her to sleep but was enjoying myself too much. I wore my eau-de-nil.

16th August:
St Paul's Tennis Match. Lil and I went to town early. Bought stuff for an opera cloak each. Lil red plush, I white cashmere and swansdown. I also bought a new dress, pale grey, one of the new spring colours. In afternoon Lil, Rose, Ada, Blanche Curnow and I went to see tennis match Avenue v Paul's at the college. Mr Lopez and Bode sat with us, the others were playing and only came up occasionally — D. Windeyer, Hunt and Taylor. Ada told me Mr Curlewis wouldn't go to Paul's dance because he knew I wouldn't speak to him.

22nd August:
At night went to Hague Smiths, Mr Curlewis called for us and we met Nina and the Maynards. I liked the dance very much, the rooms very, very crowded but it was lovely in the grounds. I danced with lots, then in the garden Mr Curlewis told me something, I could never like him in that way though but I am sorry, so sorry it has come to this. He wants me still to be his friend, but I know it is not wise.

29th August:
Sewed a little and idled a great deal, I have never spent such a lazy week, I feel so restless and idle, it is quite demoralising. Ada came at night.

30th August:
Idled, sewed — it is fearfully hot. Caught the 2.30 pm boat to Watsons Bay and walked from there to Bondi arriving about 5 pm, there were about 20 of us and we had tea, strolled and sat in the moonlight. I was with Mr Russell most and a good time with Mr Curlewis, we are always going to be good friends. The strikers had a big demonstration.

1st September:
Sewed, started an article, 'Angels in Petticoats'. At night went to Women's Literary Association for first time, Mrs Gullett was in the chair, Mrs Green read papers on Macbeth which was the subject of discussion. I like it very well and have joined as a Junior Member.

2nd September:
Morning read Spectator *and wrote a few lines. Afternoon Lil and I to tennis at St Paul's College. I liked it very much indeed, played one set with Mr Milner Stephen* and one with R. J. Millard. There was a riot today in Sydney and 2 men killed, it is a fortnight since the strike started. Wilfred Nathan came in evening and said he had heard that I was engaged to Mr Curlewis and asked if it was true. Ada said so too. O, this is awful, I don't know what to do, I must never be seen with him again, that is very certain.*

4th September:
Wrote to H.R.C. I shall not go to the Race with him, but on Mr Thomas' invitation. Went to sleep in afternoon, I did not feel well. Rose went to Confirmation Class. H.R.C. came up in great excitement this evening. Lil and I were alone, he only stayed about a quarter of an hour — un mauvais quart d'heure.

5th September:
Sewed at a blouse in the morning. In afternoon I went alone to call on the Hague Smith's. Curlewis saw me and jumped out of the train to speak — it really is exasperating.

6th September:
Etc. etc. all the morning. Afternoon Lil and I went to University Boat Race, without a chaperone too. On the boat I was mostly with Mr Thomas and Mr Roseby — I hardly exchanged a sentence with Mr Curlewis — it is better so. The Varsity was beaten by nearly seven lengths.

9th September:
Etc. etc. all day. Night went to Buttercup Spinsters' Ball at Needs and wore my pale green. Left early to catch last train. Someone told me H.R.C. stands outside and watches our house at night sometimes.

10th September:
Wrote the first social letter for the Tasmanian Mail, *we are to get £5 a quarter for a weekly letter. Night went in to Weiss' and played cards — scandal, etc. I got it pretty warmly at scandal, especially about a piece of poetry H.R.C. put in the* Parthenon *'There is none like her, none'. (See Appendix III.)*

19th September:
Sewed, idled. Went to St Paul's in afternoon to play tennis. At night went to Art Society, it was an awful crush, very fashionable. I was introduced to several artists — Mr Lister Lister, Percy Spence, Mr Lionel Cowan, Mr J. Ashton, etc. etc. I did not care for

---

*Later Mr Justice Milner Stephen.

it very much. XX was in the tram but did not speak to me, only said so I could hear he was going to enlist as a special constable tomorrow. There was a big riot today, the strike is awful.

20th September:
Idled and thought all morning, I have never idled so fearfully all my life as the last 3 weeks. In afternoon went with Ada to Mrs Wolstenholme's at Dulwich Hill to see if she could chaperone our moonlight picnic. Saw X, he bowed very coldly.

22nd September:
Mr Brock will not let us have the ballroom for our ball and the invitations are nearly all out. O he is a wretch. We spent the whole day in calling him names and thinking what we could do. Rose has chicken pox and is in quarantine in her room. I bought a new white veiling dress to-day. I'm dying for the Government House Ball on Thursday.

25th September:
Morning wrote the Tasmanian Mail *letter. Night Mr Cope, Lil and I went to the Ball, it is the first Gov. House Ball I have been to. I danced with several German Officers off the* Leipzig.

5th October:
Rose, Mr Cope and I went to hear the new bishop, Saumarez Smith at the Cathedral and it was so hot and crowded that I nearly fainted. Afternoon I read a little of Boldrewood's Squatter's Dream *and had a little dream on my own account.*

15th October:
'Court Maidens' Dance. All day we set tables down at West's Rooms and did various other things. At night went to the dance — we all wore powdered hair and patches, I wore my white veiling and Maud Freeman and I received the visitors. It was a lovely dance although I think I have enjoyed others more — it has cost us about 30/- each. Everyone said the dance was a great success and we were very plucky girls, etc. etc. Came home in a cab about five of us, all very weary.

18th October:
In the morning had a game of tennis and wore a cambric dress for the first time this summer, it is so hot. Lil and Mr Blunt sat talking earnestly all the time, she had told him. I think he is a scoundrel, I wish I were a man that I could horse whip him.

26th October:
Cooked, etc. in the morning and afternoon read and dreamed, night went to St Stephens. Mr Curlewis was at home when we got back and he has copied out half of Swinburne for me, a sort of expurgated edition because Mother won't let me have the book complete.

27th October:

Read Swinburne, it is glorious — 'The Triumph of Time' carries one away. Tennyson's loves seem quite feeble after this man's. Went to town and walked as far as A. Horderns and bought the Parthenon Waltz *to see if it can be published. Booked seats at Palings for Dramatic, some person or persons unknown had kindly sent us tickets. Played tennis and read poems — sat outside in the moonlight and went to bed early to have a good think.*

28th October:

Half made a black lace hat. Mrs Thompson and Katie have asked Lil and me to go to the Mikado *with them to-morrow night. Played tennis and at night went to Fullford's Dance at Hurstville. Waggonettes met the train and it was an exceedingly nice dance, I had my programme filled in a few minutes. I had a long talk with Mr Carruthers* and he is going to do us an article.*

1st November:

Lord and Lady Carrington left Sydney amidst great demonstrations. At night when we were dressed and ready for University Dramatic night, there were awful shrieks in the Avenue and Rosie was carried in by 3 gentlemen (Mr Blunt one) with a dislocated leg. She had fallen backwards over a fence. Dr Kingsbury and Service came and they put her under chloroform while they set it. We put her on a bed in the drawing room and Lil and I sat up half the night each. I think 2 such frights would kill us all. Curlewis came up after the theatre to see how she was.

4th November:

Finished off my blue skirt and it looks so nice, quite plain with a tiny crossway frill at foot and a straight back rather full and knotted at top. Annie Summerbelle came up to bring us Myee, a waltz she has composed — she played it for us and it is very pretty. She wants us to give it a critique in the Parthenon. *Afternoon went to University Athletic Sports and walked with Mr Bode a great deal and hated it. After tea I went up the road with Rex for something and met Mr Curlewis, he walked with us and bought Rose some lovely flowers.*

11th November:

Lil and I went for a bathe to Lady Robinson's beach and ate our lunch there. Came home and May and Ethel Maynard came to call. Lil had a row with Mr Cope and has answered an advertisement for a governess. I shall go too — I would like it far away on a station. Louie Mack** wrote me such a nice letter, I had sent a note of sympathy after her father died — she asked to be friends again and forget the past. I wrote to her, dear little thing — it is nearly two years since we 'fell out'.

---

*Later Sir Joseph Carruthers M.L.C.

**Louise Mack was one of a family of 13 children and daughter of a Methodist minister. She had an unhappy marriage and left Australia to live in England and the Continent for many years. During the First World War she was a war correspondent in German-occupied Antwerp.

13th November:

Mrs Christian wrote to say poor little Annie is terribly ill again. She has two doctors and a trained nurse. They fear a clot of blood has gone to the brain or an abscess is forming. She was taken worse on Saturday and woke in convulsions which have recurred twice and her side is all paralysed, we are all so miserable. I worked hard at Algebra all morning. I am going to work up my lessons again and try to pull myself to standard same as when I passed my senior, it's surprising what a lot one forgets.

15th November:

Lil went to see how Annie was — she is just the same, no worse. This anxiety is terrible. The doctor wants to perform an operation and they won't let him.

16th November:

Annie is dead. Mr Cope went out by 6 o'clock and she expressed a wish to see him. He went in and while he was there they thought she died. Lily and I went out there at 3 pm— the poor poor father and mother, oh their grief is terrible. So small and still and white she looked — O God, it seems too awful.

20th November:

Louie Mack sent us a card of sympathy. In the morning the dressmaker came, she is to do the bodies of our dresses and we shall make the skirts ourselves, it will be something to do this terrible week. In afternoon worked some quadratics, they are splendid things for occupying one's mind.

23rd November:

Lil and I went to St Stephen's in the morning and then Mother and Mr Cope went out to dear little Annie's grave. Met Curlewis and he is so very sorry about Annie. He said he knew we should not feel inclined to write, and offered to do something for next issue.

25th November:

Painted most of the day. Dora and Ethel Garnsey called in the afternoon. Ethel is engaged to Mr Lopez only it is a secret yet. I suppose I ought to feel sad 'cause he used to make pretence to be in love with me once, a little. Got a very excited letter — a love letter I suppose from C. I couldn't help laughing and yet — oh I don't . . .

27th November:

I have finished the painting, it looks quite presentable, a little rustic cottage, trees and bridge and a sunset sky. After tea I went out to post a book to Kentish. Met Curlewis, he is going to copy some more Swinburne out for me, I can do with any amount, I wish I was allowed to read it all.

29th November:

I had to go to town, for Rex a suit and Rose a knee cap. Her leg was taken out of plaster of paris today. It was a horrible dusty burning hot day and it seems hotter wearing black. Met Louie Mack, she of course is in mourning for her father.

4th December:
Lil and I went to town, I bought a large canvas 22 x 16 and a copy to paint for Mr Cope's birthday. Then we went to the Clairvoyant's but she was engaged, then we went to the Waverley Cemetery to Annie's grave, it looks so lonely and neglected. Then to the Christian's — poor Mrs Christian looks years older — everything in the house brought little Annie to our thoughts.

20th December:
Morning wrote Tasmanian Letter, and sewed. Afternoon went to Dawes Point to go on board yacht. We had a perfectly grand *sail, only it was not rough enough.*

24th December:
We all went to town shopping, bought cruet stand for Mother and Mr C. a song, scent for Lil, music for Rose and gave Rex 2/6, and Minnie a blouse. Had lunch at Fresh Food and Ice and met Curlewis and Sid Mack outside and talked a little. It was a long tiring day — got a good many cards and posted them.

25th December:
Read Mill on the Floss, *chatted, idled, etc. Night went to the Henry's, there were quantities of children there and we danced with them and helped entertain. Rose got a dear little sewing machine and Rex a boat, whip and bird.*

31st December:
Got up this morning, first time since my illness. Mr Cope gave me a lovely present, a very very fine white muslin for a dress and a black liberty sash, he gave Rose a black and white cambric and sash, and Lil a lovely floral white pougée silk. At night I started Homepapers No. 1, we sat up and saw the new year in. This year has gone very quickly. It will be six weeks on Sunday since darling Annie's death, oh we do miss her so.

I haven't a thing to show for this year, no new language or science started, I've gone back in my studies except English. Its been a profitless frittered-away year. It's very easy to make new resolutions for the new year but I don't suppose for a minute I shall keep to them — I do want to try to keep 3 — 1. to be a better home daughter, 11. not to be caddish if people are below me, 111. and chief one. To be 'larger' — I do hate pettiness and littleness of all kinds. Then be noble and singlehearted. Dare to be all that is good and womanly and Christlike.

THE *Parthenon* case had been quite an experience for the young authors but they remained quite firm in their stand against the young girl from Manly. They showed no compassion or sympathy and in fact often reprimanded their young competitors for not enclosing coupons or complying with their requirements.

She records writing at *Bobbie* during 1890 but for many years did not complete it, as the book was not published until 1897.

1891

The Course of
True Love Never Did...

Parties and tennis and a gay life are all exciting and enjoyable to Ethel, and Mr Curlewis' name is starting to appear rather frequently in the diaries. He is undaunted by her frequent and unpredictable rejection of him, and she accurately predicts her stepfather's reaction when Lil appears to be falling in love with Mr Blunt.

She is devastated by the death of Annie Christian, probably her first experience of losing a very close friend. I wonder did this, only two years later, influence her emotions and thoughts when she wrote about the death of Judy.

7th January:
Lil and I went down to Manly by the 2.30 pm boat and Amy met us and took us to Glendore, it overlooks Ocean Beach. At 5 pm we went for a picnic, two boats' full to North Harbour, such a jolly time we had. Mr O'Brien brought us home right to the door. Wore my white muslin and black sash for the first time. Louie has asked me down to stay about a week, I'm going on Saturday.

10th January:
In afternoon caught the 4.30 pm boat. No one was there to meet that boat, I had missed the other so took a cab. We talked most of the afternoon, I like the girls and Mrs Mack so much, Alice is very pretty. In the evening we went to the Pym's and had a dance in their big dining room. I rather liked Mr Hilhouse Taylor, he is a very clever, thoughtful man; he is very interested in the Parthenon *and is going to write for it. Madame Summerhayes, her daughters and Mr Nichols came and we had some very good music.*

11th January:
Mother and Mrs Davis have started a Sunday School for the Avenue children in the ballroom. I have the head class — 5 boys and 1 girl. In the afternoon Earnest O'Brien came down, and he and I and Louie went for a long walk over the rocks. They tease him and call him Wild Dog, he is so good-tempered.

12th January:
At night Mr Curlewis, Louie and I went to the Corso and coming back sat down on the beach, Louie went to sleep and in whispers he told me about Miss Hawley — I think I like him better for telling me. Suddenly Louie fainted, we were so frightened, he got water in his hat and brandy from a hotel, she was so bad, we were nearly an hour getting her home.

13th January:

Mr Curlewis and I went for a walk and sat out on the rocks all the morning. He told me lots of things — I believe I like him a little better, it's a puzzle to me how he likes me so very much.

14th January:

Louie was ill again, I sat with her for some time. Mr Curlewis came down, also Mr Conlon and Mr Rutter, and we went for a picnic. It was awfully rough, Sid Mack and Mr Rutter were in our boat and the latter couldn't row, we heard afterwards that we had been in a dangerous position, I wasn't a bit frightened, neither was Lil; Alice, Louie and Mrs Stephen were though. Coming home, just as we were in the boat, 2 broadsides came over and swamped us, we were all soaked. C. had just saved the boat and Amy, Gus and Norman from being dashed on the rocks. We got in at about half past 8 put on dry things and went to the Pym's for a dance. Sat with C. in garden sometime. Danced with Mr Grant, Taylor, F. Mack, C. and others.

15th January:

Louie, Lil and I had breakfast in bed we were so tired. Louie and I had talked all the night. She told me about herself and J.B. I was surprised. Lil and I caught the quarter past five boat home and I was so sorry to go, I have scarcely ever spent such a delightful week.

29th January:

Worked and read Robert Elsmere, *the theory seems strangely true, still . . . I do wish I had someone I could talk to about these things. Went up the road to buy a painting copy, met Mr C. coming from tennis at the University. He asked me to show any kindness I could to a Mr Creed who has just come to board in the Avenue. He is just from England and is studying for the Bar and seems lonely.*

3rd February:

Worked and sewed. Afternoon played tennis. Lil tumbled down and Mr Creed was sitting talking to Rose, it was awful. Was introduced to Mr Creed. He takes off his hat with such a sweep, one could fancy him living in days of three-cornered hats which were flourished off and put under the arm. I rather like him, though I fancy he is a bit conceited and pedantic. Mrs Daintrey wrote to ask us up to Picton.

9th February:

The new servant Harriet came. I went to town, payed Froedel, went to Dymocks and treated myself to some new books — Selections from Robert Browning *—* Life of Rossetti, Ivanhoe, *bought Marston's* Song Tide *for Lil, bought a piece of opal for painting, also a big canvas and 2 copies. Read Browning.*

10th February:

Started a large canvas in oils, rocks and a waterfall, painted for three hours. Afternoon sewed and read Swinburne, learnt 4 verses of 'Forsaken Garden' and read two chapters of Ivanhoe.

14th February:

Morning Tasmanian letter, etc. etc. Wrote one chapter Young Rebel. *At 3.30 pm went to picnic, it was a very nice one indeed and they had three boats. Going over I sat in the bow and a big wave came over and drenched me to the skin. I dried a bit at a house at North Willoughby. I was with R. J. Millard mostly coming home. I walked through Domain with C. and I was* horrid *to him, when he said he loved me, I told him I detested him with all my heart — and so I did, I don't like him an atom.*

16th February:

Lil and I went to town and had another sitting for our photos at Kerry and Jones — bought chiffon fan, etc. Afternoon played tennis. R. J. Millard played with us.

17th February:

Wrote, corrected proofs, etc. Amy Mack came for dinner and afterwards the play. It went off very well, they laughed and clapped a good deal, everyone congratulated me on my part, then I went to put on my white evening dress — I had worn a plain white liberty trimmed with chiffon, white hat and poppies for play. Going over C. was waiting, he begged me not to go in just then and at last I yielded and walked about on the far path to escape Mr Cope — suddenly Mother confronted us — she was angry. I went in and we had dancing. I danced with Mr Campbell, H. H. Russell, R. J. Millard, Curlewis (2) — I don't know what to do about latter, he is getting awful, I do like him but not in that way an atom. He says it is driving him mad. I wanted to tell him to go away and never see me again but I simply couldn't, he seemed to feel it so.

18th February:

Packed my portmanteau, etc. etc. and Lil and I caught the 5.17 pm to Picton. Miss Bennet from Campbelltown got in and we went up together. Got there about 8 pm and went to bed early.

19th February:

Mrs Daintrey and Miss Bennet went to the show to judge, so Mr Daintrey saddled one of the horses and Lil and I rode about the paddock in turns. It is my first time on for ages. At 10 o'clock we went to the show and were introduced to Mrs Rotton, Miss Selma Antill, Mrs Cowper, Capt. J. Antill and others. Sat in a buggy to watch the jumping.

20th February:

Went to the show at 11 o'clock to see the ladies riding. In evening went to Jarvisfield, met a lot of new people. Had a long talk with old Mr Antill, we are quite good friends. Danced with Capt. Jack Thompson — he took me down the garden. I like him very much but I'm sure he's an awful flirt. He gave me a rose and is going to send me a horse of his own to ride on. Miss Bennet drove us home at 12 o'clock.

23rd February:

We were going for a ride but a heavy thunderstorm came up so I got under the table instead. Read some of Queen's Gardens *(Ruskin) and wrote to Louie.*

24th February:
Mrs Daintrey and I rode for six miles, cantering part of the way, it was lovely, my first time out on the road.

27th February:
Lil and Mrs Daintrey rode and I painted at my waterfall. Wrote to Tasmanian editor in reply to his letter telling us that our work was falling off and he would have to get someone else at end of the year. That's cause we scribbled it off so. Wrote a poem from the French of Victor Hugo. Read Swinburne. I know the 'Forsaken Garden' by heart, I do love it.

2nd March:
It teemed with rain, got a letter from Mother saying she does not want us home. There is something in the wind I'm sure, I believe they're moving, they are so mysterious.

4th March:
Walked the two miles to get the letters. One for Lil from Wilfred and a lovely long one for me from Louie, she writes splendid letters. Posted a letter to Curlewis that I wrote on Sunday telling him we must have nothing at all to do with each other, it only makes people talk and is no use — I do like him, but I am sure it is not in the right way and the only thing to do is not to see anything of each other. After I posted it, strangely enough, there came a letter from him, such a nice letter. He said Mr Creed was always asking when 'Miss Cupid' was coming home. He wants to ask me again in a year if I liked — I think not, it's not fair to him either. In afternoon Mrs Daintrey and I rode 16 miles, as far as the Barker's on Oaks Rd. Night we packed up.

5th March:
Caught 9.15 am train home and got to the Avenue about lunchtime. All the house was topsy turvy, carpets up and servants gone. They are having a lovely new carpet fitted down right through drawing room and dining room and the green carpet is for our bedroom. I am glad to be home.

6th March:
This morning there was a letter from C. such a dear letter, so manly and yet — I feel so miserable about it all, he is feeling it very much. He is going to send back all the letters I have written him by Mr Creed. I think that is nice without being asked, though there is nothing in any of them that all the world might not see. Worked hard all the morning, the man laid the carpets, they look lovely. After tea I went out for a game of tennis, Mr Creed handed me a parcel from C. I went and opened it and there were every single letter I had ever written since Jan. 1889 — 18 in all, answers to invitations and such mostly. Also all the programmes at dances with my name on. Also two withered roses and the little verse book and card I sent at Xmas to him — And there endeth the last chapter.

Mosmans in 1880.

Mosmans Bay, 1880. Ethel often caught the ferry here at Mosmans Bay wharf. This bay was used as a whaling station until 1851 and the two-storey stone building is the only remaining structure of those early days — it is known as the Barn.

The footbridge was built in 1880 by a Swedish mariner who used rough planks and made the handrails from bamboo, but it was replaced in 1902. This was the scene of a walking party described by Ethel in 1890.

Dance programmes with tasselled pencils were carried by the young ladies at a ball, so that the various dances, which included Waltzes, Scottisches, Quadrilles, Mazurkas, could be booked in advance by the gentlemen. It was every girl's aspiration to have her programme filled early in the evening.

Back: *Rose, aged 16, half sister of Ethel and Lilian.* Right: *Lilian aged 22;* Front: *Ethel aged 20.*

Louise Mack: Ethel and Louie were friends and rivals at Sydney Girls High School. She was also an authoress and wrote amongst other books Teens *and* Girls Together.

St Pauls College, circa 1870. *The scene of some of Ethel's social life in her late teens.*
By kind permission of the Fisher Library, University of Sydney.

The students of St Paul's College 1891, many of whom would have partnered Ethel at the tennis parties and College balls. Certain traditions are still maintained at St Pauls and one requirement is that academic gowns be worn to dinner each evening.
By kind permission of the Warden of St Paul's College.

Inglewood, where Seven Little Australians *was written. This home was extensively renovated for Mr Seivers around the time of the First World War. It is still standing today, and because of subdivision its present address is 1 Werona Ave Lindfield.*

7th March:

I have put my days and dreams out of mind
Days that are over, dreams that are done.

Wrote Tasmanian Letter, I am doing good ones now it is too late I suppose. Worked, etc. The drawing room looks so pretty with its new carpet, drapes and the easel with my waterfall picture.

9th March:

Wrote an essay on Friendship for Literary Class. In afternoon went to Mack's and had a long chat with Louie, she lent me Keats. In evening talked literature with Mr Creed. He lent me his Rossetti, first making me promise only to read what he had marked.

10th March:

Read Rossetti, etc. started a story which I am calling 'Five Sweet Symphonies, not to mention the Discord'. Wrote a good deal of it. Read and wrote most of the day.

11th March:

Idled and read poetry. Lay on the floor and tried how many poems I could say from remembrance — 'Fears', 'The Oblation', 'Forsaken Garden', 'Indian Serenade', Arnold's 'Self Dependancy'. Afternoon went to class, afterwards into town and got 2 Review of Reviews, *they are going to send them regularly.*

12th March:

It rained and then cleared up. The washerwoman did not come and the clothes were all in soak, we did not know what to do — at last we three set to and did a copper-full — Mother washed, we rinsed and pegged out. My first washing! I felt a little mauvaise *— afternoon had a fearful headache. Read* Wormwood *then and all evening; it is a horrible, fascinating, powerful kind of book, but phew, the taste is in my mouth yet. I wouldn't have written that book for anything. Marie Corelli is only 24.*

13th March:

Mother and I went to Government House to see Lady Jersey about the Parthenon, *she was just going out. Did some shopping. Night wrote Varieties and reviewed* Wormwood *and three other books. Played tennis in afternoon. F. H. Smith wrote to ask Lil and me to go to Hawkesbury for a week at Easter with a lot of them, Nina, Louie, etc. It would be awfully jolly, but Mr Cope! Saw C. when I was going to town, he looked nicer than usual, we bowed in the most commonplace way.*

16th March:

Nellie Hague Smith came down this morning in a great state. Mr H. Smith objects to other gentlemen being asked to the Camp except brothers, it is vexatious — only Mr Wilshire, Mr Fairfax and their married brothers are to stay in the house it seems. I think a good many are going to camp at Broken Bay and come over to see us. Afternoon read and wrote.

17th March:

Wrote my essay, 'With Infinite Diligence, With Infinite Love', it is the class motto. In afternoon did puzzles for Parthenon. *At night Florrie, Nellie, Louie and Amy came and we had a meeting in our sanctum. Sid and Mr C. came to fetch the girls, when we were outside, I shook hands with C. and found a note in my hand. It said he will never give me up whatever I say and that he was mad when he said he wouldn't trouble me again and sent back the letters — he shall never give up trying. It doesn't alter things a bit. I have a voice in the matter and I shall* never *change. In afternoon I was talking to Mr Creed in our drawing room and asking him some quotations, at same time I asked him 2 words of Greek that were in an envelope C. sent back, I said I had come across them in reading — he said 'I will ask Curlewis' — it couldn't have been worse.*

18th March:

Worked and read Dolly *a delightful book by Mrs Burnett. Afternoon went to Government House. Lady Jersey received us in the red drawing room, she was so nice, not a bit stiff and enquired about advertisements and subscribers list of* Parthenon, *she is going to write and let us know if she will write for us. Did some shopping — at tram C. came up and shook hands, I felt quite angry, he said, 'have you been asking Creed for any more Greek?' — I hate them both.*

20th March:

Lady Jersey wrote us such a nice letter and says she offers a prize for an essay.

21st March:

Went to town in morning. I saw an advertisement for a governess £80 a year and was mad for it. Saw a Mrs Dent at the Metropole, after a long talk she asked me to play and said I would do, I was to teach French, Latin, English, Music, Euclid, Algebra, Painting and Drawing to 3 big girls and a boy for £60. I said I would let her know. Mr Cope was awful about it, he swore if I went he would set a detective after me, I was under age, etc. etc. In afternoon went out sailing. We had a glorious sail, went across the heads to Manly, back to Cremorne where we had tea and then home by moonlight at about 10.

22nd March:

Tied up books and dressed dolls for hospital in morning. Night started to write Goethe essay, did proofs, etc. and wrote to put Mrs Dent off. After all I suppose it would be rather idiotic to go, we have a beautiful home, our own little sitting room, very little to do, a fair amount of money and good deal of gaiety.

25th March:

Caught train at 9 o'clock, Lil, Lucy O'Brien, F. and N. Hague Smith, Mr Fairfax chaperone and Rob and Clive. Got to Milsons Island at 1 o'clock. It is such a lovely place and such a pretty comfortable cottage, we have brought no servant, but there is a girl here to do odd things for us and the rest we shall do ourselves. That Louie has had a row with those at home and won't come, indeed can't come.

26th March:
Pulled about — read Two Masters, *had music, there is a piano, an organ and a concertina, cooked and did a lot of things. I am so vexed Louie couldn't come — and I should like it better I think if there were more gentlemen down — however it is great fun and such a lovely fresh place.*

28th March:
We all went for a sail down to Peat's Ferry. Mr Fairfax is very jolly, I like him. Sid and Lucy* are gone on each other. We played a lot of tricks on the boys, apple pied their beds, sewed the sheets together, etc. etc. I am enjoying myself greatly.

29th March:
Pulled, read, walked, the boys put a huge toad in our room, we did shriek, then in the middle of the night they rang the dinner bell down the chimney and did other things to pay us for our tricks.

1st April:
Got up very late. Nellie and I went to the top of the island. In afternoon Sid, Lucy, Flo, Nell, Gertie, Lil, Norman and I went for a pull, such a jolly one. I jumped into the water getting into the boat, I'm always doing it — they call me the 'duck' and 'Mrs Amphibious' because of my affinity for water. At night we all sat on the verandah, I said aloud Swinburne's 'Forsaken Garden', some Tennyson, Mary Queen of Scots, etc. and we all told stories.

2nd April:
It poured with rain, so we hung about all day. It is intensely amusing to see Sid and Lucy — he is awfully in love with her and can't help showing it. Caught the 5 pm steamer and got to Peat's Ferry, then had to sit on the station in the rain until 8 o'clock, we were soaking. Lil and I got a cab at Newtown and arrived home at about 10.30 pm at night. Tasmanian Editor has given us another quarter and sent our last cheque.

3rd April:
Lil and I went to town saw Maclardy Troedel, settled various matters. Went to Fresh Food for lunch. Curlewis wrote again to Rose asking her to Boat Race and sent two tickets. I shall buy a ticket, I wouldn't go on his for worlds though he has begged me to. Met Miss Windeyer, she is sending me two cards for the conversazione. There is such a row in the Avenue between Brock and Alexander, libel case coming on. Everyone has notice to quit — some legal technicality which means nothing. Night sewed chiffon, wrote, etc. There was a fearful torpedo accident at Middle Head, two officers Hammond and Bedford and two men blown to bits.

---

*Sid and Lucy: Sid Mack (Louie's brother) and Lucy O'Brien

4th April:

Afternoon Mother, Lil and I went to the Boat Race. It was very exciting, Sydney went away like wildfire and kept ahead the whole way, Melbourne 2nd, Adelaide last but A had to pull with a fixed seat as they broke a slide. I knew seven of the nine pulling for Sydney — Lopez, Sawyer, R. J. Millard, Scott, Dick Thomas, M. Stephen, Conlon and other two were Helsham and Cox. We went on the Pheasant *which was the grand boat having the Jersey party on board — the* Birkenhead *was the jollier boat though I am sure. When we got home Rose said Curlewis had been and tried to persuade her to go to the Race, Ruby Christian was with her and she couldn't.*

7th April:

Worked in morning, then to town and bought a 'dainty dot' hat, went to Louie's on the way home for afternoon tea. In train I saw C. Talked to Mr Creed after tennis. Ada told me that Mrs Minns, the artist's wife, says Mr Creed is always talking to her about me. He says 'I am one of the nicest, dearest little girls he knows, so pretty and like a sunbeam' — I did laugh for I didn't know he liked me at all.

9th April:

Lil went off by 8.45 am to catch the Maitland train, she is going to stay with the Coopers of Gostwyck for a fortnight to see if it will do her good. I wrote most of the day, did 'the Home', etc.

11th April:

Wrote Tasmanian Letter. Afternoon Rose and I went to Eveleigh to call for Macks and then to University. Just like other Commems the students made a big row and interrupted Lord Jersey and Sir William every second. Louie formally introduced me to Nina Russell again. We went to top of tower, I had on Sid's graduate's gown, C. came too, he looks nice in his gown, I didn't speak to him at all, I daren't, Louie chaffs so.

12th April:

Read, wrote, etc. At night Rose and I went to church. On the way I lost Mother's watch, there was a fine to do. Ada and I went down to Herald *office and put in an advertisement offering a handsome reward.*

13th April:

Went to town to Troedel and took M.S.S. met Louie and went first to Fresh Food for lunch and then to School of Arts. When I got home there was my watch, I was glad — a man had picked it up — it has cost me 15/- to get it back. I am going to have a four o'clock tea party on Friday, I sent out notes, tiny 'Come Early' paper with a tea pot or cup on. Invited Ada, Blanche, Louie, Alice, Lucy O'Brien, Nina Church, R. J. Millard, Mr Creed, Sid Mack, Wilfred, Mr Grahame, Willy Curnow, Mr Pickburn.* Put on them 'Tea and Talk, Parthenon Sanctum Friday 4 p.m.' — Mr or Miss Fiddlesticks?

---

*Later Judge Pickburn, Industrial Arbitration Court.

15th April:

Wrote prize page, Varieties, Here and There. Then went to town. Saw C. in the tram, we just bowed. Night wrote last of Parthenon *for this month. Tidied the sanctum a little, cleared out a lot of old papers. Mr Creed wrote, sent me Literary Puzzles, also two poems of which he disclaims authorship.*

17th April:

Made the sanctum look sweet. Put my best paintings on the easels, verse books, etc. all about and arranged my tea tables. The weather was very showery. Mr Grahame and Mr Pickburn arrived first and I had to talk to them alone until I was quite desperate, then all the others came. Everybody talked a great deal, no one seemed stiff, though Ada was rude to Mr Creed and laughed, he came in evening dress as he was going out to dinner. Alice sang 'Ora pro Nobis' and Sid sang too.

18th April:

Wrote Tasmanian Letter. Idled and day-dreamed a good deal, C. figured in those dreams very much I am ashamed to say. Someway I can't help thinking of him. Read a stupid story. Evening dreamed again — I want shaking.

20th April:

Pouring with rain. Took into my head I would see if I could make a fortune by writing for that sweet paper The Bulletin. *Composed forthwith a vile parody of 'Come into the Garden, Maud'. Night went to Women's Literary Society class, subject 'Is Realism in Literature Desirable?' Very good evening, excellent papers.*

22nd April:

Went to town, saw C. in tram, he was smoking like a chimney as usual, it disgusts me. Shopped and called for Rosie and we went to the Art Gallery. Saw the cast of the Ghiberti gates for the first time. Also a big picture in water colour of a girl in Grecian dress, done by Shepard and supposed by a lot of people to be just like me. I have been asked if I had sat, or rather stood for it. I should be conceited to think it like me.

23rd April:

Did my bedroom thoroughly and the sanctum badly. It gets into a most confusing, if picturesque, state of untidiness. Read two children's stories. Blanche Curnow wrote and asked me to ask a lot of people for Saturday so I did.

25th April:

Did Tasmanian Letter, packed basket and went for 2.30 pm boat to Lane Cove River. It was a lovely picnic, I enjoyed it intensely. In afternoon we played rounders, then had tea in the pavilion, such a pretty table set. Ellie Curnow and I poured out. Then we made programmes of visiting cards and danced all the evening. Talked to Mr Creed for a long time, I do like him. Talked to C., I am going to be his friend, it can't hurt me and it helps him he says.

26th April:
Nina came up for afternoon, also Louie, the latter stayed and slept, we talked to nearly 5 am this morning. She says C. was awfully miserable last night and confided in her — she says he cried — great dry sobs. Oh, I do feel a wretch and yet I can't like him if I can't, it is a miserable affair altogether. Louie says he has always had a hard life of it, it does seem too bad of me.

27th April:
Afternoon went to Literary Society meeting. I read a paper, 'Literary Debauch', for the first time. It was quite a success, I got enough compliments to turn my head, some proposed it for a discussion. When I had got into the tram to come home, in jumped Sid Mack and Curlewis, I had to talk to them all the way to Newtown. Lil came home, she looks so well, I am glad to get her home.

9th May:
We are going to the Cricket Match, Zingari v H.M.S. Fleet — Lord Jersey, Lord Ancrum, Mr Goschen and others were to play for Zingari. Everyone at home said it was too cold and wouldn't go. I went to Louie's for tea. Curlewis, Sid and Pickburn had been sailing and came home for tea, I hardly spoke to former. I had to let him bring me home though and . . . I can't write it down. Lay awake nearly all night.
*   I am frightened at what I have done, and yet so happy . . . I never really thought I cared for him till tonight.*

12th May:
Got ballroom ready for our Four-O'clock Tea and Dance — set tables, etc. — scones, sandwiches and cakes of every kind. At 3 the 'party came in' or detachments of the party. Altogether we had about 70. I introduced a great deal and was quite a good hostess in fact. Half the people went at about 6.30 but half made a good T and stayed till 9.30. It was very jolly everyone said — a good original idea.

14th May:
Wrote various odds for paper, etc. etc. Went to Miss Josephine O'Reilly's about Singing Lessons. She tried my voice — I told her I hadn't an atom but she says I've more than I know how to manage. I'm afraid however I know better — I don't care, I will learn.

16th May:
Wrote Tasmanian Letter. Lil and Mr Cope had an awful row — he behaved horribly, kept puffing smoke in her face to aggravate her, and when she got angry, taunted her about Mr Blunt. She said she would go out of the house, and he said go, so she packed her portmanteau and cleared out. I told him I thought he was a coward and a cad, so I do. Went to Mack's to tea and came home early with C. He gave me such a sweet little book — Old World Idylls *by Austin Dobson.*

20th May:
Dressmaker came and I helped her make me a brown cashmere trimmed with fur — at least I didn't do much. Night read and idled.

21st May:
Read, went to Paul's in afternoon and wore my brown dress. I liked it awfully. Willy Windeyer introduced me to Mr Mills — one of the nicest men I have met I think — but there, what have I to do with other men now —

22nd May:
Went to town, saw C. in the tram, bought a song, etc. and he was in the tram going back. Also he walked to my lesson with me — Camdenville, and waited while I had it and walked back. I'm getting downright wicked but I do like being with him and after all there's no harm, we're going to tell Mother soon, I'm dreading it.

23rd May:
Tasmanian letter in morning, afternoon I went to Five Dock. It takes a fearfully long time to get there. There were a lot of people there, it's such a nice place, such a lovely old fashioned garden and the river at the bottom of it. Mr Creed, Pickburn and others there — C. of course. We let off fireworks, danced and strolled in the garden. I did the last most. He made me promise unconditionally what I half-promised before. I couldn't help it, he is awfully determined and has a very strong will — I wouldn't like him though if he was weak. I feel desperately frightened sometimes at what I have promised.

24th May:
Read, etc. went to Mack's for tea and then to church. I was disappointed rather in the sermon for I had expected something splendid. The church was packed. C. brought me home and we walked.

26th May:
Morning nothing in particular. Afternoon very much the same. Mr Creed came for dinner — I do like him — Mr Cope does too. Louie came after and gave Rose and Rex their music lessons. In evening Sid Mack and C. came up. I liked him better than ever but it's horribly uncomfortable with Mr Cope.

31st May:
Morning read, afternoon thought, night read and built dream castles. This sort of thing quite destroys the even tenor of one's ways — all the same it's a sweeter, happier, if somewhat perplexing, state of existence.

2nd June:
Went to singing lessons, coming back I tripped on some mud and twisted my knee, C. was there and walked to tram with me, he gave me a letter from his Mother — such a sweet Motherly sort of letter, I do want to see her now. He came in about 1pm with plants for Mother and I gave him a note back. My knee was so swollen and aching I had to go to bed, they have sent for Dr Quaife. I wrote a note to C.

3rd June:
In bed all morning, Dr Edwards came, he says I have twisted a ligament and can exercise it if I like. If!! I was up and dressed in no time though it hurts to walk much.

4th June:

Wrote, sewed, etc. all day. C. wrote me such a nice letter, I had to answer it, he was quite anxious. We have promised to go to the O'Brien's on Saturday, his Mother is to be there, I do wonder what she is like, she is a lady, I can tell from her letter. Dr Quaife came and said I am not *to exercise my knee, to use it as little as possible.*

6th June:

Wrote, Tasmanian Letter, afternoon Lil and I went to Five Dock. C. was in the tram — also *his Mother and a young sister and brother. I have felt perfectly miserable all day about it, I knew Lil was taking stock, and oh I don't know what Mother and Mr Cope would say to her. She's educated and all that, I'm sure, but she was frightfully dressed and seems worn out and unmindful of herself with drudging after all her boys. I'm awfully sorry for her for I believe what with being so poor and having no daughter to help her, she must have an awfully hard time of it. I do hope C. is good to her. There was a hobbledehoy school boy brother of his too — Dolly is alright and Rex a dear little lad. Lily seems perfectly aghast and says I'm doing a nice kind of thing. I can't help feeling miserable about it, though I suppose it is caddish of me and after all* he's the *same, and can't help his family.*

10th June:

Sewed at my dress, it's not pretty a bit I think, the heliotrope looks quite grey at night. At night we went to the June Bachelor's Ball— it was raining so we had a cab, I didn't dance, my knee was too bad, I don't want to make it worse, I filled my programme however and sat and talked and met a Mr Hungerford, such a nice man.

12th June:

Talked about going to England till we worked ourselves into the wildest enthusiasm, if Mr Cope would sell a piece of land at N.Shore we could go. Went to singing lesson, Miss O'Reilly has gone to Queensland for a holiday. C. went with me and I told him about England. Then we went in tram and I got out at Horderns, he waited and we came back together. Scarndalous! as Lucy O'Brien would say.

13th June:

Did accounts, talked England. We all went on board Victoria, it is lovely, it made me wild *to go, it would be £105 return each, even Rosie, and then travelling and sightseeing on Continent. Went to Gardens for a little, then to Free Library and read for an hour.*

17th June:

Read, idled and sewed. It is a public holiday on account of the general election. Afternoon at 5 went to the Doaks at Neutral Bay, dressed there, I in my eau-de-nil and Lil in pale blue. Very jolly dance indeed though I had to sit still and talk to my partners because of my wretched knee. One blessing though, I don't limp.

19th June:

Went to town and bought a new evening dress to wear at Government House and went to dressmaker's and back, made lobster salad and helped with oyster patties, cakes, made claret cup, etc. and set tables for our little dance at night. Wore my old red evening dress, and enjoyed myself 'mensely.

23rd June:

Went to Mrs Dixon's to be fitted for my new dress, it is so pretty, soft white crêpe de chine. Mrs Curlewis, Claude and Rex were in the next car to me, talked to her a little, I think I might get to like her. She said she was sorry to hear about us going to England. Night went to Musical at Government House, Lady Jersey asked us if we had got the portrait alright. About 250 were there and I liked it very much. The young pianist Ernest Hutchinson played — he was splendid. Mr Cope was horrid.

25th June:

Afternoon had a headache and went to sleep, I don't think I ever was so deeply asleep, I seemed to have gone quite off this planet, such a strange sensation it was. Mr Cope has been home all day headachey and queer. Dr Quaife said it was only a chill, not typhoid fever which we were afraid it was.

4th July:

Wrote a little at the Young Rebel. *Read Morris,* At the Roots of the Mountains. *I don't know what is the matter with me lately, I believe I'm a bit disappointed, I thought perhaps love was more lovely and sweet than it is. It is horrid of me though, for he is all and more than he should be and loves me more than I thought anyone could. It is one of Earth's good things I think to be able to know that one person loves you more than all the rest of the world.*

5th July:

Morning read, afternoon went to the O'Brien's, went on the River in the boats. Night went in garden, C. and I came across a charming little tableau in the shape of Mr Creed embracing Louie. I knew it would come. Dear little Louie, she was fearfully excited upstairs after with me, she didn't seem as if she knew what she was doing.

6th July:

Lil and I went to town shopping. I tried to get white satin shoes and couldn't in my size anywhere. In afternoon went to Girl's Common Room at University for tea, lots of old High School Girls there. Got up a present for our old teacher Miss Walker who is just married to a Mr Garvin. Night to Hague Smith's. Nell and I had a long confidential chat. She told me that she liked H.R.C. better than any man, though she wasn't in love. Of course, I didn't tell her about us. . .

9th July:

Went to town, C. was in tram. I am never going in it with him again, people will talk.

10th July:

Morning wrote. Afternoon Rose and I went to Mack's to go to Boat Race. Creed confided in me a good deal about Louie and I was listening attentively when up came that Lopez and presented me with a cup of tea and two spoons in the most marked way. Idiot! And once upon a time before he met Ethel Garnsey he used to like me, of course not as much. Poor little me, and now we always rub one another up the wrong way. At night Louie told me all her secrets.

11th July:

Lil and Rose went to Hague Smith's. Night we went with them to Halle's Concert. It was glorious, Lady Halle's playing on violin is exquisite. Mme Fillunger has the loveliest clearest of voices and Mme Burton's too is beautiful. Met Louie after. She says Nellie Hague heard some of our confidences last night. This is fearsome!

13th July:

Louie came up to say she wouldn't go to Manly, we had such a quarrel over it, of course I wouldn't go alone with C. so I wired to him and she put Creed off. Night went to Cleopatra to see the divine Sarah Bernhardt — it was divine, I could follow her pretty well, not the others. I fell in love with Marc Anthony, I wish C. was just like him, I wish we had lived in olden days, everything is so set and conventional nowadays. I'd like to be a great success, anyone great and clever, anyone but just me. Oh C. is love the same off the stage and on, mine's not like that I know, I believe his is though.

17th July:

Went to see Louie off to Quirindi, I shall miss her fearfully. Afternoon C. came to see me and we had such a catastrophe, the Bristowes and Maynards came and he had to go in sanctum till they had gone. Mother says she can't have it like this, I believe she's right. It's horrid for her, she feels going against Mr Cope and I think it is hardly nice for C. We were alone for a long time, I wouldn't break my promise for all the world now, it would hurt him so and he's too dear and good to be hurt. But I wish I could feel wildly in love with him.

20th July:

Morning read and wrote. Night went to Literary Society meeting. Subject was 'Influence of Women's Suffrage on Politics'. Its horrid to see the way some of them go on about their rights and wrongs, its old-fashioned of me I suppose but I do think it would take from the womanliness of a woman to be in Parliament.

23rd July:

Morning nothing in particular. Afternoon went to sleep for half an hour. Night went to the Paul's College Ball. We both wore white, Lil with silver girdle, I with crêpe de chine. I enjoyed it immensely and danced every dance, it did my knee good I am sure. Partners — Sawyer, Scott, Coyle, Abbott, Russell (3), Craig (2), Macarthy, Doak, W. Doak, Jo Wood, etc. 2 Barn Dances. It's lovely to be dancing again, Paul's is a splendid place for a dance, all the students' rooms to sit in between dances and the corridors and libraries. Three girls came home with us to sleep. Mrs G. Waldron chaperoned us. I liked Mr Bob Craig, Mr Sawyer and Coyle best.

30th July:
Afternoon idled and read. Night wrote an article on Women's Suffrage 'How it strikes a Non-Advocate' — (misself). It seemed mad when I read it so I sent it to Mr Creed to read for me.

4th August:
Mother ill in bed all day, it is really getting serious, we have been talking of going to live at Ryde or some such place for her health*. Mrs Weiss begged me to join her painting class free gratis, of course I wouldn't, I wish I could afford to learn though. Painted some tall arum lilies up the side of my opal. Mrs Daintrey came for the day, they are going to live at Gunnedah.

9th August:
Got up at 11.45 am. Scandalous! Wrote article on 'Hidden meaning of Pagan Myths' for Australie, *idled, etc.*

13th August:
Night went to Dulwich Hill to the Hague's dance. It is only a year since Addie was married to Mr Fairfax and she was there to-night so sedate and so very much married — playing cards, while we were frolicing through the Barn dance! I never, never want to be married; it gives me a funny choking kind of feeling even now to feel I am no longer free and what would it be then.

17th August:
Morning read Homer, translation of course. Night went to Literary Society meeting. Someone proposed that 2 papers of last year — notable papers, to wit Miss Scott's 'Individuality' and Miss Turner's 'Literary Debauch' form subjects for discussion.

18th August:
Etc. etc. which being interpreted meaneth idled about. Sid came up at night to tell us startling news. In the awfully windy weather the Law 4 boat crew were in the icy water, after their boat tipped over, for 10 minutes. Eventually a Watsons Bay steamer came to the rescue. I felt slightly anxious.

30th August:
Went to church. Night music and poetry at the Hague's. Miss Close is supposed to be a splendid fortune teller by the hand. Mine was 'That I was very refined, spiritual, used brains considerably, clever in 3 subjects, ought to do some great "hand work" painting or sculpture. Should come to fame. Had plenty of admirers, should marry by 22 and be unhappy, marry again. Have terrible illness when 30 and never quite recover,' etc. etc. Heaps more nonsense.

---

*Ethel's Mother had always suffered from chronic asthma.

3rd September:

Night went to dance at Elizabeth Bay, couldn't find the house at first. I don't like that kind of society a bit. The men seemed to treat the girls with such lightness and the girls are so forward and horrid and say such cruel things. Mrs T. asked us to lunches, more dances and a boating party. I shan't go again.

4th September:

Morning sewed and read. At night Mother, Lil and I went to Government House Ball. Cab again. I'm nearly bankrupt. It seems rather strange to see Lady Margaret and Mary Villiers dancing away as if they were out, they're only 14 and 16 and wear their hair down.* Mr Goschens dancing or rather romping is enough to make anyone die with laughing. Everyone was talking of it.

5th September:

We have decided to go to Lindfield. I named it the Sepulchre but Mother objected so I shall call it the Catacombs. It will be like being buried alive to live in a quiet little country place after the bustle and excitement of town life. I would always like to live 9 months in town and 3 months in the country.

8th September:

Afternoon Lil, Rose and I went to Victoria Barracks. There was a Captain Taylor there I rather liked only he was so conceited because he was so good looking. Went to Horderns, did a little shopping and came home. Ada came for a time and we chatted a little, I am afraid to do more than talk commonplaces with her.

11th September:

C. came at 10.30 am. I didn't like him at all and I thought I should so very much after a fortnight's absence. Perhaps it was only 'cause he didn't look nice, he was horribly sunburnt and his coat seemed to smell of tobacco. It's stupid of me I know. 'One of my silly fastidious ways' Louie would say.

12th September:

Afternoon went to picnic at Wolstenholmes at Lane Cove. Played rounders, etc. in afternoon and got through a programme of 13 dances at night. I enjoyed it very much. Had 3 with C. liked him better, I'm terribly changeable I'm afraid in a small way, but I wouldn't break my word for worlds, even if I wanted to.

17th September:

Went to Hurstville with Ada and got crowds of buttercups and maidenhair for the table. Night Nell came and we made jellies, lemon sponge, date creams and all manner of good things. I am getting quite a don at confectionery.

---

*Hair was worn long until a young girl made her debut.

18th September:
Made trifles, claret cups, etc. etc. set the table in the ballroom, Joseph helped well. About 40 or 50 came and everyone seemed to enjoy themselves and said they were awfully sorry we are going away. They say they shall have University walking parties up to see us, everyone was so nice, I liked it muchly.

19th September:
Cleared up after dance. Wrote Tasmanian Letter. Went to sleep, trimmed a big shade hat for myself, did accounts and idled. This dance has cost us a good deal, Lil and I are paying for it by ourselves.

22nd September:
Packed books, cleared pictures. Afternoon C. came and spent an hour and a half with me. Last time in this house. We are going to write to each other every week and he is coming up to Lindfield sometimes. He liked my painting, I'm going to paint something for him.

24th September:
Mother and I went shopping all day, bought 2 pretty bedsteads for Rose and me, lots of kitchen and dairy things and various etcetras.

25th September:
Packed and worked hard all day. Mrs Payten came and helped. I rather like moving, it's great fun. Such lots of letters and messages come from people saying how sorry they are, and that they shall all come up to see us even if they have to walk. Got a long, long letter from Louie, poor little thing she is fearfully homesick and miserable about Mr Creed — everything is going wrong she says.

27th September:
Packed, etc. etc. Mother and Mr Cope had a row. Went to Hague Smith's. Everyone seems so sorry we are going and say they will miss us awfully. It's nice to feel you're not on the list of those 'who never will be missed'. Wrote a very long epistle to Louie and copied out two poems for her.

28th September:
Went to town, bought prizes, etc. In afternoon Mr O'Reilly called and I entertained him among the packing cases. At night Lil and I ran down to the summerhouse as I had promised for five minutes to say good-bye to C. He gave me a lovely little book of poems: Austin Dobson's At the Sign of the Lyre.

29th September:

Watched our household goods being hoisted into the carts, bade adieu to the Weisses and then Lil and I left. Had lunch at Fresh Food and then went to Lindfield. I liked the place awfully. It is a pretty square house with a long balcony and verandah, honeysuckle and white roses creeping up. The drawing room is a nice long room with 4 windows and pale blue walls, we can make it very pretty. The dining room is rather small and there is a little room that we are going to paper and transform into our sanctum. Upstairs 4 bedrooms. Rose and I sleep together, downstairs kitchen, servant's room and various outhouses. The garden and drive are very much neglected but the roses are lovely. There is a big piece of orchard but it is also neglected. *

2nd October:

Invitations came for a lovely dance, 'the Leonidas Dance' that all our friends in Sydney have been getting up to give us, it's to be on 16th. Oh it is too lovely. I didn't think we had so many friends. Ada told Lil before and Rose, and they never even told me a word until yesterday.

6th October:

Rex started school at Gordon — the public school, he can't go to any other until he is old enough to go to town. Lil and I went for a tremendous walk and kept calling at cottages here and there about fowls and other livestock. Everyone made such a lot of us, and told us their family histories and troubles and everything. There is a poor Mrs Nash has had a fearful amount, very poor, sick husband and a lot of children.

8th October:

Gardened. I am trying to clear the aphids off my rose trees, it seems hopeless. Afternoon the Rev. G. and Mrs Crisford called, I rather like them. They have enlisted us for a bazaar, both to work for it and help serve. I thought we had left such frivolity behind us in Sydney. Night wrote Young Rebel, *Chapter XIV — a chapter on smoking. Taffie has done every possible and impossibly naughty thing, I don't know how to keep him going to the end of the year.*

11th October:

Lil, Rose and I went to church at Gordon, such a funny little church. Mr Crisford preaches very well. Three Pockley girls and one boy was there. Afternoon read Sin in a Lifetime. *Night finished copying out my prize tale to* Illustrated London News Competition. *It's cheek of me to compete I know, but I'll have a try.*

16th October:

The Leonidas Dance given in honour of 'the 3 little Miss T's'. Gathered roses, went maidenhair hunting and then to town at 4.15 pm, got to Ada's about 5.45 pm. We went

---

*This house is still standing today, but it would be difficult to recognise as the one in the photo. Its present address is 1 Werona Ave, Lindfield, it is named Woodlands and is owned by Mrs Patricia Mills. The original home was built between 1884 and 1887 for George Braham but it was extensively altered by Mr Andrew Sievers about the time of the first World War.

in late, Mrs Bennett took so long and they were all waiting, they wouldn't commence dancing till we got there. It was a divine dance, everyone was so nice and made such pretty speeches to us, it is lovely to have so many friends. Danced with Curnow, Flavelle, Lopez (2), Dudley Ward, Manning, Russell, Wolstenholme, Flatt, Pickburn, Creed, Fred Mack, etc. etc. C. of course — three or four times. I felt quite shy with him again, it's a month nearly since I have seen him, it doesn't seem real at all. It was so hard to keep dances for nice ones, and refuse others, we were so rushed. Lopez and I were quite friends again.

18th October:
Got up at 11, Nina, Lil and I talked dresses and suchly till dinner, Mr Dice was there still. He asked us to go and stay with them at Drummoyne. Nina told me a little of the talk there had been about Lopez and me, Ethel Garnsey was jealous, and Jo Wood used to tease Lopez up at Newcastle.

21st October:
Painted a little in the afternoon — a water mill scene on a tambourine for the bazaar. I hate tambourines and frying pans and such painted. It seems a debasement of Art. Heigho, I wish I could paint well.

22nd October:
C. came up by 10.15 am train. I felt awfully shy at first again with him. He brought me 2 books to read Autocrat of Breakfast Table *and William Morris'* Howard the Halt. *We went for a walk and got quite lost, getting home to lunch after 2. He caught the 4 train down. I believe I am just beginning to be really and truly in love. He has some trouble I fancy, he seemed older and graver but said he wouldn't tell me cause he only wanted to think of pleasant things all day. It was lovely being together all day. I am so glad, glad he loves me as he does. Love is even more beautiful, more infinite than the poets say and Life is very beautiful.*

25th October:
Read a great deal of Oliver Wendell Holmes, I love it. Made and spoiled a cake. Night sat out on the lawn and talked theology with Lil and Mother. I wonder what I should be called if I had to be classified in some religious sect. Free thinker I suppose, though like many others I go to Church of England. God I believe in and trust with all my heart. God and good, and I think man is man and master of his fate. As to heaven, I don't think it is just a place for good people. But just God the great essence of Life and all life, after death merges in him.

28th October:
Sewed at blouse, held a review of my wardrobe, heaps of dresses nearly all shabby, I'll have to get some new ones — exchequer permitting. Letters from Illustrated News, Tasmanian Mail, *etc. Another bad thunderstorm, I do hate them. I generally bury my head in the sofa cushions till it is over.*

1st November:
Painted a little and finished second tambourine for bazaar, lengthened a white muslin dress, finished and copied out a little article on picnics and sent for approval to Sydney Mail. *C. sent me a little book* Pirated Poems, *they are so good.*

3rd November:
Mother went to town to engage two new servants. Put up valances and mosquito nets. I have been quite industrious to-day. Six fowls (15/-) came for Lil and me, we put them in the fowl run we have had wired off, it only cost us about 30/-. Oliver the gardener left.

9th November:
Nell and I were idling about when suddenly we saw two figures coming up the line, I went down to meet them. It was Sid and Louie. *I never had such a lovely, lovely sudden surprise, for I didn't expect her till Xmas. We all took afternoon tea to Gordon and sang and talked all the evening. Louie and I slept together or rather, occupied the same bed and talked nearly all night.*

12th November:
Went to stay with Macks arriving at 12 noon. C. was there and after tea Louie, he and I sat in the drawing room, Louie went out for a little, a very little time and I was horrid to him. I am the most stupid little donkey when I get these moods. Shook hands quite coldly when he went. When we went to bed Louie wrote Mr Creed an enormous letter so I wrote C. a wee note, saying — oh never mind.

14th November:
Started my blue skirt, poultryised and did various household things. Afternoon Lil, Rose, Rex and I went to the Bazaar, a frightfully sick affair. Spent a little money in duty's cause and returned home thankfully. Night wrote Wayside Notes, started Chit Chat, etc., did accounts. I am in such a state, C. is coming up on Monday and Mr Cope has calmly and deliberately announced his intention of staying at home that day. No answer from C. to my letter.

16th November:
Mr Cope stayed at home so in despair I packed up secretly a picnic basket and set forth to meet C. and his little sister Dolly. Got into the train with them and went to Gordon. It was a terrifically hot day, we picnicked down in the gully. He brought me some very nice sweets and The Days of a Lazy Lawyer. *We had a very pleasant day despite the heat. Sid forgot to give him the letter that's why he didn't write. I do love him and I'm going to try not get stupid fits again. I left them at Gordon Station at 4 and walked home. He says he and Creed are going to come and camp here in the Vac, and I am to ask Louie here to stay and then!! Night did accounts, etc. It is just a year to-day since dear little Annie died, just a year since the passing of the sweetest soul that ever looked with human eyes.*

'The dear little General was sitting next to his stern father.'
Seven Little Australians

Ethel Turner at the time Seven Little Australians *was written, aged 21. This photograph was printed in* Review of Reviews, *20 November 1894.*

H. R. Curlewis was admitted to the Bar in 1893. Ethel and Herbert were secretly engaged for five years.

Sophia Curlewis, Herbert's mother referred to in the text as 'Marmee'.

Frederick Charles Curlewis, Herbert's father who owned the Warren Brickworks.

18th November:

Painted for an hour or two, an opal for C., picture of a girl in a cornfield with a harvest moon behind. Mother and I left cards* at the Pockley's but they were all out. Read and finished the Bondman, *it is a splendid book.*

27th November:

Morning read A Hardy Norseman *by Edna Lyall. I went for letters and was caught in a horrid thunderstorm, it was lightning so I went to the hotel for shelter. Had a letter from C. I feel so anxious about him — he wrote it from bed, it seems when he was capsized in the Boat Race he hurt his side and now has to have an operation and stay in bed for a fortnight. He wrote me such a dear letter and wants me to send him just a line or two to read every day. Of course I shall.*

30th November:

Morning, etc. etc. we are without a servant. Afternoon went to the post. There was a letter from Herbert, also one from his mother to me and one from him to Mother, all asking for me to go down to him, he is so ill. Just as I got home Louie came, she had come all the way from Sydney to fetch me. I just crushed some things into a gladstone and went off with her by next train. After tea at their house we went out to see him, I was awfully trembling and frightened when I got to the house. He had an operation on Saturday, and was weak and upset from it and so glad I came. I stayed there till 10 pm. I liked his Father very much, also Mrs Curlewis and the five other boys.

4th December:

Got to Hermsley** rather late. Spent rest of day with H. he is getting on nicely, I have to go home on Monday, I ought to have gone yesterday. We have had some lovely hours together this week, I have read some Law to him Pollock on Torts, *it's quite interesting and also parts from* The Gadsby's *by Rudyard Kipling. Had a letter from Editor of* Illustrated *saying that though my Mutable Maiden story had not won the prize it had gone very close and he offered me two guineas if I let him publish it.* Avec plaisir, monsieur.

7th December:

Went to see Herbert, spent from 11 am to 4 pm with him. It will be as bad for me as for him to go home. O I do love him so very very much. I haven't a thought now that isn't his. I caught 6 pm train home, came up with Ella Pockley. It seems good to be home again at Inglewood, I love it here. Night did accounts, etc.

---

*Visiting cards were used frequently as an expression of welcome and friendship. It was considered polite having received a calling card to return the compliment, and even if you lived nearby it was also correct to wear hat and gloves.

**Hermsley: the name of the Curlewis family home at Newtown.

8th December:

Wrote the last and final and concluding and end chapter of Young Rebel*. I am glad. Started puzzles for* Parthenon. *Night darned and had a 'think' walk by myself.*

18th December:

Decided at the last minute that I would go to the University Dramatic Old Soldiers, *went to Mack's for T. Herbert was there by a strange coincidence, dressed there and went to the play, he didn't come, I thought it would be better not to be seen together too much.*

25th December:

Idled about, had a big dinner, Mr and Mrs Board and family came for afternoon to our surprise though not to our pleasure especially. Herbert sent me the loveliest edition of Browning, a little booklet and a letter I wrote to him but I'm afraid I can't give him the picture I painted till I see him, as it's opal and would smash in the post. Wrote also to W. Curnow and Louie and finished Tasmanian Letter.

26th December:

At 9 am I thought of a little story and wrote at it for nearly an hour. Afternoon finished 'Jerry' and copied it out. I'll send it to The Bulletin *and see if I've any luck.*

Ethel's lifelong love of literature comes to us most forcefully in this chapter — when she gave herself a treat she went to town and bought some new books and one can feel the intense pleasure that she experienced from receiving a book as a present.

(In my childhood days I clearly recall many birthdays and Christmas presents from my grandmother, or Nan as I always called her, and many a time it was a well worn and well read and greatly loved copy of an old book with slightly yellowing pages. In an attempt to make it look a little newer, Nan would glue some cream patterned wall paper on the cover and then cut out a picture to stick on the front. Inside the cover was a loving message 'To my darling Philippa on her 8th birthday. This that belonged to Nan and then to her father, is now hers for keeps. With a kiss from Nan, Dec. 1940'. Perhaps in those young days I must have shown a fleeting glimpse of my disappointment, that it was not new and shiny with crisp, clear pages, but now I realise that this was the most precious thing that she could give me because she loved it herself.)

The year is filled with undulating emotions — she wants to experience the love that she has read about and in the way that the poets tell her it happens. She loves and hates C. alternately and it is probably all summed up when she says 'I feel desperately frightened sometimes at what I have promised'. The temptation to reply to the advertisement for a governess is surely seen as a way to escape from the present, decisions and the sometimes stifling home situation.

She displays her wicked sense of fun when she was staying at the house party at Milsons Island on the Hawkesbury River — her obvious delight in the pranks and antics of applepied beds and toads, etc. Many a similar situation is related in great detail in a number of her books.

---

*This story, as far as we can ascertain, has never been published.

1892

He Would Far Rather Bury Me

The secret meetings with Herbert were a trial to Ethel and her mother, but Mr Cope's intolerance and infatuation with his step daughters necessitated a furtive relationship between the three girls and their suitors.

The *Parthenon's* voyage has lasted for three years and has been a great challenge for the young editors, but troubled waters are ahead. Ethel is not too discouraged however, and she searches for new seas to sail in.

24th January:

H.R. Came. Rex acted the part of adhesive plaster so we did not have much time together. H. brought a hypodermic syringe and strychnine in case of snake bites and gave to Mother 'to protect his property' he said. For my birthday he gave me a lovely copy of Shelley in red morocco.

29th January:

Mother and I went down by 10 am train, she went in omnibus, H. met the train and he and I walked down to meet Mother and Mr Astley for a long consultation. Mr Astley says the Parthenon *has a great future before it, that* The Bulletin *people and other journalists say that as a literary production it is really very good, but that the business part is badly managed. He says they would like to buy it or the copyright. He took* Young Rebel *home to read. Did a lot of shopping, cashed the cheque and went back to Hague's to sleep. I do like Nell, better than Louie I think, she is truer.*

30th January:

Left Hague's at 11. Went to Curlewis' as promised, saw Mrs C. for a little time, she had a bad headache. Their drawing room looks very neglected and untidy. It wants a girl's hand about it. Then went to town and H. took me out for a pull in a University skiff. Terribly wicked but no one saw us. In the domain after Ada Weiss saw first him and then me! She can add two and two I am afraid. Then we crossed to North Shore. Took the tram and walked to station getting there at 4.45 pm. From there we missed the train purposely accidentally and walked right home to Lindfield, then he had to go back, poor fellow, alone.

2nd February:

Had a long letter from Astley, he eulogises Young Rebel *very warmly and says it is 'peculiarly worthy of publication in book form and is a charming, natural tale and would, he believes, be very successful. He says if I offer it to Ward Lock they would only give me £5 or £10 perhaps and advises me to keep it till negotiations are concluded about* Parthenon, *as his principals would most likely publish it as it would 'well introduce the series of books they had been intending to issue'. He made several offers, or rather suggestions about the* Parthenon, *asking how much we would sell for and still retain our post as Editors at a fixed salary or if we would sell copyright for two years. We don't know a bit what we ought to say, not having business heads. Mother is going to town for advice.*

3rd February:

A terrible thing has happened. Alice, our new servant, a pretty, nice girl of 17 or 18, went off early this morning or in the night with her lover Alec. We are so troubled about her, they have both disappeared from Lindfield and our enquiries and searchings are of no avail.

Mother went to town and saw Mr Kettlewell of Edwards Dunlop, also Ward and Lock. They seem a bit doubtful about Astley and have given us various pieces of advice, they all say the Parthenon *is a good little property and are going to write further to us. The manager at Ward and Lock kept* Young Rebel *to read. The* Review of Reviews *mentions my 'Hidden Meaning of Pagan Myths' among the noteworthy articles in the magazines. Mrs and Miss Pockley, Mrs and Miss Crisford called and I had to entertain them.*

4th February:

Sewed all morning and nearly finished a white skirt. Read Barracks, Bivouacs and Battles *by Archibald Forbes. Alice's father came to see Mother, we are all so troubled and sorry for the girl. Mother has determined to allow her to come back. I am so very glad, it seems so wicked of people not to give her a chance, she is only 17. Everyone here says let her go, but Mother says if she can possibly save her from future wrong-doing she will, they wanted to put her in one of those horrid Reformatories for three or four years.*

5th February:

Neglected everything to read a highly sensational book, A Slender Clue *to the bitter end. It was very exciting and really well written.*

6th February:

Mrs W. brought Alice back this morning, poor little thing. I never felt so sorry for anyone in all my life, she looked so utterly despairing and wretched. She says she would rather come back here than go anywhere, for wherever else she goes she would be taunted. A police constable came and talked to Mother and Mr Cope, he says the young man Alec has been put in prison. Mother wants him to marry Alice and he is willing, so it is settled they are to be married in Court *on Thursday next and then he will be released. We shall start them in housekeeping things if they can afford to take a cottage. I expect Alice will have to stay here till she has earned more money. She looks such a child, oh it is a shame. She has had no chance, no good home or friends and she is so pretty and of course has not had the help of education.*

Sewed, etc. Had a letter from W. Curnow. Wrote to Nell and H.

8th February:
Painted a little at the background of Red Riding Hood, I have not touched it for a week. Afternoon sewed and watched the eccentric behaviour of a savage kind of cow that arrived today. Mr Langan of the Daily Telegraph *wrote to say all he knows of Mr Astley is he bears a good character but has no money, we had asked his advice.*

9th February:
Lil and I walked up to Stoney Creek Road — about three miles and back to find the laundress and tell her to come. H. came for the day, we went to the post and had letters from Nell, Louie, W. Curnow and also Blanche asking us to Brush Farm. We had such a nice long day, I don't think I have ever liked him better. He is going camping tomorrow till Tuesday. Night wrote letters.

12th February:
Sewed at camisole, read Austin Dobson. *Mr Cope went to Court, and Alice and her lover Alex were married after at the Registrar, poor little thing, I do hope she will be happy. Invitation to Ethel Pockley's wedding. Afternoon went with Mother to call on the Pockley's, Ethel got a lovely present and lots of letters while we were there. Our drawing room is horrid compared with theirs and yet lots of people think ours is pretty. Night did Tasmanian Letter packed my gladstone, Rex is coming too.*

13th February:
Rex and I caught the 8 train to town. I sent him on to Dulwich Hill and shopped all the morning and read at School of Arts. Met Mr E. Wilshire, he walked up King St with me and was embarrassingly empressé *in his manner. I don't know what was the matter, he was so stupidly complimentary and flowery and 'couldn't he see me again while he was in town, wouldn't I make just a little opportunity — well might he ride up to Lindfield'. Then I walked a little way with Guy King, he only came down from Parkes yesterday and I was the first person he knew. Went with Nell to painting lesson at St James chambers, Mr Howes is rather a nice man. His pictures are very good, but he is what he calls an impressionist and paints in that quick, rough, style that catches the effect immediately, to us used to smooth painting it seems rather as if he squirts the tubes of paint at the canvas. Only three other students.*

14th February:
Went to church. Afternoon read Proper Pride *in the hammock, then Louie and Sid came up, also Addie and Mr Fairfax and John Hyclif Fairfax junior whom I call The Morning Star. Louie and I had a long talk then Sid disburdened his conscience to me after tea in the garden. He is really in love with Lucy, it's not liking only, he says he has proposed to her and wishes she was in love with him. Nell and I read in the evening and talked nearly all night.*

16th February:
Morning started an opal for Ethel Pockley — a girl in a moon-lit harvest field. Worked a tobacco pouch for H., initials and a University cross, plush is awful to work on. Afternoon started writing a tale that I think I shall call Tekel. *Night wrote to Astley (wretch) telling him we were waiting for his reply, also did accounts and found I had 18 pence and sundry items owing at Farmers, heigho for a shower of almighty dollars.*

19th February:
Tidied my bookshelves and added another shelf, I think I like books better than anything on earth. I have about 30 really good ones, the poets, and odd volumes and about 25 or 30 miscellaneous. A very poor library Ethel chérie. *It will have to be less chiffon and such and more books. Some bound volumes 91's* Parthenon *arrived. Night did Tasmanian Letter and wrote to H. He is coming up on Wednesday, wonder if I shall like him as much. N-n-no, perhaps not, or perhaps more.*

24th February:
Herbert came. He wanted to tell Mr Cope at once, I wanted him not to just yet. He says it is dishonourable and puts him in a false position. I can quite see that, but telling him would be misery for months as well as a public engagement. I asked him to let me be quite free for six little months more, then it wouldn't be deceiving Mr Cope or anything and I would do what he liked after. He said that it would be as bad and that right must come before even love. If I thought it wrong I would never ask him to do it and oh I can't be quite engaged *yet, I feel it would choke me, I must be free a little longer. All my life I shall be bound and I will have six more months. He says I don't love him properly because I confessed I loved Mother more and would rather give him up than her. Haven't I known him only two or three years and she all my life and isn't she my own Mother? What 'Properly' is I don't know, I have never loved anyone at all, he is the first one but I do like Mother and the girls and Rex more. I can't help it. He says he loves me well enough to give me up and he feels it would be best for me. For four hours we were at it, both miserable — he loves me far too much, but I* couldn't *give in and the result is we have completely parted, for ever and forever. Everything is at an end. I shall burn all his letters. I wanted to send the books he gave me back and he said 'for God's sake don't, — burn them. It would be sacrilege, book burning,' I will send them back in about a week. I don't think I am wrong in this. If he is willing to give me up just because I don't want Mr Cope told, how can he call it me giving him up. Anyway I don't seem to care a bit, only I hate to make him feel wretched — I feel so hard-hearted*

and hate myself for giving him so much pain — his reason is purely conscientious and oh, he does love me. I won't *give in.*

25th February:
Morning nothing, afternoon daubed a little at Red Riding Hood for appearance's sake, also got his letters all together to burn. Mr Cope came home at 6 pm and brought me a letter from Rose who is staying in town the night. Rose enclosed a letter from him, he had given it her at the boat this morning, oh such a letter. I do hate myself. He says he is wrong and that I shall have my six months, oh I am a hateful thing to have hurt him so much. I wrote to him.

26th February:
I am sorry I wrote, I have been thinking it over, he assumes I shall be ready to go back the second he likes. As though I haven't an atom of pride. I wrote again and said I had considered it and everything must be completely over. It is pouring with rain at last.

27th February:
Caught the 10 am train and had to run all the way and then fainted in the train or went unconscious. H. was at the station and Rose, I gave him the note I wrote yesterday, he hadn't got the other one, I am so glad. The bus had gone so I was obliged to walk to the tram and he came too. He begged me so hard all the way not to break it off, it was hard to hold out, but I did. Went to Troedel's, got cheque, shopped, had lunch at the Cascade, went to painting, only Nell and I there. Nell was ill and went home early. At 5 pm went out to Louie's, it was too wet for picnic. I promised to give him an answer tomorrow night, he wouldn't take this morning as final, it will be just the same though tomorrow. Louie says that I am heartless and he has been so awfully miserable. I gave him a promise that I would think well about it tonight.

28th February:
I couldn't do it. Oh, I have been proud and horrid, I seemed to see it all in the night. I got up and wrote him a note — he had asked me to forgive him, I asked him to forgive me which was far more as it should be. I dreaded the thought of him going out sailing in the rough wind without knowing so I got up early and went out to Stanmore at 9.30 am intending to give a child the note to take in, I thought he would be in bed. And just as I got to the street who should come up but himself. I did wish for an earthquake. Everything is all right, we had the Mack's study to ourselves all the morning and part of the afternoon. I shall never doubt again that I love him and I will never hurt him again by saying things, I didn't think I hurt him so much.

2nd March:
Painted, read Pickwick Papers *again, quarrelled with Lil in morning. Evening sewed, read and made up with same young person. I don't like the way she treats H.*

3rd March:

Wedding of Ethel Pockley and Dr Hinder. Mother, Lil, Rose and I went to wedding. Mr Cope didn't. It was very nice indeed, crowds of people, 7 bridesmaids and everything en règle. *When I am married (how strange that sounds) I should like a big ceremony I think, it is the great day of one's life, and it is nice to have all one's friends to wish one Godspeed on the strange new voyage. I believe though I should be afraid and do the 'disappearing trick' at the church door. A special train took us up to Lorne, some 140 or 50 guests, where there was a swell breakfast and afterwards at 3.30 pm the 'happy couple' departed, among showers of rice and shoes, for Hobart.*

7th March:

All my world has gone wrong and I feel as blue as — oh there's no simile. Kismet *and yet they're only small things I suppose. First, the* Parthenon *will probably publish its own funeral number this month and what will the Turners do then poor things. I shall go out and be a governess I think, I can't live on £10 a year and I won't let Mr Cope keep me after being independent for over three years. Second my* Young Rebel *came back from the publishers — a good story they say but it doesn't pay them to publish local things, of course too, it's not a book, only a bit of one. All these things are against me.*

11th March:

Caught the 10 am train to town, shopped in morning. In afternoon went to Hermsley as promised for an hour. Then to the Ackman's, it was pouring wet. They gave a dinner party in honour of my small person. They have everything very nice, butler in attendance, numberless courses, etc. of course it's easy when one has the money. A Musical Evening. Hannah entertained, she is bright and clever certainly but hasn't a scrap of shyness or reserve, she is a precocious young thing too, 16 and a good deal older than I. Still I like her.

13th March:

Went to picnic. Steam launch round the harbour, and then we had a champagne lunch. After we all went back to the Ackman's and the singing was divine, Travaligni especially.

14th March:

Left Ackman's at 11 am. I like them fairly but they are rather overpowering and always in a state of beatific complacence at the marvellous cleverness of their children. Had a horrid fainting attack in the School of Arts, the room was close and misty with the pouring rain. I suppose I had a headache. Didn't go to Mrs Creed's, met Mother and came home. Oh, so thankfully. Dear old Inglewood I do love it. Got a new photo holder also two easels. Lil and I are wondering if we could get a small class together here instead of being governesses.

16th March:

H. came for day and Rex was at home! I read Law to him in the drawing room, it is his exam tomorrow. Night corrected proofs did accounts. I am going to save up for a horse.

22nd March:

Had two letters from H, one by the post saying he would know the result of his exam today. Then I saw it in the paper — he has passed, got his L.L.B. and third class honours. Oh I am so very very very glad. He sent a second letter by Rosie telling me and saying he is coming up tomorrow, that he is possessed of 70 devils and has an intolerable longing to see me. I am to exorcise them. Oh I do want to see him and I'm afraid Nina and Ethel Garnsey are coming up.

23rd March:

H. came, we had a little picnic at the top of the hill and then suddenly decided to tell Mr Cope at once, I gave in at last, Mother wants it too. He went down to the station when Mr Cope's train came in and said he wanted to speak to him. Mr Cope said he wouldn't hear of anything, he wouldn't listen and snapped his fingers at him. He has not been violent since he came home, but just in a white heat, he won't open his lips to me but wrote me two notes both saying he distinctly and utterly refused to sanction an engagement, that nothing would make him change, after I was of age he supposed I could do as I liked. Everything is lovely.

24th March:

Nina and Ethel Garnsey came up and we had a pleasant day. Rosie brought me a note from H. and I got two more from him by the post, one written at 8 and the other at 11. Mrs Montgomery called and is going to send her two little girls to us to be taught for 3 guineas a quarter. Fancy us teachers!

26th March:

Lil and I went down by the 8 am. H. and Pickburn met us and then the Mack's and we all went down to Double Bay. Then we went on board and sailed down the harbour, some of the girls were a bit squeamish, I wasn't a scrap. Had lunch at Middle Harbour, played quoits and sat about. Then came back, it was lovely and rather rough which I liked.

27th March:

Morning talked to Louie. Afternoon to Herbert in the study. At night we two sat on the back balcony. I never loved him so much. 'Que splendid spirit, your soul and mine'. That is what he said and what I felt.

30th March:

Finished painting opal for Nell. Mrs Bear is coming to me for painting — two guineas a quarter. Painted a little picture, then Lily and I quarrelled and she kept on nagging and nagging at me till I threw the canvas at her in a fit of temper. Of course it missed her and fell on the carpet and spoiled. She is perfectly hateful today and always is throwing Herbert and Louie at me 'cause she knows it vexes me most.

31st March:
Took a big basket of food and groceries to Alice. They have a wretched little shanty cottage with one room divided into bed and living room. They seem happy though and look ridiculously young to be married, just like a boy and girl. Mother has sent them a little furniture up and they are getting a little more comfortable. Had a letter from H. Mr Cope has not addressed a word to me except he snapped out that H. could come to Inglewood so long as he didn't offend his eyesight. That is because he knows we would meet outside. Night darned and idled.

1st April:
H. came, we had a lovely morning together over the hills and far away. He says he has taught me to love him at last and indeed he has, I really date my real love for him from last Saturday night. We told Rex and that young person said he gave his consent. Mr Cope came home at 3 pm which considerably surprised us. He would not go into the drawing room however and kept sending Mother up to chaperone us, he wouldn't have us left together. Night read and wrote Tasmanian Letter.

4th April:
Morning our two pupils came, Florrie and Alme Montgomery. I taught them, it seems so funny to be teaching, it is interesting though and they are very nice little children. Night started a new story. I'm not sorry the Parthenon has gone, it is such a relief. Forced writing is bad I am sure.

11th April:
Sewed, walked and read. Mr Cope is still horrid, he never opens his lips to me and looks at me as if he hates me.

18th April:
Packed a picnic basket and caught the 10 am train to Gordon. Louie and I had arranged a quartet picnic, she and I, Mr Creed and Herbert. And Leslie came and Mr Creed didn't, we were all so vexed, I was sorry for Louie. We stayed till 8.30 pm had a perfect day. Mother was frightfully angry with me for staying out. I did get in a row.

21st April:
I am having a serge dress made at home to save my pocket but being near hopeless ruin with it, Mother came to the rescue. Ruby is staying with us. But I feel as if my heart would break sometimes when I look at her and catch a little gesture or look of Annie's. Oh the awful silence of Death, 'is there never a chink in the heavens above where they listen for words from below'. Mother and I went to Government House Garden Party in afternoon. Crowds there I knew, liked it very well.

25th April:
Mr Cope and I had a fearful scene, he says he will compel me to do just what he says, that he won't let me go to town to stay for two or three days, that he'll write to Mrs Mack, that he'll make me prove my age by law, etc. etc. etc., it was awful. Then Mother

and Lily quarrelled with me, it must be all this wretchedness that is making me touchy, Lily is always saying things about Herbert and taunting me with only liking him and no one else till she gets unendurable. I never was so miserable in my life, I shall leave home and go and be a governess somewhere, Mother is very cold to me and says she hopes I will go, everything is wretched, wretched, wretched.

26th April:
Taught Florrie, made a serge under-skirt and did some things I shall want when I go away. I wouldn't stop here. Had a letter from H. oh such a nice letter, I don't know how I could stand everything if it wasn't for him.

9th May:
H. came, his eyes have been troubling him and as he is to have a holiday Mother says he can come up as often as he likes this week.

14th May:
Etc. etc. in morning. Afternoon Herbert came, Mr Cope wouldn't put in an appearance. H. and I sat out on verandah for two hours in a very wild dog manner, he smoking, I embroidering; then we had afternoon tea and he went home. Mr Cope sent word that he was to come to dinner next Saturday and was to walk up with him! Are the heavens going to fall?

15th May:
Finished Through the Dark Night. Read Mirage and In a Grass Country. Had literary indigestion and went to church at night. Came home with Pockleys and went to supper there.

16th May:
Taught, sewed, afternoon painted from the top of the hill. H. wrote to Mr Cope thanking him for his concession. Mr Cope said it was 'very decent' of him; he is facetious now and keeps making funny remarks, but won't speak to me.

21st May:
Lucy and Earnest O'Brien came for day at 10 am and Herbert for dinner. Mr Cope didn't come home until 6 pm but when he did he was quite respectable, in evening he sang and we all sat in the drawing room, H. and I had exactly one and a half minutes alone.

24th May:
Afternoon went to Pockley's for afternoon tea. Lil dressed up for fun as an old lady, a friend of ours, it took Harold in best of all, he was talking to her quite a quarter of an hour before he knew her. We did have fun.

29th May:

Mr Cope is the most inexplicable mystery of a man! He has been as nice as possible to Herbert, they shun the subject of 'me' and have been like dear friends all day. I can't understand him. At night Mr Cope sang about a hundred songs, then they smoked and H. left about 9 pm, we have had no time alone since yesterday afternoon.

30th May:

Taught in morning and painted a little opal and a jar between whiles. Lil came home at 6 pm. Talked to her and read The Light That Failed *— Rudyard. It is beautiful. I feel all stirred up and I want — what, I don't know, something vague and intangible.*

31st May:

I have been in a tense all day — it is more than a mood. I feel aching to go and live where life is lived, not just passed through. No, even Herbert doesn't satisfy me though I wouldn't let him know and though of course I love him more than anyone. The quiet and the gum trees and the grass are oppressive, they sink into one's soul and stifle one. I think I am growing older, my head is not always in cloudland and poetry now. I have been very young I think for 20, most girls of 14 are older. Some things are bitterly disappointing. I don't half understand them, I don't want to either. 'Life sweet as perfume and pure as prayer' — It has been and shall be.

2nd June:

Sewed, wrote a little at a tale I have just started, I tore the old one up but am calling this one Tekel, *my head is full of ideas if only my pen can catch them, it won't go quickly enough, cold-hearted little imp. Someone in* Patience *says 'Do you know what it is to seek for oceans and to find puddles, to long for whirlwinds and have to do the best you can with the bellows.' That's my case.*

12th June:

Mr Cope and Herbert made stiles over the fences, they seemed very friendly. I read Caesar's Column *(absurd), afternoon he, Rex and I sat out in the sunshine, it is glorious weather. Night H. and Mr Cope talked until late, I tendered the olive branch in the shape of a good night kiss to Mr Cope and was chillingly received.*

14th June:

Went to post. There was a long, long letter from H. asking me to try to be reconciled with Mr Cope. I want to very much for I do love him very dearly and this estrangement hurts a good deal. I wrote him, Mr Cope, a long and loving letter asking him to forgive me and be friends.

16th June:

Mr Cope's answer came. He won't forgive. Oh he is hard. He says he would far rather bury me than give me to any man, that after Mother he always loved me better than anyone on earth, etc. etc. That he should have the same feeling of abhorrence to any man. I have bruised myself against a cold stone wall all for nothing and the smart is pretty bad.

17th June:
Taught or rather 'broke the children up'. Gave each one a prize and in afternoon we had a Dolls' Tea Party.

26th June:
Mr Cope is a bit horrid again about Herbert, he hates us to speak to one another or to sit near one another. H. went home in afternoon, walked down, we three girls walked with him past Roseville and coming back were frightened by a bull.

28th June:
Made Sid Mack come up for the day, we dressed him up like a fashionable lady, he looked splendid — a golden curly wig, bonnet, veil, riding habit skirt and long jacket. Then we took him up to the Pockley's to try to take them in. They laughed till they cried over him. Harold had come up in the train with him however and guessed.

1st July:
Caught the 5.30 pm to Neutral Bay, had dinner at the Doak's, then dressed and went to the Atalanta Dance, it was very nice, I enjoyed it muchly, met lots of people I knew and danced the programme through all but one dance when my hair came down. When all was over decided I was not quite so mad after dances as I used to be.

3rd July:
Got up at 11 am. Read Two Little Wooden Shoes *by Ouida, my first, it's pretty but horrid, I don't like her. H. came at 2.30 pm, we sat in the study together and had a lovely afternoon. I am very anxious about him for he is getting thin and owns to feeling weak. At night we were together too for a little time. We are both going to make for ourselves famous names, I am to write. And I am to start Greek with him as soon as I have caught up my Latin a little more.*

4th July:
I read the loveliest book or part of it after 11 pm last night Not All In Vain *by Ada Cambridge — I think I like it better than any book I have read. A pig has been killed and all day we have been making sausages, pork pies, etc., and Mother has been getting hams ready, it's our first experience. I made some native currant jelly.*

17th July:
Herbert and Mr Cope went to Mrs John's in morning, afterwards H. was showing Rex how to tie hands together illustrating with mine — just knotting a string round my wrists. Mr Cope was so angry and told him he'd trouble him to try it on Rex's hands not mine and H. was angry. We quarrelled all the afternoon but made up later.

19th July:

Lil came back and brought little Dolly Curlewis with her to stay for a few days. She is such a dear little child, I am so fond of her. Mr Cope likes her too very much. From little things she lets drop occasionally I know they must have a wretchedly comfortless home, it is hard on poor Herbert, I feel I can never make it up to him quite for all he has to stand at home.

27th July:

Dolly went home, I shall miss the dear little thing very much. Went to post and idled all the afternoon. I am so anxious, Rose brought me a line from Herbert, he is to have the operation on Tuesday. I dread it unutterably *but daren't let him know I do, he says he doesn't care a straw.*

2nd August:

Went out to Hermsley in direct disobedience to Mr Cope but I certainly owe something to Herbert too and at any rate when he was in danger I wasn't going to let anyone stop me. He had two doctors — McAllister and Blaxland and was under chloroform. I went to him with Mrs Curlewis soon after the operation. He was quite off his head and kept calling Ethel, Ethel — where's Ethel, all the time. Slept at Hermsley. Thank God it is over.

10th August:

Idled about, I feel horribly out of time with everything, went to post and gave Miss Archibald a painting lesson.

21st August:

Talked on an infinitude of subjects — literature, love, psychology, etc. I got into a many-mooded mood. Exaltation and melancholy, excitedness and wanting-to-cryness. And he understood exactly — oh it is so nice to feel sure of being understood. We both feel it. No one on earth but I know him as he really is. He told me one secret he has never told anyone.

25th August:

Taught the children while Rex went to the post. Letters from H. 'Aunt Elgitha' and 'A Dreadful Pickle' the stories I sent to Ward Lock's a month ago have been returned. Alas! I knew they would be though. There was a great crisis this morning. Mr Cope has been as horrid as he could for these five months and then this morning he suddenly stooped down and brushed my face with his beard. I couldn't be hypocrite enough to turn and kiss him thankful for his tardy forgiveness, especially when I have done nothing to be forgiven for. I turned my head away instinctively, it was all over and done in less than a second, he declares he won't speak to me again this side of the grave.

26th August:

I wrote to Mr Cope, also to Herbert. Mother says I am to go to town till Monday each week and then go away when I have finished teaching the children in September. I couldn't go however because Mother is ill in bed, so I couldn't leave her, H. will be disappointed not to see me. Rose is so naughty, and Mr Cope is horrid, and Mother ill, and the servant an idiot, all these things are against me, and I wish I lived on another planet.

10th September:
Etc. in morning. I asked Mabel Pockley to the Australie Picnic and we caught the 1 train down and the 3 Fern Bay steamer. It was an awfully jolly picnic, I don't remember ever a nicer one. We played cricket and rounders in the afternoon, then had a nice sit-down tea in the pavilion, poultry, jellies and all, en règle, *I went in with Dr Trechman of the Varsity and afterwards gave him three dances. The pavilion was splendid, we had barn dances, Swedish, etc. etc. I danced with W. Curnow, Wolstenholme, Davis, Pickburn, etc. etc. etc. and talked to W. Curnow coming home on the boat in the moonlight. When we got to the wharf there was Mr Creed. I was surprised. He walked for 20 minutes with us down George St and I learnt afterwards from him that Herbert had been following us, ill as he was and afraid I shouldn't like him to meet us.*

19th September:
Went to bed this morning with an attack of Russian influenza, I felt horribly ill, a maddening headache, sore throat, pains in the limbs and feverish. Had to send Mrs Archbold away. New servants Amy and John came.

26th September:
Felt much better, so went to town and did a bit of shopping. A poem of mine, 'Footsteps' appeared in the Tasmanian Mail. *At night thought out a story, then started it in pen and ink, I think I will write a series, three or four of them. I have called it Sketches Behind the Counter No. 1.* The Little Duchess. *I fancy it's not bad.*

1st October:
Went to a picnic at Kogarah. Most irregular, H. and I went first at 11.30 am and waited for Louie and Mr Creed, they didn't come for a long time and we got hungry and went to a little shop for dinner — quite a lucky chance, a nice old woman who served us up hot roast mutton and potatoes, apple charlotte and nice tea. We felt quite 'Saturday People, 'Arry and 'Arriet' out together, not a soul we knew anywhere. Mr Creed and Louie both arrived later and we talked and talked. Louie gave me such a grand book, The Love Letters of a Worldly Woman.

4th October:
Did some shopping, called in to see Mr Spooner about those stories of mine and caught the 3 pm train home. H. came up to the station with me. Night wrote some social paragraphs, 'Twixt you and me and the doorpost' and sent them on spec to Mr Spooner.

7th October:
The children came for the last time, we are giving up teaching, it's too much of a tie and too little 'lucre'! I must use my pen again and see if I can get on a little that way, I'm nearly bankrupt. Gave Miss A. her lesson.

12th October:
Had a letter from Mr Spooner. Editor of Illustrated *saying the matter I sent was very good and would I write a similar column every week! He asked me to go and see him.*

13th October:
Went to town to see Mr Spooner. I am engaged to write a column weekly of chatty and personal matter. Half a guinea a column. Hurrah — it's big print and spacings. I think will call it Between Ourselves. *Went to Nina's for lunch and afternoon. Mrs Church was away so Miss Nina was entertaining* sola cum sola *(Jo Woods) in the drawing room. She was so glad it was only me. I went and read in her bedroom. Walked to train with H.*

17th October:
Sewed a little, talked to Miss Barry, gathered maiden hair and flowers for her to take home. Gave Miss A. her last lesson and she paid her two guineas and thanked me for teaching her. H. sent me a copy of the Mikado — *pianoforte score — by Mr Cope! He, Mr Cope, says he shall tell him he won't allow me to receive presents from him. I wonder what he would say if he knew about the bracelet and the books.*

27th October:
Caught the 1 pm train, shopped, met H., went to Mack's and he and I had the study, for a short time. Had tea, dressed and went to the theatre. I wouldn't let H. sit with us because of people talking. I didn't enjoy the play as much as I used to enjoy University things.

29th October:
There has been a fearful row between H. and Mr Cope, it started over a very little thing, Mr C. told H. not to come up to-day and not to give presents to any member of his family. H. asked his reasons for the latter and Mr C. flew in a fearful rage and called him some dreadful names, a . . . liar, with an epithet was one. Then Mr C. came home and had a row with Mother and me and everyone. He says H. shall never enter his doors again.

4th November:
Deb. and I got up at 5.30 am and went for a ride, I rode Elise's horse, it goes splendidly, we went about ten miles, my hair was all down my back and my hat off when I arrived home. Edie drove me to the station and I was shopping at Anthony's and in town all day.

Faculty of Law Graduation 1892. Right, Herbert Raine Curlewis, Arthur James Kelynack, Sidney Mack (brother of Louie), and John Meillon (grandfather of the actor John Meillon).

The O'Brien homestead at Bondi where Herbert Curlewis was born in 1869.

Miss Lilian Turner. A writer in The Woman at Home *said: 'Lilian has been inspired by her sister's success, but her* metier *is somewhat different. She takes social life in Australia generally for her province, and in* The Lights of Sydney — *which was published by Cassell — she has achieved at least one conspicuous success.'*

Bukyangi, Powell St, Killara, built by Charles and Sarah Jane Cope.

This photograph appeared in The Woman at Home *and in the accompanying interview it said:
'Ethel Turner, the romancist of childhood, seems in some respects little more than a child herself;
she is only in her twenties, and has the happy temperament which never appears to be "grown up".'*

*The little study in which Ethel Turner wrote a number of her early books and which was later
used as a work room by Lilian.*

GUM LEAVES

BY ETHEL TURNER

WITH ODDMENTS BY OTHERS

PICTURES BY D H SOUTER

WILLIAM BROOKS & CO.
SYDNEY & BRISBANE

Gum Leaves *published in 1899, contained a collection of poems, stories, and letters to Dame Durden*
(Ethel's pseudonym when she was the children's editor of the Illustrated News).

10th November:

Went to see Mr Spooner at 11, he had written to me to come in to see him and I didn't get the letter till yesterday. He said he had wanted me to write Social as well as my column, but as I didn't come it might be too late, he doesn't think the other lady will suit him and will let me know next week.

18th November:

Saw Mr Spooner. I am so disappointed for Lil as well as myself that he has arranged someone else to do the Social column. But I have nothing to grumble at, he has asked me to write an extra column of Between Ourselves and take complete charge of the Children's Page*. He paid me three guineas.

26th November:

My story, 'Laddie' came out in Illustrated *and the rest of the Children's Page. H. came up in afternoon and we went for a walk. We had a dreadful quarrel, my fault of course, I said I broke off the engagement from that minute and he couldn't get over it. I suppose I was a little wretch.*

28th November:

Pulled an old white muslin to pieces and half remade it à la mode. *Went to post. A note from Herbert, such a nice one. Rose brought another up from him at night, he may come up tomorrow.*

29th November:

Herbert came up and we went over the hill top, we had a little picnic and all is right again. In afternoon I walked to the post with Mabel Pockley and told her about my engagement — they have seen me so often with him they must know — she was so nice and very interested of course.

12th December:

Spent rather an unprofitable day. Painted a tambourine so badly I must do it again. Idled in afternoon and did part of Children's Page at night.

24th December:

Lil, Rose, Rex and I went to town and shopped all day. Between us we got Mother a lovely little gold brooch, a silver bread fork and I got her too a new screen of pleated art muslin for drawing room. For Mr Cope we got a Canary Breeding Cage and a silk handkerchief. For Lil I got a bottle of scent and a serge skirt. For Rose a lace cape and 1/-. Rex 1/6. Louie a scent bottle, etc. etc. My Xmas presents were, from Mr Cope 8 collars and a silk handkerchief. Mother a writing case and nailbrush, Lil Everybody's Book of Poems *and from H. Carrol's* Through the Looking Glass. *He says* The Bulletin *editor says my story 'The Little Duchess' is good and accepted, he is going to write to me. My first thing in* The Bulletin! *I believe I shall be successful in the literary line after all. I will be.*

---

*The Children's Page in this newspaper and other subsequent papers became a major part of her life for the next forty years.

Memo written last day of '92:

Last year I said I would have three of all clothing made and £10 banked. I have not quite succeeded. I am two winter skirts and three nightgowns short. In the bank I have £10.

By next year this time I hope to have deposited £50 in the bank and six of everything. To have taken lessons in Singing and Music. To have finished my book Tekel. *To have one children's book published, and have written several short stories for* Bulletin *and other papers as well as any regular work.*

The relationship between her writing and her personal daily experiences is now very apparent. Each event and emotion she puts aside in safekeeping for use at some later date, and these she will draw upon when necessary for a story not yet conceived.

The snake-bite reference in January, when H. gave a hypodermic syringe and strychnine to be used for her protection, she quickly fashioned into a short story called *As It Fell Out* published in the *Little Duchess*.

In June there was an incident recorded of Sid Mack dressing up as a fashionable lady. Here again she used the humour of that occasion in her short story, *A Modern Achilles* which also appeared in *The Little Duchess*. In this the young man dresses up and acts as chaperone for a boating picnic. All sorts of adventures befall him before he is finally unmasked.

Throughout her writing Ethel has no hesitation in embroidering here and trimming there in order to make the garment fit, and sometimes it becomes quite confusing to determine which event was real and recorded in her diary, or which was nearly real with a few embellishments.

Was she ambitious? I believe she must have been although she didn't quite know in which field — although determined to write, she wanted to paint well and sing or perhaps be a famous actress — so much for youth and its aspirations. She was one of the fortunate ones whose fame was recognised only a year or so later.

1893
A Red Letter Day

Quite by chance Ethel discovers that her gift as a writer is in portraying children. It is hard to determine whether she was able to recall her own youthful sentiments or whether she observed the behaviour and strange little ways of children she encountered — perhaps it was a combination of both. It has been said of her that she was a child herself writing about children. She had the key to unlock their innermost thoughts, and as with a talented artist, she drew her pictures vividly and realistically, with unusual and varied shades and hues. Her characters became real people painted with exquisite touches of love and humour.

2nd January:
Had a very nice letter from Editor of Bulletin. *He says 'The Little Duchess'* is a neat little story, very naturally told and all the better for being out of the beaten track of the* Bulletin. *It is to be kept for a special occasion. He sent me a cheque for £2 for it. Wrote to H. There has been a row at home between Lil and Mr Cope and Lil has left home. Story MSS's — Bobbie, etc. posted to England to Arthur Shaw, started 'On the Manly Rocks' —* A sweet small tragedy. *Our cow and calf arrived on Saturday.*

18th January:
Finished and copied out short story 'In the Coil of Things'. I may keep it for the Winter Annual *we are thinking of getting up.* I do *want* Fame — *plenty of it. Today I feel I want it almost more than anything, nothing else can quite satisfy me. If a fairy came and offered me Love or Fame, of course I should choose Love. No, I don't see why I shouldn't have both. I don't want to be married though for a long, long time, a little time ago I thought I did but I want to have a tilt with Fame first. Conceited little ape, you want your ears boxing.*

20th January:
Wrote a little, had shoals of letters for Dame Durden, read Little Minister. *It is a lovely book. Oh, there isn't anything like Love. Fame would be a Dead Sea apple if one hadn't love too, I don't know how I could have thought that Fame might be almost as satisfying, why I believe why I want it chiefly is just to make him more proud of me.*

**The Little Duchess* was included in a collection of short stories that she published in 1896 under the same title.

21st January:

Morning wrote Between Ourselves *and did housework. H. came at 2 o'clock. He gave me a lovely little pair of ivory opera glasses, gold mounted, in a leather case with S.E.B.T. on it – for my birthday next week. Afternoon we went for a walk, we are getting bold. I told him what I had thought about Fame and he said I didn't know what love was if I thought that. He misunderstood me I think, because when I hadn't just that silly fit on, I knew they weren't even to be thought of together. As to knowing what Love is! I can hardly believe I am the same girl who said she loved him a year ago, I didn't know then I own, but now!*

24th January:

Seven L. Aust. – sketched it out. H. came up for the day, we walked about, had a tête à tête *in the summer house. I am 21 today, an infant no longer. I shall have to stop Herbert calling me 'Baby' as he always does. Lily gave me a beautiful edition of O. W. Holmes* (Breakfast Table) *three blue and gold volumes in a case.*

27th January:

Night started a new story that I shall call Seven Little Australians. *I don't think I'll let it go in the* Illustrated, *if I can do without it there, I'll see if I can get it published in book form.*

4th February:

Rosie went off to Bowral to Mrs Laby's boarding school by the 9.45 am train from here. Afternoon H. came up, we wandered about the orchard and talked. Talked financial matters too. He lent his mother £25 and won't bother her for it. Though it is just what he needs to start his chambers. He may go in for a grammar school mastership. The new servants Mary and James left. My new bookcase came, a little beauty, dark wood with glass doors, the books look lovely in it. I have 68 good ones. I am getting quite anxious about one of my ears. I can't hear out of it at all and think I must go to the doctor.

11th February:

Read a little of Puck *by Ouida, it is* horrible. *So coarse and horrid, I couldn't read it all and shall never read her again. H. came at 2 pm. He had rather a bad fit of 'the blues'. He is very anxious to start in Chambers at once and had got the £25 he needs and then lent it to his mother. Now she can't possibly pay him back. I have £15 already and shall have £10 more in a week or so and shall* make *him borrow it from me. I am having a great piece of work to persuade him but I'll never forgive him if he doesn't, I should* love *him to have it from me. I shan't let Lil or Mother know.*

12th February:

Wrote out two chapters of my book – Seven Little Australians.

17th February:

Went to town by the 8 am, straight out to Dr Quaife, he examined my ear again and then sent me to his brother who is a specialist. I put in rather a rough time, it is a very unpleasant kind of operation and the worst is I have to go again a few times. Night wrote to H., a very personal letter and told him he was terribly careless about his appearance.

18th February:

Wrote and copied out before tea a story about children though not a children's story, 'Two Little Bush Flowers', I hope it will do for Annual, *I think it is rather good myself and Lil likes it very much. I wish I hadn't written H. that letter, I have sent another one to say he is not to open it.*

20th February:

H. came for day unbeknowedst to the Power that be's. He said he was pleased *about the letter! Because it showed I would say anything to him and more it was nice to feel someone took some interest in him. He* did *look nice, he had a high collar, white pique tie, new hat — altogether I have never seen him look so nice. I gave him £22 of the £25 I am going to lend him. I* do *love him having it from me and he says he shall like to feel he owed his start to me. Talked about the furniture for his Chambers, etc. etc.*

17th March:

Went to town and had my ear done, it has gone back Dr Quaife says, he gave me a kind of medicinal snuff to take. Met Louie and went to School of Arts and had lunch at Fresh Food, spent an hour at Angus and Robertson and bought three books. Went to Hermsley for evening. Herbert was this day admitted 'in the presence of the Full Court, to the Bar'. H. R. Curlewis B.A. L.L.B. Barrister-at-Law, it takes quite a lot of ink to write.

19th March:

Stayed in bed till 12 noon! I who get up at 6.30 am or 6.45 am. Mr Creed and H. sailed all day. I talked Gum Leaves *with Louie and wrote to J. Le Gay Brereton.*

23rd March:

Wrote at a story part of the day 'The Man with the Iron Mask'. I shall send it to The Bulletin, *it's rather good I think. H. was to have come today but he wrote an excited letter instead. He has got a brief!! And a splendid one too, a big one, junior to two of the best counsel against the best.*

27th March:

Read most of the day The Wages of Sin *by Lucas Malet. Louie and Mr Creed quarrelled, and Louie says they have broken it off for ever. That means a fortnight I suppose. H. won his case and Mr Brown went to his Chambers and insisted on him accepting a £5 note in addition to his fees. That is very good for a start. He wanted to be married on it right away.*

30th March:

We were expecting Rosie home today but they have written from boarding school to say that the knee she hurt will not bear the journey and she is to stay there for the holidays. All at once we decided I should go up to Bowral for a few days and see her. And then, after 2.30 pm, I wrote the whole of Between Ourselves, next week's Children's Page and a bit of the following weeks. Pretty quick work.

1st April:

Caught 8 am train to town, bought new umbrella, shoes etc. then on to train for Bowral. Mrs Laby and Rosie met me. Was introduced to crowds of girls, a Miss Dixson and several others, had a long talk to dear old Rosie.

5th April:

There is the dearest old lady here, she is 86 and her husband was Colonel Otterly of the Royal Engineers. She has lived the most wonderful life, was brought up in St James Palace where her father was a favourite courtier in George IV's time, went to India, was attacked by pirates, shot a tiger, and did wonderful things in India. I sat in her room all the evening and she told me hundreds of stories. I am really fond of the girls, they are very nice— I think they reciprocate it too. They quarrel for the last kiss from me at night, who is to sit next to me, etc. etc.

7th April:

We hastily arranged a picnic to the Fitzroy Falls. Mrs Dixson and I drove down, and hired a drag and four horses (we subscribed for it amongst us) and we went out to Fitzroy Falls — 34 miles there and back. They are really splendid and the scenery around magnificent. Had a very pleasant day and much climbing down ladders and places warned to be unsafe. Night danced and had games. Mrs Dixson and I have quite become friends and she has begged me to go and see her when I am in Sydney. They are the big tobacco people, very rich but not nouveau at all. Mr Cope would turn his nose up though.

10th April:

Caught the 9 am train from Bowral, all the school and Mrs Dixson came to the station to see me off. H. met me in Sydney and I went out to Louie's for afternoon as she is very ill and going to have an operation.

26th April:

Went to Ed. Bulletin, he has accepted Lil's story, 'Orange Blossoms or Weeds', I am glad, it's her very first. And he made me a present of mine 'In the Coil of Things', it certainly is sick. H. came to bus with me, he is very dispirited with all these losses, his family is in a very bad way, the ES, AC has stopped payment, and the Brick Company is to be wound up he thinks and Mr Curlewis will be out of employ. The London Chartered Bank has suspended payments and the distress in Sydney is getting worse, one thousand bank clerks are out of employ with all these banks going. It is worst time ever known here.

29th April:

The opening of Milsons Point Railway today. Dr Quaife sent me a bill for five guineas for my ear. It's very heavy I think 15/- a visit considering I went to him and my ear is rather worse than better.

3rd May:

Sorted out old letters, burnt quantities and ribboned others. Had a battle with the moths in my wardrobe in afternoon.

9th May:

H. came at 11.15 am as it was 'Anniversary Day'. We have been engaged two years. Took our lunch out over the hill, I had a 'Mood' — I haven't had one for a very long time now and can't think what gave it me.

16th May:

Read, wrote, sewed, etc. The Commercial Bank has gone now. I think the end of the world must be at hand. That's the fifth big one — seventh in Melbourne.

16th May:

The Tasmanian Mail *wrote to say they were retrenching and must cut off the Sydney letter — £20 a year less. I have given my share of it up to Lil so it is all her loss, poor kid.*

18th May:

Went to town to Mr Spooner. The blow has fallen, my luck was too good to last I suppose, they are retrenching in the office and are 'reluctantly compelled to do without Between Ourselves', at any rate for a time. That means £55 per annum in future instead of £110 from Illustrated. *Heigho and again heigho. At night went to University Dramatic and enjoyed myself muchly.*

19th May:

Mr Spooner introduced me to Mr Bennett, proprietor of all the three papers. He's a portly Philistine. He asked about my stories and seemed very interested. Introduced me to Mr Jeffrey of the Town and Country Journal *and I left 'Wilkes of Waterloo' and the 'Toychild' there for him to read*. He said Wilkes was an 'excellent story' — he shouldn't have thought it had been written by a woman, much less a young girl. Asked how long I had been writing, why I hadn't sent to England, etc. He's a nice man.*

29th May:

Went to David Jones' Sale, bought stuff for a white crepe kind of dress at a reduction, don't like it. Went to Farmers 20 per cent sale. All Sydney's selling off. Town was crowded with people waiting to see the new Governor arrive. Went with Mrs Daintrey to the old Daintrey's. They have a very nice old-fashioned place and 20 acres of ground right in Randwick and overlooking Coogee.

---

*Both these are to be found in the collection of short stories called *The Little Duchess*.

12th June:

I have written and suggested a Children's Page for the Town and Country, *The Land of Little People, I wish the Editor would engage me to do one weekly. Wrote at my play, I am getting quite excited about it. I have called it* The Wig. *There is nothing like cheek, when I have finished I shall calmly march down and take it to Mr Boucicault.*

17th June:

Finished my play. Hurrah it's the first I've ever attempted in my life and I don't believe it's bad. It isn't ambitious, only a One Act thing.

22nd June:

Town at 10 am with Mother. An auspicious occasion. We went to Criterion Theatre and asked for Mr Boucicault. He came in presently, a short clean-shaven man. — I, in a small voice 'I have written a short one-act play and should be glad if you would read it Mr Boucicault.' He, consolingly 'Oh, everyone is writing plays nowadays — I'll read it sometime, not for a month or two I daresay, I have a drawer-full waiting for me. Ah — good morning'. Hic jacet* therefore for the present my first play. Went to Miss Baber for my third singing lesson and she said my voice was surprisingly strong today. Rosie came home today dear child. She has improved wonderfully. She brought home some very creditable water colours, she plays quite brilliantly and altogether boarding school seems to agree with her.

24th June:

I fainted this morning for a bit of excitement but didn't like it much. 'Wilkes of Waterloo' to my great surprise appeared in the Daily Telegraph *this morning. I only gave it to the Editor about 29 hours ago and hey presto here it is, 2 columns of it. That's another milestone reached for the* Telegraph *is difficult of access I hear, it is the first I have tried.*

26th June:

Mother and Rosie were in town all day. Rex said a very wicked word, swearing and I overheard. Then he vowed and swore before heaven he didn't say it and said it was Frank and then he confessed. I feel utterly miserable about it, the child is being ruined by never being punished and all of us are responsible. We are not going to tell Mother about it till morning. 'Toychild' was published in the Daily Telegraph *this morning. I was* pleased *to see it.*

12th July:

Wrote a little of the fourth chapter of Seven Little Australians.

14th July:

Rosie and I went to town and finished getting Lil's presents. Rose gave her a Mendelssohn, Rex writing paper, Mother a tablecloth for her bedroom, an inkstand and

---

*Hic jacet: here lies.

MSS case, and I gave her a new dress, soft blue with velvet to trim it, an umbrella, a pair of brown shoes, a pair of gloves and a purse. I did love getting the things, she is so poor just now and I am pretty well off and they will set her up beautifully. H. came in afternoon, he is a long way from well. Dr McAllister told him he doesn't have enough to eat — that's the wretched state their house is in, no management or anything. It makes my blood boil to think of it sometimes.

27th July:
Wrote a short article, 'Women in Large Doses'. At night didn't go to the Dixson's Dance and instead sat in front of the fire at Hermsley talking with H. I do believe a man, at any rate a man like Herbert, feels and thinks more about little things than a woman does. When I am at all cold or have moods or anything, he says I simply can't imagine how they hurt him. And sometimes he says after I have been very nice to him, he almost makes up his mind to go right away somewhere forever just so he can always remember the last time he was with me I was nice. At times, after I have been loving to him he says, he is afraid to see me the next time for fear I shall be cold and indifferent again. I must be a very horrid girl I think.

1st August:
Started my dress for the ball on Thursday. Mr Cope has one of his periodic fits of hatefulness on him and is really unbearable. Mother is miserable about it — oh he does make her unhappy. He seems to be tired of her — and of all of us just now which is inexpressibly galling to a woman of any pride. She says she wishes she could take us all away and live away from him for a time at least. I do think mother is the very best and noblest woman on earth and oh she has suffered. He ought to smooth her path for her, not expect as he does, that she should bear all unpleasantnesses and make everything smooth and nice for him. He has been swearing and cursing and making himself absolutely odious.

11th August:
Went to town to see Editor of Town and Country *— Mr Jeffrey. He wants me to do a story for the Xmas number — 2 guineas. Then he had a long talk with me, he was* very *nice. Gave me lots of solid advice, and a sprinkling of compliments. Advised me to try a book and said I wrote as good a short story as anyone he knew and would like to see if I could sustain an interest. Mr Boucicault has returned* The Wig *with a note saying he has not had time to read it. Almost more unsatisfactory than a refusal. Night copied out the seventh chapter of* 7 Australians, *it's a big undertaking writing a book.*

6th September:
Wrote chapter XV, 7 Australians. *Lil came home and told of prizes offered in Cassell's for a story, 21 to 30,000 words, prizes £25, £15, and £10. There is hardly time to try but I shall just have a shot. Sat down and wrote hard and by 11 pm I had written 4,000 words and done Children's Page.*

7th September:

Wrote from 9 am till 12.30 pm without a break, I have done 14,000 words altogether counting 7,000 I had done earlier on Tekel. *My brain is spinning but I don't think it will be a bad story. Mr Pickburn thinks my play* The Wig *is first rate and the University Dramatic is going to play it, probably at Xmas. I am so glad.*

4th October:

Sewed at heliotrope blouse in morning. At night I was suddenly taken ill with a fearful sore throat, I could hardly breathe and thought every minute I should choke. Mother sat up with me fomenting my neck and poulticing it all night. It is quinsy we think, I thought it was diptheria.

6th October:

In bed all day but getting better. A long letter from H. written before he knew I was ill. He asked me not to be so cold and undemonstrative — he says I seem afraid of showing my affection and oh he does wish I could be more spontaneous. It's this unfortunate manner of mine.

18th October:

Morning wrote chapter XX, 7 Australians, *killed Judy to slow music. Copied out chapters XIII and XIV. I shall be glad when it's done.*

20th October:

Finished 7 Little Australians. *Hurrah. I thought I'd never get to the end. Now I have only to copy out 7 more chapters and it is ready to go and hunt for a publisher.*

27th October:

Went to Mr Jeffrey, he gave me a note — very complimentary one introducing me to the manager at Ward Lock in Melbourne. Then I saw Mr Bennett on the way back and he asked me to leave the story for him to read but he 'shouldn't pay for it if I wanted it in book form for the advertising would be enough for me if he published it'. I like that, it's remarkably cool indeed, I shan't let him have it.

1st November:

Went to town. Mr Bennett said he had read 7 Little Australians *himself (that Mr Jeffrey tells me is a great honour). He said 'It is too long, but except for that it's very good, indeed very good — after the little girl Judy goes to school it couldn't be better indeed'. He said if I boiled it down he would take it. I told him I would rather send it to Ward Lock first, so he said I could.*

2nd November:

Walked up to post and sent 7 L. Australians *to Ward Lock, Melbourne. It took 18 stamps. Posted the 'Third Great Wave' to the* Daily Telegraph. *I've got a new idea for a book* The Story of a Baby, *not a children's book.*

4th November:

Packed up and cut sandwiches in the morning. The party came at 4 pm, it was the very hottest day we've had this year, it seemed suicide to walk to the river but we did it, someway. Barrys, Austens, Garnseys, Mr Creed and Louie, etc. etc. about 40 or 50 altogether. We came back for 9 pm train fearfully tired after the eight-mile walk.

9th November:

Had a letter from Ward Lock, I was amazed to get it so soon. They say they have read my MSS and conclude 'I wish to negotiate for the immediate publication of it. That owing to the terrible depression they are using their power of selection very sparingly but if I will tell them what value I place upon the work they will write me further'. Not at all a bad letter to get from my first publisher and within a week. I can't think what value I place on it, I must get advice.

10th November:

Went to town, asked Bulletin *advice — Mr Archibald. He says it would be unwise to ask much — £20 and a royalty. Asked Mr Henderson and he said the same. Did shopping, etc. Wrote to Ward Lock and said £30 and a royalty — I am living for an answer. Poor old Rosie has failed in her matric., she will be terribly disappointed.*

25th November:

A Red Letter day. Ward and Lock have written to say 7 Little Australians is a bright story of considerable merit. They have offered me £10 for copyright and a royalty of 1d on all books published under 2/- and 2d a copy on all over 2/-. They have also made it a condition that I shall let them alone have a sequel or sequels. And have asked to see any newspaper stories of mine with a view to publication in book form. Such a nice letter it was. It is a small sum of course but then as they say 'times are bad and I am unknown as yet'. There was a bad row this morning between Mother and Mr Cope, he is in his usual Xmas-time humour. I am going to take Mother to Tasmania with the money from the book — in about five weeks.

27th November:

Another domestic storm! It is really getting serious. I had to act mediator between the two all the time. Mother was bent on going away from him at any rate for a time. She really is a good woman — my idea of a good woman. Not religious outwardly, but just doing her level best for everyone always. She deserves to be well-treated. Night wrote Chapter IV Story of a Baby. The storm is lulled and almost a peace has come. Rosie wrote to me privately in great distress, she has no money for all sorts of things school girls want. I sent her 5/- and 2/- pocket money.

29th November:

Miss Williams, a dressmaker came. Nearly made a white pin spot muslin for me — such a pretty dress. I went to the Pockley's at night, Mr Tucker was there, I like him very much. I sang 'Will He Come' and I played two accompaniments for Mr Tucker. He asked us to a picnic he's having and then said in a strange tone to me that I was to bring my 'happy betrothed' or something similar. I said I thought he must be mistaken.

30th November:

Letter from Ward Lock making a further proposal about 7 Little Australians. *They offer £15 for copyright and a royalty of 2½d on each copy sold at 2/6. They say it will be well-bound and be illustrated by a first-class artist. They ask me to be ready with a sequel by April — the book is to be published in England on 1st March and be here by the end of April and they say they are very glad to be associated with the Louisa Alcott of Australia.* Such *a nice letter it was.*

5th December:

A terribly hot day. Afternoon fainted two or three times for want of something better to do. Night started sequel to Seven Little Australians *— wrote half a chapter,* Growing Up, *I think I shall call it. Had a twelve-page letter from H. full of Sunday — Love is the greatest thing on earth.*

6th December:

Another letter from Ward Lock. Mr Steele says that from the 'undoubted ability I display for young peoples' stories there should be a very bright future before me' he said further 'I do not hesitate to confess, though I am a man of 40 and tough as business men go, that the death of little Judy affected and impressed me greatly'. I love Mr Steele.

7th December:

Another letter from Mr Steele, enclosing a book, Advance Australia *thing and saying he should be glad of any suggestions or friendly criticism for it. Offering also to send me books occasionally for review in Children's Corner. Night Herbert and Mr Pickburn came. I talked to Pickie most of the time, books and such. I like him very much indeed, there is no one I like talking to more.*

16th December:

Mr Tucker's Picnic. Finished and copied out story. Went in the electric launch, cruised about the harbour and landed at Clontarf for tea. Mr Tucker talked to me all the way down and ordered the launch to be taken wherever I said. Then after tea I went for a walk on the beach with him and we sat down at the end of an old pier. We talked of many things for a long time and then suddenly he began to tell me he loved me and asked if I could ever care for him, he said he knew it was a very short time but he couldn't help putting things to the touch. I never felt so unhappy about anything, it seemed as if I had deceived him by saying I was not engaged and yet I was not at liberty to say I was. I told him that I was engaged to Herbert. Oh I did feel horrid and he was so nice — after Herbert there is no one I like better. He was so white and strange-looking I could have cried. He says ever since the Walking Party he determined to tell me some day and when I said I was not engaged he felt at liberty to. He says there is nothing I can blame myself in — and there isn't, I can say so most conscientiously. He asked for my friendship as the next best thing I could give him and said he must always have love unsatisfied in his heart while mine is satisfied. Coming back he sat at the end of the boat alone, I had to talk to some wretched man Gibbes who never stopped. I feel so miserable about it, he seems to be taking it so hard.

17th December:

H. came for day, Sid Mack came also. H. was coming to Tasmania with us — just down in the boat and back so as to be with me, but Mother says she couldn't enjoy it because we should have to deceive Mr Cope. H. is fearfully disappointed but very good about it. This is Mother's trip altogether and I won't disappoint her in any way.

18th December:

Busy sewing at things for Tasmania, I think we shall go in about 10 days. Mr Tucker said he hoped to go down to Hobart too if I had given him any hope. There was a terrible sailing accident yesterday, the Ripple, *eight people drowned.*

19th December:

Mr Tucker wrote me and also sent 'in homage and to express in a measure the feelings that had influenced him on Saturday' some verses he had written about 'the bright sweet face of her who is, Unto, my world the sun' — to wit, me. Pretty verses — far too good for me. I detest myself. Wrote to H., or tried to, lamentable failure. I'm out of joint.

20th December:

Went to town, Mr Tucker caught me up and walked up to the School of Arts with me, said various things and gave me a little picture. Night went with Rosie to the Pockleys. Mr Tucker came and walked home with me though it was out of his way and no trains. I had a long letter from him too 'in extenuation of the verses, etc.' — a very nice one. I really like him.

22nd December:

Went to town by the 8 am and Mr Tucker walked up with us, asked us to another picnic, we to settle the day and then he would ask other people. Shopped from morn till dewy eve, got presents for everyone. Went to Hermsley for evening. Everyone was very pleased with their presents, I sent them three or four days ago. H. gave me a Swan gold fountain pen, Meredith's Adventures of Harry Richmond *and Albert Smith's* Adventures of Harry Leland.

23rd December:

Went to Louie's in morning to their new home at Neutral Bay. Another note from Mr Tucker saying the picnic was to-night and hoping very much we could go, that he wanted this opportunity so very much to wish me a happy Christmas. I was tired and Herbert was here so I didn't go (I wanted to though — just to be on the water by moonlight) Lil and Rose went and had a lovely time.

25th December:

H. went down by the 10 am, had an unChristmassy Christmas, nothing to mark it but goose, pudding and almonds. In afternoon read Some Emotions and A Moral. *Night Lil, Rose, Rex and I went to church.*

26th December:

H. came, I half made a blouse and idled. I have been in horrid moods lately — felt as if I had absolutely no capacity for feeling and as if my heart had gone to sleep. It has made me cold and careless to H. till tonight and then he told me how it was hurting him — he was nearly heart broken at the thought of losing my love. I'm a beast.

29th December:

Went to town and drew £13.7.0 out of the bank, took berths, on the Oonah *for 6th. £6 the two. Had a reckless fit of caring not for consequences and being seen by people. Met H. and we went to choose a ring at Fairfax and Roberts for my birthday — not an engagement ring. We got a lovely one, plain gold with tiny pearls and a diamond.*

Memo written 30th December, 1893:

By this time next year I set myself to have done the following things: Banked £150. Taken Mother and myself for a trip to Tasmania. Written *Sequel to* 7 Little Australians. Story of a Baby. A Children's Annual. Gum Leaves Annual. *Sketches. Weekly Children's Page. Short Stories.*

Several incidents in the diary of 1893 are certain to have influenced the story of *Seven Little Australians.* Rosie starting boarding school at Bowral must surely have prompted Judy being sent away to school, and the parallel between Mrs Cope and Esther is very obvious — Mrs Cope threatens to take her three daughters away 'for a time anyway' when home life becomes intolerable with Mr Cope, while Esther takes all the children to her parents home at Yarrahappini.

Nowadays it would not be considered unusual for a book to tell of an accident such as the one that happened to Judy, resulting in her death. But when *Seven Little Australians* was written, the theory generally accepted was that 'good always triumphed over evil'. Therefore a death such as hers would have been to point a moral, which in this case it did not do. Hence there was considerable criticism at the time as to whether Judy should have been allowed to die.

In this way Ethel Turner was ahead of her time in writing. She also captured a warm relationship between parents and children, exemplifying a frankness and equality that was not readily acknowledged in those days.

1894

Fame Seems Coming to Me

Ethel was exceedingly encouraged by the spontaneous reaction of the publisher to her first book and the newspaper reviews both in England and Australia were most complimentary and flattering to the young and unknown authoress. Coulson Kernahan, Ward Lock's literary adviser in London, made this report on the manuscript:

'Here is the Miss Louisa Alcott of Australia — here is one of the strongest, simplest, sweetest, sanest and most beautiful child-stories that I have read for years.'

She showed herself to be a remarkably astute and determined business woman, even in these early years and frequently challenged her publisher for a higher royalty. On occasions, she offered the same manuscript to several publishers to see who would give her the best terms.

6th January:

Mother and I went on board the Oonah *at 3 pm, Rex, Lil, Rose and Mr Cope came to see us off and latter was greatly agitated about the delay and none of us were dry-eyed. Talked to Dr Millard on deck till 7 pm and then went below for dinner, thought better of it and went to bed. Both ill in cabin but managed to get to sleep after a time.*

8th January:

A day of one thousand hours. Mother and I lay limp and unlovely in our berths till after 4, we simply hadn't strength to crawl out. Then I had some ice and a biscuit and went on deck to watch the Tasmanian coast scenery — simply grand, only we were past Nature. Mr Taylor was there to meet us at Hobart — never were two feeble creatures so fervently thankful. He took us to the Coffee Palace for the night and we had coffee bread and butter and enjoyed it mightily. For 58 hours I've had nothing but one small biscuit and a drink of beef tea. Mother ate things but I couldn't.

9th January:

Mr Taylor took us out on top of an electric tram to Sandy Bay, such lovely scenery everywhere and Mt Wellington with its head in the clouds. Then to Tasmanian Mail Office to be introduced to Mr Davies the Editor, such a nice man, running over with fun. I like him immensely. Had dinner — red currants and raspberries for finish and then bought big plums and cherries, marvellously cheap and went across the harbour to Bellerive.

17th January:
Started at 9 am for Browns River, Mother and I, sola cum sola. *Top of the brake we were in box seats for the 22 miles there and back. Oh the scenery along that road, on the left the Derwent, broad and blue and very calm, the fleet just coming in and on the right the mountains, blue and purple and grey and green with patches of white sunlight. It's impossible to describe it. Got there at 11 am starving and ate sandwiches and eggs and drank coffee like hungry schoolboys. I made fearful and wonderful sketches of Mt Wellington with colours that never were on land or sea.*

19th January:
Letters from Lil, Rose, Mr Cope and 16 pages from H. Finished reading The Heavenly Twins *and started Kipling's* Bridge Builders. *Watched the sun set behind Mt Wellington, orange and gold and pale yellow lights and a mist of purple over the mountains. I think I should be good if I lived here, very good. I should grow. One* can't *be small with a mountain like that behind one always.*

30th January:
Caught the Oonah *at 9 am for Port Arthur. Fairly smooth trip. It is a very beautiful place, all possible natural advantages, but I suppose the beauty must have seemed a mockery to the poor convicts. We got hold of an old man — John Best, who was a convict for 27 years. He showed us over the Penitentiary and the Church and told us all sorts of stories. Started at 12 noon for Sydney.*

2nd February:
Got up at 7 am and went on deck, we were about at Bondi. Got to the wharf at 8.40 am — 57 hours. H. and Mr Cope were there waiting. They had got up at 2 am and walked down from Lindfield. H. has got fearfully thin with the worry of me being away. It would be useless to write that he is glad to have me back. The girls met us at the station and Rex — it is very good to be home again after our wanderings. Everybody talked at once for hours of course and Mr Cope had a present for me. *

6th February:
Wrote 1½ chapters Sequel in morning. Such a blow of misfortune! Mr Spooner wrote to say that after this week my Children's Page would not be needed, the I.S.N. is going to stop publication. Exit my means of livelihood. I'm nearly penniless after the trip.

9th February:
Went to town by the 10 am. Mr Jeffrey met me in the office and said 'would I write the Children's Page for the Town and Country'! *My ill luck did not last long. I am safe once more, it is a great relief. I do like Mr Jeffrey. He says I can do it exactly as I like; terms are not decided on yet.*

---

*No mention is made of what the present was but the card found among her papers reads as
 follows: 'May your Fame as an Authoress be as
      Bright and Steady as the Light of your Lamp.
      Ethel with best wishes
      from her Dad
      24-1-94'.

George Meredith wrote to Ethel thanking her for the copy she sent him of Seven Little Australians *and saying that 'he had been introduced to a nursery of real children, whose humour, characteristics and chatter are as redolent of their stage of life as breath of the nodding meadow flowers.'*

By kind permission of the National Library, Canberra.

Mark Twain sent Ethel a very nice note saying that 'he could see in a moment that Seven Little Australians *was not going to be commonplace'. Mark Twain 1835-1910 was the* nom de plume *of Samuel Clemens the American author, whose novels* The Innocents Aboard, The Adventures of Tom Sawyer, *and* Huckleberry Finn *gained for him world-wide acclaim.*

By kind permission of the Mitchell Library.

Mr A. B. Paterson, 'Banjo' later became a firm friend and on occasions dined with Ethel and Herbert at their Mosman home. His best known works include Clancy of the Overflow *and* The Man from Snowy River. *He also wrote the ballad* Waltzing Matilda *to the tune of an old English marching song.*

Herbert aged about 26.

The boat Gipsy, *Sydney Harbour, 1885. Herbert was one of the crew members who sailed with this boat for many years.*

St John's Church, Gordon in January 1900. Ethel and Herbert were married there on 22 April, 1896.

Ethel and her daughter, Jean who was born on 7 February 1898 — this photograph was taken in the same year.

Ethel's bookplate which was designed for her by Adrian Feint.

Ethel and Jean in a photograph taken for The Bulletin. *The caption said 'It will be satisfactory to Mrs Curlewis' numerous readers to know that domestic joys have not so far been allowed to interfere with her literary work!'*

10th February:

Caught 11 am train up. There has been a fresh incident in the Lucy-Sid warfare. Sid went down to the wharf to meet her boat from Melbourne, Mr O'Brien told him not to speak to her, Sid said he wouldn't — but not out of respect to Mr O'Brien. And Mr O.B. struck him a blow in the face. H. came at 2 pm. It was very hot — he fanned me most of afternoon and sprinkled lavender water on my head. Night we walked and talked. I don't believe anyone ever understood each other as we do.

21st February:

Went to Hermsley for evening. H. has a girl to coach in Latin, and he has taken the Law book he is writing with Mr MacIntyre to a publisher and they have accepted it — at least promised to when it is finished. He is begging me to be publicly engaged when April comes — Mr C's stipulated time, I know I ought, but it is so much nicer having things as they are.

26th February:

Went to Pymble with Mother to look at some land we are thinking of buying. I like it exceedingly — so much indeed that as soon as I can get together about £80 or £90 for an acre, I shall invest in one as a speculation or to build a house upon in the far future.

8th March:

Did Children's Page. Wrote the start of a children's story for Louie, she wants to try for a page in the Mail and asked me to begin it. Also sent off £1 to Louie that she asked me to lend her 'as a great favour'. H. came in evening. There's a Classical Lectureship vacant at Melbourne University, £400 a year, he wanted to know would I marry him at once and go too if he got it. It would be dreadful I think.

13th March:

An idle day, I am quite out of the writing mood. Had a letter from Louie, such a nice one. She said I am the 'idealest, dearest little friend anyone could have' — such a lot of nice things, I was quite surprised.

28th March:

Started making a frock for a present to Dolly, fawn-coloured tweedy material with pink yoke and pink stitching. Went to town with Lil to see Mr Jeffrey and got my Dame Durden letters — at least 290 for the week, it's getting alarming.

29th March:

Read the Children's Page letters for prizes all the morning — 3½ solid hours it took me and there are three more classes. Daphne the cow had a calf this morning away in the bush and the whole family turned out to search for it, we found it far away — such a dear little thing.

5th April:

A letter from H., he has just read MSS of Growing Up, *read it with prejudice he says because he doesn't believe in sequels and Louie said it was not half so good as* 7 Little A's. *He says it is splendid, one of the best things I have written and the best of the kind he has ever read, that he read it with real interest apart from me and thinks it is artistically written as well as filled with interest. He thinks I ought to be the first children's writer in the world! Dear old boy, of course, I can allow for pink spectacles but then his judgement is always worth having and he slaughters my pet stories when he sees fit so it isn't all flattering. Letter also from Mr Creed asking my help — another cloud on the Louie-Creed horizon. Mrs Mack is a martinet again.*

This small note written by Ethel to Herbert shows her capacity for driving a hard bargain even though it was so early in her literary career.

April 10th, '94

My very dear one boy,

Just a word to let you know I have not yet shuffled off this mortal coil nor even begun to review my possessions with a view to making my will. Seriously, I am all right — I heard you say 'honour bright?' you horrid big nuisance and add nearly. But honour bright it is nothing for you to worry about.

I wanted very much to hold a consultation with you yesterday, I got a cablegram, Ward and Lock to say they would prefer to purchase complete rights to *7 Little A's* and offer £50 prompt cash if I forego royalty. What would you have done? Of course £50 is a big sum especially for a first book and a children's at that, but then again Royalty lasts so long, there is the chance that 10 or 12 years ahead some benighted children may still be inquiring for it, like *Little Women*, etc. and I should be getting royalty all the time. You see it is only £35 more than the sum promised already for copyright — if only 4000 are ever sold (the first edition is to be 5000) I get £40 more which makes £55 and there is always the grand Perhaps of Browning. They asked me to wire reply and I did — and refused — shall you call me a conceited goose?

I went to town today . . .

The rest of the page was torn off.

(At the time of publication of these diaries, 1979, there have been forty editions of *Seven Little Australians*. In paperback it has been reprinted five times and the story has been translated into ten languages. It was a stage play in 1915, a film in 1939 by O'Brien Pictures, broadcast in New Zealand and South Africa, televised in serial form in Britain in 1953, televised by the Australian Broadcasting Commission in 1973 in ten episodes and repeated in 1975 when colour television was introduced.)

11th April:

Wrote all the morning and finished the last chapter of my sequel — it is a relief, there is only the copying out now. I have been less than two months doing the whole book, started in February, after coming home from Hobart and I've done a lot of Story of a Baby *and other work as well. My eyes have gone so tired and aching, I'm not going to look at a book or pen for two or three days, I've been writing by a flickering candle too long, I'll have to go in for a reading lamp.*

14th April:

Went to town and H. met me at St Leonards and took me over to Neutral Bay. He did not go to the T party as he has quarrelled with Louie — again, Louie is getting perfectly sickening with all her airs.

23rd April:

Went to town, shopped, bought a new dress in a hurry, pale pearl grey as unserviceable as it is pretty. Went to consult Fanny Coghlan as I have felt a bit ill lately. I wouldn't go to a 'man' doctor. She says I need strength and prescribed Blands pills, iron and strychnine. Mustn't dance or walk too much but may in moderation.

1st May:

Copied out chapter IX, Story of a Baby *— I don't like it at all now and* cannot *get on with it, I'll have to shelve it for a time.*

9th May:

Three years ago to-day H. and I were engaged — privately of course. We were going to celebrate the anniversary by going to Manly, sitting on the rocks where we had sat when we weren't engaged and he was miserable, coming home, going to the Mack's old house and walking down Wilson St in the evening, the way we came the night of nights when he was taking me home to the Avenue. But it rained — so instead I went to Hermsley and he took a holiday. In the evening we had a fire in the drawing room and we sat and talked. It was one of the days to be remembered always by us. H. gave me Children of the Ghetto *and* Stories from Scribener.

11th May:

Mrs Daintrey came for day and Madge Doak for afternoon. Lily's new story, 'By the Blue Australian Mountains' began in the Town and Country. *It is advertised all over* Herald *and* Telegraph *as 'an Australian novel by an Australian author of great promise'.*

15th May:

Went to Dr Brady, my deaf ear has seemed worse lately. He says there is a growth in my throat that ought to be cut out. Whew. I'm nervous.

28th May:
Had a terrible quarrel with Rose, I don't think I can ever feel the same to her while I live. Wrote hard at Story of a Baby, *it is getting stupid and unmanageable, but it is nearly finished. I am going to send it to three publishers at the same time. Herbert came in afternoon to 'comfort' me, I had not cried so much as I did this morning since Annie died.*

29th May:
Went to town by the 8 am. I had secretly made an appointment to go with the Thompsons to Dr Brady's and have my throat operated on. I knew Mother would be nervous so I didn't mention it at home. It was pretty bad, he cauterized it five times but I wasn't a coward after all. Herbert and Lil were in the next room and Katie was with me so I really wasn't game not to be game.

31st May:
A letter from Ward Lock asking me what sum I would take for serial rights of 7 Little A's. *Went to town for advice, asked Mr Jeffrey, Mr Archibald and Mr Roydhouse. Acted on the last's advice and wrote 'Half what the firm receives'.*

5th June:
Read Jane Eyre *in afternoon. Night Rose and I went to Atalanta dance, and enjoyed it immensely. Danced with H., Mr Pickburn, 2 Pedens, Creagh, Sendall, Doak, Uther, Old, Broinoski, etc.*

7th June:
A lovely letter from Ward Lock and a perfectly delightful *notice. I must get a scrap book and some stickfast. It speaks of me with Miss Alcott and Mrs Hodgson Burnett, and says 'Judy' is likely to become as famous a character in fiction as Topsy of* Uncle Tom's Cabin. *Mr Steele says Mr Bowden was 'quite enthusiastic about the new book' and thinks it will be a big success. And they want my photograph and a sketch of my 'literary career' for the* Queen *or some other big English paper. And they want to see all my other writings at once. Oh I am so happy. All life seems rose-coloured, fame seems coming to me and money too. I will make such good use of the money.*

16th June:
Morning went to town, cashed my cheque and banked £12 of it. At night Mother, Rose and I went to the dance at Government House and liked it so so.

17th June:
Letter from Mr Steele asking me to send Growing Up *and* Story of a Baby *to him at once, he seems very vexed that I have sent the latter to two other firms. Afternoon went to see the land we have bought at last at Gordon, beautiful land, 4½ acres next to the Pockley's.*

18th June:

Went to town by 8 am, shopped and bought white merveilleux for ball dress and rose pink velvet for puff sleeves. Miss Williams came in afternoon to make my dress, it looks lovely, quite a train and such lovely silk, a baby body, and soft folded belt. At night Rose and I went to Committee meeting about the dance in aid of the Vicarage funds.

20th June:

Went to town with Rex, walked to museum for his benefit and Mark Foys for mine. Saw Mr Jerome the originator of Cosmos *by appointment. He said my fame had preceded me, and all sorts of flattering things. Asked me to write a story for it and to consider a proposition he made about being woman editor of the paper. I don't think I like him. He's a French American, clever I should say and very plausible. Night went to Walking Party. Walked and talked to Mr Tucker chiefly.*

21st June:

Did Children's Page. Had a great mending day, stockings and clothes generally. There will always be warfare between the pen and the needle with me. At night went to University Ball. Mrs Caro chaperoned me. It was a lovely ball. I danced with H. four times, Pickburn, Dr Millard, Creagh, Macintyre, Jenkins, Bode, King, etc. etc. I could have filled my programme over and over again.

5th July:

Started to prepare old story A Girl Named Bobbie *for book publication should it be required. Went to Dr Brady, he thought it would do the other ear good to have it cauterized again so he did my throat about seven times again — without cocaine. Horridly painful. We got to be quite friendly however, I like him very much. Afternoon started reading Children's Page letters, about four hundred more to do.*

10th July:

Morning started a new book I am going to write The Little Larrikin, *it is going to be very much drawn from life, Billy Curlewis is the 'larrikin', Herbert, Roger, other people real too.*

18th July:

Busy all day decorating rooms and setting tables for the Lindfield dance. Lucy O'Brien and Alice Thompson came with us. I liked the dance very much, danced with Mr Mocatta, Jenkins, H. Pockley, Old, etc. etc., three with Mr Tucker — at least, one and talked for two. He has not had the letter I wrote about the University Dramatic next week. Danced three with H. and sat out two — frightfully wicked of course but not noticeable in such a crush.

19th July:

Busy cleaning up till 12 noon. In afternoon H. helped to open 550 Dame Durden envelopes. Then we differed about Mr Tucker.

23rd July:

Had a letter from Mr Steele, he is in Sydney and wanted to see me. He arranged about Growing Up *which he likes very much, he says £25 for copyright and 6d royalty on 6/- edition, lower ones in proportion and half serial rights. He wanted me to give up* Story of a Baby *to him and not wait for Fisher Unwin's answer. But I won't. Then he asked me to let him know what they offer so that he may go past it.*

24th July:

University Dramatic Society's production of my play The Wig. *It seemed to go very brightly, there was very great applause, time after time, and when over they clapped and shouted* author! *Till Mr Davis came and told me I would have to go before the curtain. Which I did and got a warm welcome and three bouquets. Afterwards nearly everyone came up and congratulated me. Lil and I stayed till the end, then I went behind scenes with some others and had coffee and cakes. Then a dance, then home to Hermsley with H., Louie was there, had been there all the evening with Mr Creed — didn't show up at theatre.*

25th July:

Such a fearful crushing in the Herald *and not a word of good! Says the young author did not try to be funny and succeeded.* Star *crushes badly.* Telegraph *and* Evening News *rather badly. According to papers a failure. According to house last night a brilliant success. I suppose the papers are more to be trusted though. I have a slightly mangled feeling — I can't expect success in each thing though, probably this will be good for me and serve as a tonic or conceit extractor. Talked in bed to Louie till 12 in morning. Had my throat cut at Dr Brady's, then shopped with Louie.*

2nd August:

Went to Hermsley and made Claude's room pretty for him. Then did some cooking as Mrs Curlewis was ill in bed and domestic matters at sixes and sevens. Made 2 beefsteak pies and a currant pudding and pleased them all. Evening had a talk with Mr Curlewis about building, he has been up to see our land and says he is going to alter the bricks and send us red ones just for my sake, they were pink before and we didn't care for them much.

20th August:

Mother and I went up to land and gardened hard for a couple of hours. Afternoon read and did 5th chapter of Little Larrikin, *I love writing it and believe it will be my best. At night to Mrs Cornwell's dance and enjoyed it immensely.*

24th August:

To town by 8 am, bought a pretty pink chair for the study for a birthday present for Lil, also a blouse for her and one for myself then back to Hermsley. H. and I had a quarrel, I said I refused to be engaged to him — the last time I said that I promised faithfully never to say it again. I made up though and the making up made us both glad we had quarrelled. I don't think we have ever felt more to each other.

29th August:

Did Children's Page competitions for the month. Half had forgotten their 1d stamps and were disqualified so I had less to do. A letter from H. full of a wild plan about going out to South Africa. He has 2 relations there, Curlewises, one the leading barrister in Pretoria, the other the chief C. of E. parson in Johannesberg — he says there would be a brilliant opening and that the faint idea of winning me so soon makes him feel faint with a mad delight. It is too wild, I wouldn't let him go if the courts were full of nuggets. And how could I go with him.

1st September:

Morning wrote chapter V of Bobbie. *Lil had a letter from Cassells, the six-part story competition.* Lights O'Sydney *that she sent has won the £50 prize — the* first! *It is splendid. Oh she did want it, there is great excitement in the house. Lil says it is the happiest day of her life — it is her first bit of real success.*

2nd September:

H. stayed the night and we talked South Africa all day. I have given him a promise to go out to him. But I am doing my very best to dissuade him from it, I should be wretched there. I would far rather live on £200 a year here than £2000 there.

5th September:

Morning read at David Copperfield, *I simply could not lay it down, I think I read all my Dickens too young and am only fully appreciating it now.*

18th September:

Government House Ball. Read Yellow Aster — *villainous. Neither scholarly style nor humour to commend it — only unpleasantness. How I do hate this class of book. Wrote a 'slating' article on it and similar productions for Women's Dept. of* Cosmos.

21st September:

Just as I was going to town the post came — and with it — Seven Little Australians. *I think it was the very happiest minute of my life. It is in an art green cover with Judy running across it, a quaint little gilt figure in top corner, and Bunty eating bread and butter at back — Lovely altogether, beautiful type and thick paper. Made lunch of it and read it all the way down in train, the illustrations are excellent. Returned at 4 and showed it to Mother, she was greatly excited and loves the page 'To my Mother'. As she had the dedication I gave Mr Cope the first book. All the copies will be here in three weeks.*

1st October:

Mother and Mr Cope went to land. H. and I stayed at home. Had a serious quarrel but made up before he went. It is almost beyond credance the power over him I have — it sounds horrid to write it but I do it because I want to remember to be more careful. If I am the least bit angry with him it makes him absolutely wretched for long enough, he says he feels he could cut his throat rather have it again. He went home at 12 miserable — I couldn't make him quite happy again.

2nd October:

Morning wrote chapter XIV of Bobbie, *I wish the wretched thing was finished. I hate doctoring-up a story. Afternoon went to land, but Lil was selfish and wouldn't go down. I am still out of friends with her. I consider she was unwarrantably impertinent yesterday and I'm just tired to death of her. She is abominably meddlesome, surely I am old enough to do such things as walk to the station with him without bringing a torrent of abuse down upon me. Late at night did Children's Page.*

6th October:

First review of Seven Little A's *in* Sydney Morning Herald — *half a column long. Very good indeed although it points out errors. Thinks killing Judy is a fault. Objects to Pip saying 'my oath'. Says — apart from this the book is unexceptionable, healthy, gay and innocent in tone and from its construction and liveliness likely to engross the young. All who make acquaintance with the seven will want to meet them at a later stage as promised, etc. etc. H. came at 2 pm but went home at 8 pm. I am still on Arctic terms with Lily. It is the longest quarrel we have had.*

12th October:

All the family went to town together. There were some lovely desks at Bradley Newtown and Lamb that Mother wanted us to see. We liked them so much that Lil and I bought one each. Lovely oak, beautifully carved long book case with glass doors attached, pigeon holes, shelves and drawers. They had been £25 and were reduced to £8 10 0. I also bought eight dining chairs and a hall carpet as a present for Mother and Mr C.

13th October:

Morning cooked and packed up for picnic. About 35 there and we sat round a fire in the evening and sang. We all walked home from Wahroonga to Gordon. Rose made herself very conspicuous with Harold Pockley, it is getting fearful. Disappeared for two or three hours and made us all wait for her.

14th October:

I told Mother, as I had warned Rose I should that she must make Rose be more circumspect. She retorted that she was engaged to Harold. Such a storm there was. Mr Cope was furious. Mother went up to Mrs Pockley and the two rated Harold soundly. It's absurd with such a pair of babies — both 19! And Harold with £45 a year and no better prospect. He is on his honour to say nothing at all for two years.

15th October:

Rose still vows vengeance on me, she says she is never going to forgive me as long as I live on earth. Won't speak either to Mother or Mr Cope. The desks came, they are perfectly lovely. Spent afternoon in putting my books in shelves and various MSS in places.

Ethel and Jean, the latter aged 13 months. This photograph originally appeared in The Bookfellow, *March 1899.*

Jean. Herbert was very interested in photography and in this experiment he has used a double exposure on one plate.

The Neuk, with Jean in the foreground. This house was demolished in about 1938 and a new home built on the site, now 4 Moruben Road, Mosman.

16th October:
Morning wrote at Bobbie. *Rosie and I are the best of friends again, she has told me everything and shown me Harold's farewell letter — The queerest piece of composition I ever read in my life and written entirely with a view of it falling into Mother's hands. H. came in evening and we had another difference, we seem to have had a lot lately. He had been feeling that he was not first in my thoughts, that I was so full of my book — he was beginning to get jealous of it. I have never felt so in the slightest, I'm very pleased with the success of course but honestly half the time I completely forget it and shouldn't dream of letting it occupy a higher place than* he *does.*

10th November:
Morning made an art muslin valance for the sofa bed I shall have in my new bedroom. The house is getting on splendidly. At 5 Rose and I went to Mr Tucker's picnic, 40 people there and I don't know when I have been to a nicer picnic. And such a tea! It must have cost him quite a fortune, fowls and ham, lobster mayonnaise, strawberries and cream, beer, etc. I had a long walk with Mr T. up a long way past his house which is a very pretty little place. It is nearly a year since he told me he loved me, he says it is the longest year of his life, to me it has been the shortest. Walked with H. for a long time, oh there is absolutely no comparison between the two men, although Mr T. is very nice. H. is craving again to be married.

My portrait or rather caricature is in Daily Telegraph *today with a very laudatory notice. It says some of the brightest sketches that have appeared in the D.T. were from my pen. It says that* 7 Little A's *is a pronounced success, there isn't a copy left in Sydney. Letter from Steele. (see Appendix IV.)*

12th November:
Afternoon went up to land and settled where wardrobe cupboard was to go, and also shelf in my bedroom. It will *be nice having it to myself although it is only an attic. But the* two *windows and low window seats redeem it. Letter from Mr Tucker thanking me for my note and saying he had been feeling very depressed for the last day or two 'weakly dwelling on might-have-beens'.*

17th November:
Lily, Rose and I had a great quarrel— I am utterly tired *of Lily's exasperating interference and remarks about H. and me. Today I got at the end of my patience and in such a temper I let the nail brush fly at her like a washerwoman might have. Of course it went yards over her head, she picked up my favourite blue vase and smashed it. Recriminations on both sides followed, Rose siding with Lily. An edifying spectacle. Mother and Mr Cope interfered, Rose made mischief and had a separate quarrel with Mother and we all three declared we were going from home. Altogether a lovely day. H. came and made an oasis in my desert. He asked me something. I am going to answer him on Monday.*

22nd November:

Lounged on bed and idled. Afternoon Ella and Flo Pockley came and discussed the burning question of Rose and Harold. Really, Rose is making the house wretched with all her tempers and overbearing. She fancies herself martyred whereas she is very well-treated. The restrictions have most of them been rescinded at our intercession, they can speak, be friendly anything but lovers for two years!

23rd November:

Dolly and Billy came for the day. I looked after them and played with them generally. But my little larrikin was too well behaved and shy to appear to advantage. He sang Daisy Bell for us in a very small voice but he wasn't the larrikin at all. In evening went to Louie's at Neutral Bay. I enjoyed the evening very much, all very literary and artistic! I talked to Mr Chris Brennan, said to be a genius but slightly mad. Splendid to talk to though. And a Mr Clegg who had been reading my book and came to meet me. The nicest man I have met for a long time and the ugliest. We talked together nearly all the evening, on passages favourites with both, on Browning, Meredith, Omar Khayyam, etc.

3rd December:

Sewed all day, made the blouse body of my new muslin, it looks such a cool simple dress, yet quite stylish and has cost the large sum of 4/6. I shall wear it with long heliotrope ribbons from the waist, a black lace hat with violets in, neat shoes and gloves and look 'charming' for the least possible expenditure. Went to land, the house is finished, all but.

7th December:

Went to post. Letter from H., he has the blues badly — cause he has been doing extraordinarily well. It's very odd but he never gets them when he's in low water — says he has too much to think of and at other times it is reaction. Letters from Steele, he says a second edition is being printed in England and book doing well. Went to house, almost finished.

13th December:

Rosie and I went up to Pymble by the 10.30 am to look at the Burnett's buggy that is £20 but it is too high and uncomfortable. Then we went to Darling Pt to see a village cart — But I wouldn't go to a cat's funeral in it. Xmas Bulletin out, my story, 'The Little Duchess' is in it illustrated by Percy Spence. Louie and I are the only women writers. Mrs Tange asked me to a bush tea, and did not mention Rosie or Lil. Just because she thinks I can give her sister a lift up the literary ladder. I don't drink tea in payment for that.

17th December:

Went to town by the 12.30 pm. To Manly and back just for the trip with H. — then we went shopping, together to buy each other a Xmas present. He got me the loveliest gold brooch with a careless crossband of pearls, and a book, The Black Poodle. *I got him a Swan Fountain pen and a pocket book. Went to Hermsley for night — altogether we had an exceedingly happy day.*

18th December:

Moved to new house. A wild confusion of wardrobes, chairs, vans, crockery. After weeks of dryness it began to rain to get the bedding wet. It is the worst remove we have had, but the new house is beautiful and nothing seems too hard to do in it.

21st Decmber:

Met Lil in town and we shopped together. Tried all over to get a buggy — phaeton rather, that would come within our means. Abandoned it at last and resolved to give usual Xmas boxes and save up to a bigger sum for something better.

25th December:

Had a quiet happy Xmas. Put all the presents in the study and all unwrapped together. Lil and I gave Mr Cope a hall lamp, I gave Mother and him between them a new tapestry table cloth for dining room and six afternoon teaspoons and sugar tongs, apostle shape, etc. etc. Morning made my dressing table look pretty and afternoon read Our Mutual Friend, *ate almonds and raisins and dreamt dreams. Steele wrote to say he had had an order from a Sydney bookseller for three dozen copies of* Story of a Baby. *This is a great mystery — I don't think six people know of it and I'm not going to have it published yet.*

29th December:

H. came and worked like a nigger fencing for the cattle. Had a sudden storm with Mr Cope but he tendered an olive branch after in the shape of a kiss, so we are friends.

Breathtaking scenery, colourful sunsets and the wonder of nature often moved Ethel very deeply. The magnificence of the sun setting behind Mount Wellington in Tasmania moved her to say 'I think I should be good if I lived here, very good'. In the book *Miss Bobbie*, Bobbie also says these very words when overcome by the magnitude of the Blue Australian Mountains.

In a short story, 'To The City of Raspberry Jam' published in the *Little Duchess* collection, she relates her agonizing sea trip to Tasmania with her mother and in the story she refers to herself as the 'Girl with Imagination' and her mother the 'Person of Importance'. It is written in the present tense and is really quite amusing though there is no plot or climax — it is merely a brief chat.

Growing Up, the sequel to *Seven Little Australians*, or as it was later called, *The Family at Misrule* abounds with climaxes and anti-climaxes. However in a large family it would be reasonable to expect that this would be a normal course of events. Each personality is developed and the characters mature in this book, though little mention is made of Captain (now Major) Woolcott. Nell's short-lived repentance after her dinner party at the Fitzroy Browne's shows an understanding of human frailty and the unintentional breaking of good resolutions.

The Story of a Baby depends mainly on character studies of Larrie and Dot, a young and immature couple who find the responsibility of a young baby a great trial. Dot is an aspiring singer (one of Ethel's ambitions) and her career and family commitments are in frequent conflict.

Letters from Mr Steele, Ward Lock's representative in Melbourne, were arriving at least weekly and sometimes twice a week — he advised her, encouraged her, bargained with her and on occasions reprimanded her. He felt that he had 'found' her, and was offended if she even contemplated another firm publishing any of her work.

' "Dear old Suds," she said.'
Miss Bobbie

1895

We are Going to be Very Poor

Now that she has nearly overcome her doubts and uncertainties about marriage, Ethel obviously delights in writing *The Little Larrikin*. It is largely biographical as she admits, and it is entertaining and most revealing in many ways, as it is really a re-enactment of her romance with Herbert, who has always been devoted, patient and long-suffering.

2nd January:
Went to town by 11 and had my portrait taken again *at Creelman's, — this is the third sitting, the other two were no good. The man took me four times, twice full length with my white silk train spread out dignifiedly, twice bust. H. came in evening, he is moody again and full of resentment against the whole world that he cannot marry me straightaway.*

6th January:
Went to church. Mr King spoke very strongly against those who came irregularly and took communion seldom. Afternoon I went to him saying why I didn't and giving my views a little on religion, he be [page torn].

7th January:
Morning wrote — very slowly — a couple of pages of ch 15, Larrikin. *Afternoon a few words more, my pen won't run, and went to Lorne for tennis. Mr King wrote me an exceedingly nice letter, 12 pages long, and 'thanked me sincerely for giving him the opportunity to write'.*

12th January:
Idled shamefully. It is growing on me fearfully — I don't seem to be able to sit down and work, I keep sauntering about the garden, reading — anything but writing. Very bad week. Afternoon lay on the bed and thought out a new book, Under Twelve *I think I shall call it — if I write it.*

22nd January:
A deluge. I almost decided not to go to town it is such a long way to the station. However I donned my macintosh and set off and a hundred yards off found Herbert trudging towards me. We shopped together and I went with him while he bought my birthday present. Very unorthodox lovers Rosie would say, but he says he likes it twice as well when I help him to choose. He got me a sweet little pair of gold sleeve links. And a big comfortable 'Grannie' wicker chair for the study.

26th January:

Windy and wet — we almost stayed at home, then decided to risk it and went. About 27 of them had also ventured. H. looked so nice in his sailing cap and macintosh. We had a lovely day — landed at Taylor Bay and had lunch under the yacht awning. Lola told me a lot of things in confidence. I rather like her but she certainly is an empty-headed little idiot. She makes Bert look ridiculous too twenty times a day and shows him off as if he were a pet poodle instead of a man. She had told the Thompsons 'she really couldn't go if Mr Curlewis went, it would be too awkward to meet a man who had proposed to her four or five times!!'. A bit absurd, when he was only a schoolboy of 18 or 19 at the time he imagined he was in love with her. Of course Lola doesn't state this when she boasts of him among her other conquests. Landed about 6 pm, had tea on the shore and caught train home.

27th January:

Read Louis Becke's By Reef and Palm. *Idled, stuck cuttings in my Newspaper book. Wrote to George Meredith.* * *And wrote to, and posted to Lewis Carroll book — Seven A's and a letter. I am waiting to get Meredith's address. Boldness is no name for it.*

29th January:

Mr Steele sent me first number of The Windsor, *it really is an excellent magazine. Wrote to Mr King continuing our theological discussion. Afternoon went with Lil to look at the half-acre blocks near, we have a great — and vain — idea of buying one, putting up two or three summer cottages on it and making our fortune! I have the magnificent sum of £100 banked and she has about £25 left when Cassell's £50 comes and she has paid me back all she owes! Night did fashions and trapped my finger in the window so hard, I had to go out and do a little weep in the moonlight. A letter from Clive Curlewis at Coolabah, he says he doesn't feel at all flattered by hearing he is meant for Clem or 'Ruffy' in* Larrikin.

7th February:

Read Omar Khayyam for an hour or so. I had a 'wildly dear' letter from a girl in the backblocks of Queensland. It seems she has had a great struggle and can't get any writing accepted. So she calmly asks me if I would have one of her books published under my name to give her a start! I am sorry for her and will write her a nice letter about publishers and other advice, but that proposal is a little too beautiful. Lil came home with very saddening news. Reconstruction is at work in the Town and Country *office and with many regrets, they are going to dispense with our services. Thirty shillings a week lost to me and a guinea to Lil! I shall have nothing but book money. Mr Jeffrey says the truth is we are too good for such work, any common-or-garden dressmaker could do Fashion and social. Consoling but not purse filling! We feel very blue for we have been spending extravagantly.*

---

*George Meredith, 1828–1909 was an author who wrote novels, poems and ballads including the titles *One of Our Conquerors* and *Modern Love* and *Poems of the English Roadside*.

Departure of the N.S.W. Contingent for the Transvaal outside Victoria Barracks Sydney. The influence of the Boer War was very noticeable in Ethel's book Gum Leaves *which was published during this year 1899.*

By kind permission of the Mitchell Library.

Ethel and Herbert with a party of friends with whom they went sailing, on 26 January 1900. Ethel is seated second from left, with Herbert immediately in front. Ethel records 'had an exciting adventure — went to the rescue of a capsized crew and took them all into our boat'.

Jean's birthday party, aged two.

Henry Lawson with his daughter Bertha. Henry Lawson 1867-1922 was born at Grenfell, N.S.W. His books published in 1895 While the Billy Boils *and* In the Days When the World was Wide *typify his style and give a vivid picture of the struggles of the man on the land. He had two children James and Bertha. Henry often talked with Ethel about the problem they shared as they both suffered from deafness.*

By kind permission of the Mitchell Library.

A gathering at the Spit welcomed the first tram from Spit Junction on 27 October 1900. The steam punt seen in the distance was the only link with the northern beaches.
By kind permission of Mr R. B. Sturrock.

A horse-drawn wagon laden with bricks going on board the punt at the Spit.
By kind permission of Mr R. B. Sturrock.

Parriwi Road Mosman taken before the extension of the tram line down to the Spit.
By kind permission of the Mitchell Library.

8th February:

Went to town and saw Mr Jeffrey, he wants me to keep the Children's Page, says he wouldn't like anyone else to do it. So I have £1 a week still. Poor Lil has nothing from it but she says she doesn't care, it was a fearful nuisance to do and took a lot of money running into town.

9th February:

H. and I to Mosman's Bay where the Eula *lies for Mr and Mrs Moor's picnic. As soon as we got fairly in the boat and started, a squall struck us and the rain came down in the most blinding torrents I have ever seen. We were drenched to the skin in five minutes. As soon as they could they put the girls off in the dinghy. Then we had 20 minutes' walk uphill in the downpour. Mrs Moor had to provide everyone with a complete set out which occasioned a good deal of fun. Chatted and had music in the evening.*

11th February:

Went to see Mr Steele and of course in the end he got his way. I promised him Story of a Baby. *I'm to have 10 per cent and half serial rights.*

13th February:

A cyclone with Rosie, she spoke abominably to Mother and said things that made her cry. It's an awful shame that any one of a family should make so many disturbances. Rose is really a firebrand. Lil and I have been talking of going up the Mountains for three or four weeks. It would be heavenly. Neither of us feel at all right, and we should take plenty of paper and our fountain pens and write in the interval of climbing. I don't know what H. will say, he can't bear the idea of even a fortnight. Miss Arquimban, one of my 'literary protegées' came. She is twice as big as I am, or nearly twice. I felt somewhat embarrassed. She seems to think a surprising lot of my stories, says she reads everything I write. Had a literary talk with her in the study and gave her back her stories. I don't wonder she can't write, she has read scarcely anything, no poets, no Meredith, Carlyle, Kipling, anything, didn't know some of the best authors by name even. I promised to go and see her. Night read Keats and wrote about ten lines of the Larrikin.

19th February:

Letter from Mrs Crisford asking me to buy her Picturesque Atlas — *nine guineas, and her buggy, ten guineas! An impression seems getting abroad that I am making a fortune. Went to town and saw Mr Steele, he asked me to let him send* Bobbie *to England, and I did so on the understanding that no arrangement was made and if I wished it they were to forward it on to any other publisher.*

24th February:

Morning sewed a little, rested a much. Sid Mack came up to dinner — as might be expected. Mother and Mr Cope went to see the Reids, we three girls melted away and Lucy and Sid had a long time together — they too strayed gullywards. They are engaged — very secretly at last — I am not supposed to know but I do. The Stuckeys told H. and he told me. Lil has no idea. Night went to church.

27th February:

Lil and I went to Neutral Bay to have a bathe. on the way back I lost my purse with a great deal of money in it. And going from place to place about it and losing boats and trams made me two hours late in getting to Hermsley. Poor H. was half wild with anxiety and had just gone out in search of me. He even went up to Gordon to see if I was at home, and hearing I wasn't made it still more dreadful for him. I have never seen him so shaken as when he got back at 10.30 pm, he couldn't speak. The E. Curlewises are in great trouble — baillifs in the house and all sorts of other things to follow.

3rd March:

Morning, etc. etc. Decided — almost — about going to Blackheath. Night had an intangible fit of the miserables and walked for a long time on the tennis court in the dark. Life seems to frighten me.

5th March:

Wrote at Larrikin. *Mr Cope came home early in a very excited state. A man, Mr Blaxland — there is ill blood between them — struck him in the street. And Mr Cope struck back. It was in the Cricket crowd at the* Herald *office. I never* heard *of such a thing — two married men in silk hats acting like schoolboys. It was too short to attract notice, but they each have a slightly blackened eye. It really is rather funny.*

18th March:

So to Blackheath. Caught the 8 am train down, then a cab to Soul's to see about chloride of lime cure for the snakes that H. is sure are all over Blackheath. He had a bad fit of the blues at the idea of me going. The train left at 10.15 am and we got to Blackheath at 2 pm. All the way I looked out of the window, the scenery was lovely. The Ivanhoe is the nicest hotel I have ever stayed at I think.

19th March:

Louie, Mother and I went to Govett's Leap, it was really glorious — it is no use however attempting to squeeze any descriptions into these little spaces. It is very cold indeed and we have found such appetites.

28th March:

Started off early for a grand day. Drove first to Sublime Point, a magnificent view, then to Katoomba Falls which we reached at 2 pm and had dinner. Went down to Falls and to Orphan Rock and Ida's Glimpse, had tea and started home. One of the horses fell lame and we had to go slowly — about 13 miles back. Got in at 7.30 pm frightfully tired, had a hot bath and went to bed. Letter from Warne refusing Story of a Baby *after a long delay. It must certainly be a poor story — I am half sorry I accepted Ward and Lock's offer, I think I ought to have published it in the fireplace. Also letter from* Harper's *refusing short story, 'About a Midget' and from the* Idler *refusing 'A Saucepan Sketch'*. The tide of luck seems turning.*

---

*This short story appears in the collection *The Camp at Wandinong.*

5th April:

Morning went to Mermaid's Cave again and got a few ferns. Afternoon drove to Minne-ha-ha Falls, at least as far as we could, then walked on a long way till we found them. Night played chess.

8th April:

Rosie and Rex went with the others for a drive to Lithgow. I packed up all morning, it was terrible getting all my things into my gladstone and dress basket. Caught the 1.30 pm train home and H. met me at the station. Had a long evening together, it is very sweet to be wanted so very much. We made many vain calculations as to how much two people could begin life on. I have promised to be married before very long even if we have nothing — the longest shall be Christmas year — a year and nine months off — we are going to be very poor but that I don't mind even if we only have £100 a year.

5th May:

Played tennis in the morning, we are going to play on Sundays despite the horror of the Pockleys and the Kings. It keeps Rex out of worse mischief and does no one any harm in this quiet place.

9th May:

Afternoon Mother and I went to Dr Emily Ryder's lecture — much of it was on marriage. I have always had a shrinking from physiology but really every girl ought to know certain things. Ignorance is not innocence, I should be a good deal stronger woman today if I had known the importance of taking care of myself before instead of being reckless as I have been. Mother spoke to Dr Quaife too about Lil and me, he says we'll break down with nervous exhaustion if we keep up such a rate of writing, that we must slow off and take lots of rest and recreation. Night went to Hermsley, it is four years today since H. and I were engaged, had the first fire of the winter in the drawing room and a long evening together and H. gave me a dear little letter balance.

10th May:

Afternoon made scones for the bazaar and did other things. Night went up to the bazaar and helped with tea room, a very poor attendance. Bought a multitude of the usual useless things 'for the good of the church'. A long letter from Steele, enclosing one from Windsor Castle acknowledging Seven Little A's for Prince Alex. of Battenburg. and one from Duchess of Albany ditto. He says they are sending copies to children of note. But that though book is going fairly well, he hoped it would do better, its merits deserving more, etc. etc.

22nd May:

Morning did Children's Page. Afternoon sewed, went with Mother to pay calls. Mrs Taylor, ill — Mrs King (Parsonage) ditto. Mrs Callegan, in but not interesting in the least. Waste of time.

23rd May:

Had a letter from George Meredith. A lovely one — he says that unlike many of the books he receives, mine has given him pleasure. That he is introduced to an ideal nursery of real children, whose humour, characteristics and chatter are as redolent of their stage of life as breath of the nodding meadow flowers. That this claims his gratitude and he renders it warmly, with the certainty that my hand will not fail when I try it upon larger themes. As I will, for evidently, I have the literary gift. Of all my possessions this letter will be the dearest, there is no one in the whole world I would rather have had a letter from.

Steele wrote — there is another book called Growing Up. *I have to alter the title and let him cable it to London. I can't think of a good one so quickly — only* Growing Older. *I got in a very bad temper, Rosie left some red dye stuff on a seat and I sat down and ruined my very best Sunday meeting frock. And I had just got a new pretty brown velvet hat to wear with it.*

28th May:

Had a wire from Steele saying the trade did not like At Misrule *title and would I change. Wired back* Family at Misrule. *Night wrote a long letter to Steele and a sharp one. I told him I really must rebel at being so perpetually reminded of all he had done for me, etc. That I consider things are equal, my business is to write as good a book as I can, his, to engineer it as well as he can.*

15th June:

H. came at 12, quite knocked up. He had a very stiff brief with Rolin as opposing counsel, Judge Windeyer and several advised him to settle it, that there was no chance of a win, but he determined to go through with it; he fought hard all day and about 4 pm got a verdict for his side, everyone says it was a splendid defence. Afternoon went for a walk gullywards and talked of ways and means, the unpleasantness of butcher, baker and co. We shall be very poor but I shouldn't like to begin rich, there would be no variety then, unless one got poor. But we shall be together and that is everything in the world. Have promised to be married in March.

18th June:

Left the Hague Smith's at Strathfield about 10 am and walked from station to Quay shopping on the way. I had two or three hours to wait for Lil and occupied myself by going over to North Shore and seeing what cottages at 15/- or 17/- a week are like, I don't see how we can afford to give more. The most wretched little places, not ideal at all — poky and common and washerwomany. Why ever can't landlords build small places fit for people who have more 'sweetness and light' than cash. Rustic weatherboard with red roof and casement windows would cost little and not be so mean and wretched-looking as these.

20th June:

Wrote the last word of The Little Larrikin. *Oh I am glad too, it doesn't matter about being conceited in one's diary, and I do feel it's good. At any rate, it's the best work I've done and perhaps shall do. There's only to finish the copying out now and generally revise it.*

28th June:
Shopped all morning, evening dress things, programmes, etc. I really wish I was out of the dances, they take up so much time, cost so much and are not so madly enjoyable after all. I'm losing my zest for them. Afternoon covered a pair of black shoes with pale pink satin so the most expert of judges could not tell — a saving of 6/6 in hard cash but an infinite waste of time. Talked to Louie about royalties and literary stuff — and the possibilities of marriage on nothing per annum. Louie says she and Mr Creed are going to pay 8/- a week for rent — H. and I are thinking of the princely sum of 15/-.

13th July:
North Shore Spinsters' dance. Morning went in early to help decorate, cut sandwiches, etc. Night went to dance and wore pale salmon pink crepon with big satin sleeves, and pink shoes and stockings. Enjoyed it muchly and danced with H. a shocking number of times, also an orthodox number with Mr Tucker, etc. etc.

15th July:
Morning H. and I went to Mrs Soderberg's for lunch, I was quite vexed with her, she had gone to so much trouble. H. made a martyr of himself, he hates fried fish, but there was nothing else, and she had been to so much trouble, I told him he must. So he had two servings followed by charlotte and whipped cream and tarts, another thing he hates, and said he felt poisoned. Then I went for afternoon tea with Louie to the Thompsons. Mrs, Katie, Fred and Lil there (I am beginning to suspect those two, Fred was very nice but not nice enough for dear old Lil). The water famine is really very serious, they are measuring the drinking water, by cupsful, to buy it is 10/6 a small cask. No washing can be done or anything.

24th July:
A doleful letter from Mother saying it's no use to come home yet, not a drop of water. Also she wants me to lend her £10 quickly — I went all the way home to give her a kiss and cheer her.

8th August:
Wibigilla dance. Wore my white silk with scarlet poppies and white shoes and stockings. Really felt too tired to enjoy it. Danced with Mr Sendall, Dalton, etc. Sappho Smith came up to me and renewed an acquaintance — I was introduced to her about five years ago. She said she had read my book from cover to cover and was charmed with it, that she had heard I was engaged to a 'very clever, ambitious and good looking man'. 'Whatever do you want to be married for' she said 'why don't you stick to literature, you can't do both'. I said I fancied I could. She was introduced to H. too and had a long chat. He said he was afraid a time would come when he would be known as 'Mrs Curlewis' husband'. She said 'not you'.

17th August:

Morning finished Dolly's pale blue frock for her birthday. Afternoon started a short story, 'The Child of the Children'*. In evening H. and I went along Newtown Road to the Avenue and he showed me the log where he used to sit five or six nights a week and watch my study windows before we were engaged.

26th August:

Started Zola's Downfall, the first of Zola I have ever read. It is luridly magnificent and horrible, read till I was fairly shivering with fright. Mother went to H's. chambers. A great revolution has taken place at home — Mother has tackled Mr Cope, told him she has consented to my being married in April, that he is to give me away, and not make my life miserable until. And at last he has given way!!

28th August:

Cut out calico and sewed all day. Nearly made a heliotrope stripe blouse. I am going to buy a machine and work at Hermsley since there seems no prospect of an end to the drought. The first copy of Story of a Baby *came — beautifully got up — art green and gold — the daintiest little book I have ever seen; but I* detest *the story now, and am expecting very scathing reviews.*

30th August:

Went to town with Mrs Soderberg to choose a hand machine — new they were eight guineas but we found a second-hand one for £3 10 0. Now I will do some work. Lil came to see me, we sat and talked in my bedroom for two or three hours. She told me about Fred Thompson — they like each other, stronger verb indeed — have confessed it, but are not engaged pending Fred getting something to do, he won't ask her to be. And poor boy, it seems pretty hopeless.

16th September:

It rained, actually rained, I felt I wanted to put up my face and drink the sweetness of it. H. and I went to the Whitfield's dance — not very good, no swing about it. Professor David, Mr Garran, Mr Atlee Hunt, Broinoski, Bensusan, others there.

20th September:

Came home at 10 am. I was so glad to be at the dear old place again after nine weeks away, though of course it has been very nice being with H. so much. A letter from Frances Hodgson Burnett!! Such a lovely one, she says she has read 7 Little A's and felt she must write to me herself to tell me how good it is. That it is 'a dear story and it is beautifully told, that at 20 you can write a thing so full of real sweetness and pathos'. That I have the rare power she always expresses by calling the 'real thing' — lots more beautiful things. That the chapter 'When the Sun went Down' is so good, so real and simple and heart-wringing. And she sent her love and told me to believe in myself and have courage!!!

---

* *The Child of the Children* was published first in *The Windsor Magazine* and later appeared in the collection of short stories called *The Camp at Wandinong.*

26th September:
Looked through the Larrikin *with an eye to attacking it. I shall half rewrite it, Martin I am going to make quite a different character. Mark Twain sent me a very nice note — he said he had only just dipped into* 7 Little A's *yet as he was very busy but he could see in a moment it was not going to be commonplace, etc. etc. A letter from Steele, he entreats me to postpone my marriage and go to England with my next book, that it would do me all the good in the world. What would H. say to that I wonder? A State child came to-day as servant, Clara. And the new man for the garden.*

17th October:
Went to Hermsley for lunch, talked to the 'mad uncle' as they call him, Frank O'Brien — I liked him very much. The poor man has just been 'sold up' however and is very down. Went to Horderns for a tent for Rex's birthday.

19th October:
Went up to the store very early, my heart in my mouth. I could hardly open the Herald *and* Telegraph. *And then, after all my fears and certainities of harsh critiques both gave splendid notices. Both found* Story of a Baby *a 'decided advance on* 7 Little A's*' and said all manner of good things. I am a lucky girl, really very very lucky, for the book is not much good I feel certain. Poor old Lil is very depressed, it all seems waiting for her and it is very galling for me to keep succeeding and her, the elder sister, be behind. I wrote to Steele and begged him to hurry up and read her manuscript. Sewed most of the day — finished and put away a hemstitched sheet for the Cottage of Futurity.*

24th October:
The first copy of Family at Misrule *came this morning, it was lovely to handle it, the cover isn't as pretty though as* 7 L A *or* The Baby *— I think it is my best so far. Mother and Lil again pressing me to put off my marriage and go to England first. They say everyone is saying it is absolutely suicidal for my career.*

27th October:
Morning wrote at Larrikin, *I've nearly finished it again — Unless I pull it to pieces once again. Afternoon read Meredith's* House on the Beach.

2nd November:
Morning sewed. Mother and Mr Cope quarrelling again, he is really very unkind and inconsiderate to her, starts 'nagging' early in the morning and keeps it up all day — I never knew such a man. And yet he has his 'better parts', plenty of them. Mother was going away for a day to get out of it all but it rained so she merely stayed in my bedroom in hiding and he thought she had gone. He was frightfully angry and went off to town swearing. But at 9 pm he came back just so H. shouldn't have the excuse of staying the night.

3rd November:

Mr C. still raging. Mother quietly upstairs. It was like a scene in a comic opera to Lil and me, for he came in my bedroom once and we were shaking for fear Mother would cough or sneeze. Then as he was getting miserable and seemed more in sorrow than in anger, we made Mother put on her bonnet and come in, as if she had come home by train. Really very funny but rather ignominious. Still different people, different ways — and one can't act to him just like a rational being. Still I can't help liking him and being sorry for him when he's sorry. He's like Rex when he's been naughty.

14th November:

A dreadful day. Rosie ill in bed, she fainted last night at the Flower Festival and had to be driven home. Lil in bed with threatened influenza. Mrs Urquhart and Mrs Payten to spend the day, everything upside downside. I took command of the kitchen and Clara and tried to send in a nice little lunch but the curry was doubtful, the buttered eggs queer, the rolls burnt and only the junket right. Mrs Pains, 4 children and nurse then arrived and made pandemonium. William and Colin gave notice. Mrs Stewart groaned over the big ironing. And Clara set fire to things, and dropped plates and forgot cheerfully everything I told her. And of such is the kingdom of home on occasion.

20th November:

Weighed myself this morning 6st 12 — I've lost 4lbs lately. Did a competition for Golden Penny, *there's a £5 prize for 500 words describing a settler's life — did mine in verse. Night there was* another *delightful scene — really the home is getting wretched, he came home from the office and just because Rex had a half holiday began to swear violently. Lily suggested* she *had not given it and that he should go and swear at Mr Robson, whereupon he swore at her fearfully. Then Mother heard and came in and it got worse — he actually caught Mother by her throat, and lifted his hand. Sometimes I honestly think he is going mad; he's like no one else in the world. It's bitterly hard for poor little Mother, he's really shortening her life for her; she talked seriously to us about getting a separation, says she really* can't *bear it much longer. And yet, as she says, even apart from the soul-scarifying publicity, she couldn't bear to think of him going to ruin as he would. For he's without doubt very fond of her and absolutely couldn't live without her. Late at night Lil took him in hand and he was very repentant, and promised faithfully and 'before his Maker' to 'keep the peace' for three months.*

22nd November:

A column and a half splendid review of Misrule in Bulletin *— their reviews are good, so to the point. There are none I like better. Louie came up for the day — the first time we have seen each other since the quarrel. How we talked! I like her better than ever — there's* no one *just like Louie for a friend, we seem to have been through so many things together and are so entirely in sympathy. Such news — she is going to be married on 7th or 8th January — six weeks off!*

1st December:

Read The Man from Snowy River *and enjoyed it* immensely. *Wrote to Mr Paterson to tell him so. Wrote letters most of the afternoon, one about the widow of Marcus Clark, there is an appeal for her as she is destitute. I thought of getting up a book of short stories — getting Louis Becke, Boldrewood, etc. to write and giving proceeds to her.*

3rd December:

Wrote in the morning very slowly. I am starting a new book, a pot-boiler to help with the furniture of the cottage to be. Had a very nice letter from Mr A. B. Paterson*, he said he was very pleased to get my letter as my 'appreciation was of more value than most people's'.

6th December:

Went to Mrs Soderberg's for lunch then to Chatswood with Louie. We were both greatly excited — almost ran along the road to her cottage. The exploring was lovely, six little arbors in the garden, grape vines, strawberry plants, cape gooseberries, apricots, everywhere. And the dearest little cottage. We sat in one of the bowers — mine, at least Herbert's and mine, it is to be sacred to us. And we talked and talked and talked. And then came a rumble along the road and we darted out to meet the first of the furniture, for Creed is to come and live there from tonight and take care of it. Such a white sweet little kitchen table and safe, such a ridiculously small and interesting dining room table — a sideboard — £2 15 0 but full of grace. Even the kettle and saucepan and frying pan were romantic and delightful. Caught the 5 pm train home and idled all the evening. Such goings on are not conducive to hard work. Herald *and* Telegraph *both speak of my suggestion about widow of Marcus Clarke.*

16th December:

A terrible, awful, terrific day. The hottest I remember. Shopped and hunted for a servant from morn till dust dry eve — got blown nearly out of the world by a southerly buster. Had lunch at Quong Tarts and back to Hermsley in evening.

24th December:

Poor Children's treat. Very busy all day getting ready for the children. They came at 4 pm, such clean, respectable little things, very shy and eagerly expectant, some 'rich' children too — the three little Sargoods and Miss Oldfield, the Kings, Pattisons, etc. We played games in the paddock with them, then they ran races till everyone had won a doll or prize. Then they had cakes and tea and sweets. And then we showed a living Punch and Judy show through the study window. Rosie made a really splendid Punch, I was Judy with my nose and cheeks painted scarlet, Lil combined the duties of Policeman, Doctor and Devil. Had a splitting headache after and went to bed at 8 pm.

---

* *Mr A. B. Paterson, 'Banjo', 1864-1941 was born near Molong N.S.W. He was educated at Sydney Grammar School and studied Law at Sydney University. He wrote ballads, verse, novels and stories about the Australian countryside and his writing reflected the more cheerful and idealistic aspects of shearing, droving and bush life. In 1899 he went to the South African War as a correspondent for the* Sydney Morning Herald.

25th December:

Went to church, Mother and the four of us, in the morning. Spent a quiet pleasant day though I was forced to do a little work, having forgotten my Children's Page for the week. Such funny 'domestic' presents I got, everyone giving with an eye to the April cottage. A very nice glass dish from Mother, a glass jug from Rex, a rolling pin from Lil, 4 table vases from Rosie and from Mr Cope a handkerchief and a piece of heliotrope belting. H. gave me a Walker's Letter Copying press, it will be very useful I have so many business letters I ought to keep copies of.

31st December:

Made 'little lists' and thought out schemes of colour for the rooms — it is an endless source of delight. Went to post — again no letter from H. who is sailing at Broken Bay, but it is once again fine and sunshiny, after the thunderstorms, and no yacht wrecks are given in the paper so I am not so anxious now. Night did accounts for the year — I've made £818 altogether up to now by my pen, received £377 this year but of course the £210 is very much in advance.

In her book *The Little Larrikin* Ethel disguises herself as Linley, an aspiring artist (another of Ethel's ambitions) and she portrays Herbert as Roger, a struggling law student, father figure of a family of five boys. Herbert confesses to a jealousy of her writing and for her own good, offers to release her from her promises to him. She recognises and acknowledges her many inconsistencies and frequently resolves to be kinder to him. On the other hand she also realises where her strength is when she writes, 'Linley could paint children; she caught them on her canvas somehow with a flash and quick flutter of brushes and they laughed out at you, or were thoughtful with young sweet gravity, looked angel-like, mischievous, penitent, loving — true children, truly painted'. This assessment could apply equally as well to Ethel's own characterisations.

'The Child of the Children' referred to in August tells the story of a committee of rich little girls adopting a child from poverty-stricken surroundings, educating, clothing and trying to present her in society as one of their class. The plan seems to be progressing well until they try Flip at a birthday party. She can't resist smuggling delicacies out to her poor and numerous brothers and sisters and she is eventually exposed — much to Flip's relief.

In 1958 there was quite a stir when an article, about the above story, appeared in an English newspaper. Author James Bennett suggested that George Bernard Shaw had stolen his idea for *Pygmalion* (first performed in London in 1914 and later turned into the musical, *My Fair Lady*) from Ethel Turner's story *Child of the Children*, which was published in the *Windsor* magazine in 1897. There are indeed some remarkable similarities.

1896

And the Morning and the Evening were the First Day

Warnings from friends and her publisher that marriage would be suicidal for her career must have caused Ethel much soul-searching. She frequently admitted to a feeling of apprehension about being married and her own parents' difficult relationship must have influenced her greatly. However, she finally made the decision and the devoted Herbert was rewarded for his patience.

Once the big step was taken, all misgivings vanished and she settled down to a state of 'marital bliss'. Visitors and callers were an interruption to their lives, and by the end of the year they were longing for more time to themselves.

8th January:
Louie's wedding day. Caught 2.45 pm train down, and H. and I went straight to Neutral Bay. Such a dear little bride she looked — a very simple white dress trimmed with chiffon and a white flower in her hair. She wasn't a bit nervous, very bright and talkative and laughing. They were married in the drawing room, standing against a three-legged gipsy table — we were told off to be bridesmaids at the last minute, Alice, Florrie, Amy and I. Eddie gave her away and H. was best man. After the service Herbert, Eddie and Sid disappeared and I heard later they had gone off and shut themselves up in the bathroom and had a smoke — to relieve their feelings. Then Louie handed cake round and refused to be a little tin god. Then the cab came and we all threw rice and rose leaves at them.

13th January:
A terrible day — the very hottest known in the annals of N.S.W. It was 108° at the Observatory and 112° in the shade at the Post Office. I sewed for a time, at least, guided the machine while H. turned the wheel, but after a time just gave up and lay down on the matting and gasped.

20th January:
Shopped in morning and bought a dream of a 'robe de nuit'. Afternoon went to Chatswood to see 'the little bride'. She is absolutely brimming over with happiness — I am the first person who has been admitted since they drove there after the wedding. How we talked! Perhaps being married isn't after all quite so to-be-trembled-at a thing as I have been thinking. We calculated to a nicety by the bills just how much it costs to keep two people from starving, £3 a week. Then we drove to look at a cottage for H. and me, so we should not be out in the cold — a wonderful little Queen Anne place at the ridiculous sum of 13/- a week. I am wild to have it.

21st January:

Mother came down with me to Chatswood to look at the cottage, she throws cold water, finds the washhouse too close to the dining room and the necessity of building a servant's room and paying 13 weeks' rent to retain it, as drawbacks. H. came up to see it and likes it very much, we should have much more to spend on books and luxuries if rent is low.

22nd January:

Lil and I went down by the 11 to see the cottage, I couldn't keep away. And some wretched barbarian had actually snapped it up — bought it! I could have cried all the way home. Lil comforted me by saying it was poky, but it wasn't. Went to see another, a little beauty with every convenience, only it's £1 a week and travelling would be another 5/-, too much for the likes of us at present. Caught 2 pm back and idled and rested from the disappointment the rest of the day.

24th January:

My birthday. Twenty-four summers gone over my head. A fiercely hot day to make me remember it — got out Bobbie *and tried to think of new ideas for it. Tried writing in my bedroom in airy attire with occasional refreshment in the way of putting my feet in cold water. Result less than a page.*

30th January:

Had another bad night and felt still more of a wreck — my nerves feel like fiddlestrings. I have been worrying about the accumulation of work that has, someway, to be done before 22nd April. At 2 pm Fred Thompson came and he and Lil went to find our *gully. Fred stayed to dinner and afterwards had it out with Mr Cope about he and Lil — Mr C. is really improving, Fred didn't have half the bad time H. did, or even Harold.*

7th February:

Sydney Girls High School Prize Giving: years since I have been in the gate — Mrs Garvin introduced me to the Minister as her 'very distinguished old pupil'. when I went into the school room there was a lot of clapping and about five minutes after Miss Bruce told me it was for me *— I never dreamt of it and took no notice whatever. She said they were very proud to have me as an old girl; I felt quite embarrassed.*

13th February:

To Mrs A's at Potts Point for lunch. Didn't enjoy myself particularly, flattery very delicately applied, one is not above appreciating, but when it is laid on with a trowel, it nauseates. A woman sculptor Thea Cowan was there, very clever I believe but her skirt and blouse had parted company, pins were visible and her hair obtruded itself. Why can't women work and take an interest in their clothes too!

18th February:

Started chapter 3, The Camp at Wandinong, *but had to hunt after a stupid servant so much, I could hardly do anything. Domestic routine would kill inspiration, I'll have to*

*get a capable servant if I am to do anything in days to come. Letter from The Banjo —
he says he shall be glad to help in the Marcus Clarke project. I like Mr Paterson
exceedingly.*

3rd March:
Tried hard to write 'School At Jimbaree' * but I can't put any heart into it, writing
feels almost hateful just now. Afternoon Blanche Curnow came and at night the
Sargoods — I have asked Marian to be one of my bridesmaids. A letter from Mr
Paterson saying he can't get manuscript for the Marcus Clarke, and from what he hears
the object is not a worthy one and he thinks we had better let it go. It's a great relief, I
am so pressed with work I didn't know how I was going to keep up the meetings and
write a story for it.*

13th March:
*Sewed nearly all day. H. came up at 5 pm— couldn't wait until tomorrow. He says it is
harder to wait now than it has ever been, that the five weeks to the wedding seem an
eternity.*

19th March:
*Met Lil and shopped. Bought my wedding dress material — an ivory white merveilleux
— no looking back from the plough now. Wrote to Mr Tucker to say after all we
cannot go to the picnic on Saturday — we shall have to be househunting.*

28th March:
*Had a great clearance of pigeon holes and cupboards and sent about a ton of rubbish
out to be burned. Miss Roberts the dressmaker came and I was fitted on and measured
and pinpricked most of the afternoon. Letter from Mr Tucker — he says for reasons
better understood than stated he should not like to witness my wedding. H. came up for
evening and showed me a letter Mr Cope had sent him — a horrid one.*

31st March:
*Children's Page competitions in morning. A letter from H. asking me to come down at
once. I went by the 2.45 pm, we went straight to Mosman's, and actually and at last
took a cottage for a year. It won't be finished till 1st May, but it will be a very nice
little place — Queen Anne style, red-tiled roof, pretty finishings. And in the place we
want most of all, the top of Mosman's — lovely view and Balmoral five minutes away.
Rent a guinea, and water and sewerage rates. More than we meant but it is not dear.*

2nd April:
*Mother marked all my linen and house linen and we packed one big trunk. I cleaned
out drawers full of rubbish and got so tired out and worried I had a fit of crying and
laughing together — the second lately — I've never been like it in my life before, it's next
door to hysteria.*

---

*'School at Jimbaree' was a short story published in *The Camp at Wandinong*.

3rd April:

Good Friday. Went to church in morning. Afternoon made a 'Wedding day bonnet' for Mrs Curlewis, she is getting a new dress and mantle so I wanted to save the bonnet expense.

4th April:

Went to town by the 8 am and shopped with H. at Horderns. Afternoon we went to see the 'Chalet' — the place he has found for the honeymoon. It is really a delightfully romantic place — it overlooks Little Sirius — it is really only about ten minutes from Mosman and yet as lonely as if we were one hundred miles away. Five acres of garden — quite a wild Swinburnian garden. And a stretch of beach and beautiful sea at the bottom of it. Quaint rooms with harmonium and a very old piano with a very tall back — a summer room enclosed with glass and a splendid view. I shall love it, and it will be fifty times nicer than travelling after the tiring, exciting day.

6th April:

H. came up. I sewed all morning — thinking I had done with evening dresses for a little time I cut the pink satin sleeves out of my only respectable one to make a cosy; and now I have to stitch them in again for the Sargood's affair. In afternoon Sid Mack and Alan Uther came. They tell me they are 'going to get themselves up something 'orrible to do me proud' on the wedding day, that they can think of nothing but tall hats and wedding garments. Captain and Mrs Taylor sent us an exquisite pair of real silver fruit spoons in a case, and Ella and Flo Pockley the loveliest bread platter and knife.

16th April:

Town, shopping hard all day, bought a wardrobe, dressing chest, washstand, the veil and 50 other things. Mr and Mrs Curlewis have given us such useful things — a wire mattress, a kapok mattress, a pair of blankets, a quilt, mosquito net, etc. Florrie and Nellie Hague Smith a pair of silver entrée dishes, Mr and Mrs F. O'Brien a breakfast set.

17th April:

Stayed in bed till 11 am, I feel I am getting completely knocked up, if I'm not careful I'm afraid it will be serious, so now I am going to let everything go and rest till the day of days. Herbert is seeing to everything needful. Such hosts of presents! A real silver card case from Mr Tucker, silver entrée dishes from Mr and Mrs Sargood, etc. etc. and many more. H. stayed the night — I had a queer kind of faint and when I came round cried for long enough — I shall be glad when all the worry is over and I can rest and get normal again.

19th April:

I had a nest of cushions put under a tree and lay there all day. H. stayed all the morning and calmed me and soothed me till I felt happy again. In the afternoon he went and then Mother came and lay down with me and Mr Cope and Lil came and we spent my last Sunday at home very peacefully and happily under the gum trees at the end of the tennis court. It was a perfect day.

20th April:

Packed all day and did various little finishings. A beautiful silver teapot came from Mrs Church, a silver dinner gong from Dr and Mrs Pockley, darling Mother two dish covers and the beautiful cake basket, dear old Lil my table silver.

21st April:

Packing, etc. etc. The big ship's awning is up on the tennis court. Mrs Soderberg is here, everything is getting shipshape, crowds more presents, I've quite lost count. The study is brimming over.

22nd April:

My Wedding Day: all this is written up from memory a fortnight later. I stayed in bed till 10 am for last night I did not shut my eyes till 5 am. Ella Pockley and Flo Barry came to help. It rained just a little now and again, not enough to wet anyone. All the morning the erection of arches and flags and the setting of tables went on. At 12.30 pm I went to dress, Rosie did my hair, Mother fastened my veil and put on my wreath. Had a fit of exceeding trembling at 1.30 pm but was calm at 2. The carriage came, Lil, Rose, Dolly, Marion and I someway squeezed into it. Had no time for nervousness. Rosie was so busy giving us our cues and we were all so anxious to keep ourselves uncrushed. The church crowded to overflowing — beautifully decorated (at least the papers said so after, I did not see). Up the aisle on Mr Cope's arm, caught a vision of W. Curnow, H. Wolstenholme and Dr Barry, and said to myself mechanically their faces looked familiar. Then a glimpse of poor little Mother with tear-wet eyes in the front pew. Then Herbert looking anxiously at me (I was so pale he said). The beautiful service — only once or twice my thoughts wandered and I couldn't realise that I had to listen especially. The plighting of troths — we both spoke up bravely. Lily taking off my glove. Herbert taking my hand — putting on the new strange little ring. Mr King's voice again — then a burst of organ and Herbert lifting my veil for the first kiss — and Mr Cope brushing roughly up, pushing him aside and taking the first before anyone could recover from the surprise — it was cruel, wicked. Then Herbert then Mother. Then down the aisle again through the sea of people into the carriage. H and I, no-one else. On the way home we were so happy we decided to forgive even Mr Cope. Out of the carriage, a second into the bedroom for my veil hung perilously off. Into the dining-room for vestry business — signings of names, etc. Into the drawing-room for the reception, nearly an hour shaking hands, laughing, talking, being congratulated by a hundred people. I lost my nervousness, even got a bright colour with the excitement they told me. Then away to the marquee to cut the cake, knocked the ornament off and broke some icing, then Herbert came to the rescue. Stayed about half an hour there, and enjoyed it thoroughly — we never thought we should find our own wedding real fun. Everyone was so nice. Talked to Mr Carruthers, Mr Rolin and a few others. Then to dress — Mother helping me. Down the stairs — the hall and verandah thickly lined, then a wild plunge to the carriage through a blinding shower of rice and flowers. Cheers in the air, then off, even down to the gate they pursued us with pellets. Then on to the Lane Cove road, and calm and quiet. It was the loveliest drive in the world, about ten miles — as we went the rain clouds cleared and the most glorious sun came out. I have never seen a sky more perfect. The Chalet, and only to find that though at the beginning we had untied one shoe, another one still dangled. Hence those smiles on the way. The old housekeeper had everything ready — Mrs Curlewis and Miss Bickle had put white flowers in all the rooms and all was welcoming and cheerful as Mother had thought impossible. And the loveliest moon in the evening. And the morning and the evening were the first day.

3rd May:

All this time from 22nd to 3rd our beautiful halcyon days. We had perfect weather all the time, sunshiny cool days, and moonlight nights lovelier than ever moonlight nights were yet. Rowed on the harbour in the moonlight. Lazed on the balcony on a heap of cushions. I don't know how newly married people can go to crowded hotels. Here it is perfect, we have seen no one but Mrs Brookes all the time and yet have any amount of space and ground to wander about in. Just ourselves for the dear little meals. No appearances to keep up, I wear my tea-gown and pretty dressing gown half the time. Sometimes we go down to the beach. Once I paddled and H. amused himself by trying his revolver that has lost its terrors for me, I have even fired it once myself.

6th May:

A day of visitors. Dear old Lil came at 10 am. I went to the top of the steps to meet her, being too shy yet to venture as near to the public gaze as the wharf. Had a lovely morning together. After an early lunch Rosie and Rex came — dear old lad, they say he misses me dreadfully and kisses my portrait every night with tears in his eyes. Had a jolly afternoon together. And then H. came home — it is so lovely when 5.30 pm comes round and the evening is astretch before us.

8th May:

Louie came early and we chattered like magpies. Afternoon took the electric train to North Shore — my first venturing among mankind again. Kept my veil down and was terribly nervous at the thought of meeting anyone. Bought an armchair for the kitchen for poor old Mrs Brookes — a straw palliasse for her instead of the wire one I had ordered — 'I hate them slippery things' she said 'I'm always fallin' out of bed'. Came home terribly tired at 3 pm and hungry!

9th May:

Got up at 11 am. Made lists and wrote notes of thanks, I'm nearly at the end of the wedding present list thank heavens. Did my first married cookery, a veal ragout — and H. wouldn't touch it because a carrot lurked within.

13th May:

First day in Yanalla*. It really is a dear little cottage — plenty of sweetness and light and not particularly small — I shall make it very pretty I hope, it is delightful work — quite puts literary things in the shade for a time.

---

*This house is thought to be No. 11 Harbour St, Mosman (near Spit Junction).

Jean and Adrian. Ethel's son was born on 13 January 1901.

Jean and Adrian. Ethel continued to write when her children were young, adding to her responsibilities as a young mother.

The building of Avenel at the address 17 Warringah Rd, Mosman.

Adrian at the Spit. The start of a lifetime interest in beach, surf and sun.

This photograph appeared in The New Idea, *1 April 1903. Taken in the garden at Avenel it shows a pleasant camping-party scene, with Ethel, Jean and Adrian.*

Ethel Turner in her drawing room at Avenel.

When Jean was 4½, Ethel wrote in her diary 'Her chief delight is stories. Stories, stories all the day. I am also introducing her to Tennyson and her appreciation is great of The Lady of Shallot, The Revenge, *etc.'*

23rd May:
Mother and Rex came at 11 am though it was pouring wet, then later — Mr Cope! Who was never going to darken my doors if I married! After tea it was too wet to think of them going so Mother and I made up beds for the three and rummaged up warm things for blankets and managed as best we could. At night we all played chess and bezique and were quite an amicable family party. Mr Cope seemed quite to like being here.

30th May:
We carpentered all day, at least H. did and I painted a table. And when I was particularly black-handed who should Mrs Brookes come and say was in the drawing room but Mrs Garvin! I scrubbed at my hands, donned a clean housewifely apron over my paint and received her — my first ordinary visitor — a nice way for a bride to be caught. After she went I fell to work again and at 5 pm another knock. I told Mrs Brookes I was 'out'. It was Miss Cousens and the two Austens. Ungracious of me I'm afraid, Miss Cousens is old and it is a long way; my conscience reproaches me but really I was too grubby, and I hate rushing in to change my dress while people wait. I wish they wouldn't call yet.

6th June:
Caught the 9.45 am train home — at least, for Herbert says this *is home — to Gordon. It was so funny to be walking down the old line again and up the paddock to the house as if nothing had happened. Saw Mother and Rosie straining their eyes looking for me but I had got in the shelter of the bushes and was hiding — then they ran to the front to see if I had come and I slipped in and was lying on the dining room sofa when they came. Such a lovely day we all had together. H. came up by the 1 train just like olden days and in the evening we all sat round a big log fire in the dining room and chatted. Mr Cope was very affable and seemed to like having us. Went home at 9 pm heavily laden with flowers, butter, cream, my wedding dress, etc.*

10th June:
Mrs Soderberg came to lunch; and after a drawing-room full of visitors — Mrs Shaw, Florrie and Nell Hague Smith, Mrs Stuckey, Mrs O'Brien. I dispensed tea from the cosy corner (thanking good fortune that it was finished) and did my best to be a good hostess and make conversation general — it's a little hard though having no mother or sister to help. At night I curled up in the big armchair before the fire and read Mr Jeffrey and Louis Becke's new book A First Fleet Family, *while my patient and long-suffering husband sat at the table and sorted out the Children's Page Competitions for me.*

20th June:

Women's Literary Society to welcome Louisa Macdonald. Wet all day, till night when it cleared. We went to Literary, a big crush of fashionables. I wore my wedding dress turned evening fashion, and H. looked awfully nice and we were both proud of each other — our first appearance in Society since our wedding. Such a bit of electricity, Louie's book The World is Round *was reviewed in this morning's* Telegraph — *it said she had not done herself justice, and that it was far too personal, that there had only been* one *Women's Literary Secretary in Sydney, who was also the daughter of a Supreme Court Judge. It really was cruel of Louie, she devoted two or three scathing pages to poor Margie Windeyer — held her nose and eyes and mouth and brain up to public ridicule and ridiculed the time at the Literary that Margie stood up and recited 'Twas Roses Roses all the Way' and then forgot the next line. And tonight up bounded Margie on the platform quite quivering with wounded pride and bravado and recited 'Roses Roses all the Way' prefacing it with remarks. My hair fairly stood on end. Everyone was talking of it and blaming Louie.*

23rd June:

It has been lovely having Lil to stay all this week, I don't think two sisters ever were as much to each other as we are.

This seems an appropriate opportunity to insert a letter of dedication to Lil on the opening page of *The Camp at Wandinong.*

It seems but yesterday when you were fifteen, I not far behind, and one of us was suddenly seized with a desire to write something.

And immediately the other was seized with the same overwhelming desire — had we not all our little lives done everything together and cared for nothing the other could not share?

We used to lock the bedroom door and write at the old marble washstand that was so generously roomy; no housewifery has ever been able since to take those ink-stains from its surface. Do you remember the characters we conjured up? Our heroes with their proud black eyes, etc.

Oh the paper we wasted and the lessons we left undone that we ought to have done. Oh the candles that burned to their last breath, and used to flicker and go out near midnight, just when the whispered reading of closely written pages reached the most thrilling point.

You were never satisfied with your stories unless you could work in a murder, and your most harmless people used to kill each other for entirely insufficient reasons. I was never happy unless my favourite character or characters had died on beautiful death-beds to slow music.

Our faith in each other in those days made out mutual criticisms gentle and our admiration boundless.

This plain little tale bears your name, and gleans its grace in bearing it. So the gift must make you as a child again, blind to all faults and pleased to offer praise.   E.T.

28th June:

Engaged a new servant Louisa to come next Wednesday, I had to give Mrs Brookes notice, she is too old and she won't let me do things in my own way. Mr Jeffrey enclosed a cutting from English Daily Mail *saying 'Miss Ethel Turner was a very pretty and young Australian girl who had just come to London and was chaperoned by Mrs Frances Hodgson Burnett — and that, unlike Olive Schreiner who hadn't a dress to wear, Miss Turner's frocks were particularly gorgeous affairs, etc.' What things one does hear about oneself.*

8th July:

Louisa left and the new servant Minnie came. Morning very busy cooking, making rooms pretty, etc. A crowd of callers in afternoon, Mrs Raymond King, Mrs Wilshire, Mrs Christian and Ruby, Mrs Bristowe and Tonie, Mrs Parker, Ethel and May Maynard. Then to dinner came Mr Uther, Mr 'Billy' Creagh and Sid Mack, Rosie here too, quite a little dinner party — everything passed off without a hitch, in the evening we had a big fire in the drawing room and the men smoked and we all talked. Herbert was very pleased with the way I had arranged everything.

11th July:

Odds and ends in the morning — which means alas no writing. Afternoon Mr and Mrs Ormond O'Brien called — they seem very nice indeed — but oh, we should like to have some time to ourselves, it's visitors, visitors every day.

15th July:

Afternoon went to Mrs Todd's At Home, it was a pretty terrible afternoon, a stuffy little drawing room packed with strange-looking females. Night wrote at Bobbie, I am practically at the end of it now, it only wants 'fixing up'. Ran in to see Mr Cope at the Lands Dept., he has been reduced £11 a year and is wildly angry — still I quite expected in this universal retrenchment he would have been 'dispensed with'.

21st July:

Wrote all morning, free, fast and furiously. Writing comes easier than ever now, just the words I want rush to the end of my pen and I can't go quickly enough. Night did accounts, we are spending too much — when we put it down on paper we estimated our housekeeping at £150 a year, we are spending at the rate of £250 to £300. H. suggests — almost with a break in his voice — perhaps we had better not have quite so many puddings. H. made a dresser for the kitchen today out of a packing case.

30th July:

H. brought home my copies — 16 of them — of The Little Duchess *it is very prettily got up. The review in the* Bulletin *said it was a 'disappointing book and the characters like pretty, delicate china'.* Town and Country *finds it very good. But I trust* Bulletin *most. Felt very lonely today, it is a long time from 9.15 am to 5.30 pm and no one to speak to; even writing doesn't quite banish the loneliness and I keep wishing H. would come home.*

31st July:

Rained all day. Wrote nearly all the time, and finished the last chapter of The Camp at Wandinong — *that's not* bad, *nearly a book since I was married — certainly there's very little in it, only about 25,000 words. I am very eager to get it off to a publisher, and start* Three Little Maids, *I have such a lot in my head for it.*

1st August:

Morning nothing in particular. Afternoon went to Hermsley. I felt quite unmarried again as we went down the old street and in at the gate, quite as if presently they would all dissolve away and leave us the drawing room to ourselves. Instead we all had tea together, Marmee, 'Dad', Claude, Clive, Leslie, Bunty, Dolly, Billy, H. and I. Then we had a pleasant evening by the fire.

18th August:

Took a brand new exercise book and started a brand new story in it Three Little Maids — Lil, Rose and I when we were small. Went out to Crown St and called on the Stuckeys. I couldn't* live *in such a neighbourhood — so dusty and noisy and dirty; everyone seemed dingy and careworn and miserable. It was lovely to get back to fresh, sweet little Mosman again. Night we played chess, started on our tournament, H. gives me queen and move so far, but I am improving and intend to scorn it. If I get six out of eleven, I shall only take a rook. We won a game each tonight.*

22nd August:

Mr Curlewis and Claude came to dinner, Marmee was ill again and couldn't. H. is 27 today, just six years ago tonight he told me he loved me — at the Hague Smith's dance. And I told him I would be his friend — or 'sister' — but could never, never, never love him.

4th September:

I wrote a little — a few pages more of 'The Child of the Children' for the Windsor — *can't get into a writing mood again, there have been too many visitors and distractions. Wrote to The Banjo in answer to his letter and also sent him my* Little Duchess.

18th September:

Went to town early and bought strawberries and hyacinths, and went out to Waverley to leave them for Sappho Smith and ask after her. She had had a bad night and was no better. Such a dusty, noisy house right on the street — the sister keeps a school and a child was having a music *lesson — poor, poor Sappho. I'd like to die among green fields or with waves near — not shrieking trams and an excruciating piano.*

23rd September:
The Herald *announces the publication of Lil's* Lights of Sydney *by Cassells — the first intimation either of us have had; I felt like standing on my head with joy and I suppose she must be feeling the same, dear old girl. In afternoon came May Maynard, Nellie Hague and Blanche Curnow, also Mrs John Meillon, she seems very nice indeed and is thinking of taking the cottage next door — the junior bar is getting thick over here.*

25th September:
Phyllis and Guy Pockley arrived at 12 noon, such quaint little morsels — Phyllis is so precocious she would be dreadful to live with, but for half a day very pleasant. And Guy is a loveable little lad. We had a merry little lunch — red jelly, meringued tart, gingerbread rabbits and wafers, then went off down to Balmoral Beach. I got them masks and hidden treasures on the way and they fairly bubbled over with excitement. We all paddled and they looked for starfish, etc.

6th October:
Wrote a 2000-word story for the Sunday Times *'A Mist and A Vapour'. Afternoon with H. to Government House Garden Party. A very brilliant assembly, Rosie and I enjoyed it very much but H. said it was 'very terrible'.*

14th October:
Etc. etc. all morning. Afternoon went to call on Mrs Meillon. She has a dear little baby, four months old. Called also on Mrs and the Misses Hooke. Wrote an 'encouraging' letter to little Muriel Clarkson, who wrote to me about her stories and also to Mr Steele.

23rd October:
Went to Gordon by the 10 am train. Lil had some good news to tell, Mr Soderberg is taking Fred as pupil to dentistry and says the premium can be paid any time. Now there is some prospect of that dear little girl being married.

31st October:
Minnie left — she said she was very sorry to, and the new girl Alice came, I think I shall like her very much. Afternoon went to return Mrs Cullen's call. She showed me all over their grounds — they are lovely inasmuch as they have left them almost as they found them, there is a lovely gully and waterfall — a big piece devoted to flannel flowers and all the native trees. A thunderstorm came up so I had to stay a long time and had a pleasant hour playing with the baby and little Cliff, a darling boy of three.

6th November:

Went up to Louie's for morning and lunch — the little cottage is beginning to look shabby already and there's no money to replenish, they are very hard up just now, so far Louie says they have only spent £37 on all the furnishing. We've been much more extravagant and spent about £120 and that lots of people would laugh at. I wish wish wish I could give Louie a help; next story I get paid for I'll try and get some little things for her house.

Then at 2 pm I caught the train to Gordon to kiss little Lil and congratulate her on her first book. And a terrible fright I had, a man on Gordon station came up to me and said there'd been a terrible accident by the 10 am train — that a Miss Turner had been cut to pieces. It never occurred to me to stop and make enquiries, I just started running, madly up the line towards the house. He shouted after me not to get 'excited' as it might be no relation, but I couldn't stop. I ran and stumbled and stumbled and ran all the way to the house, my heart in my throat. And Lil came to meet me halfway down the paddock. The reaction was so great I fell down on the grass and cried till poor old Lil was quite frightened for I couldn't tell her. Then we sent Joseph off post haste to the Pains to see if Rosie was all right. And she was. It was a Miss Turner of Wahroonga, a woman of 50. A fright like that is enough to kill one. Came home at 5 pm a feeble wreck.

18th November:

Tried to write, I am quite out of the mood again and feel I'd rather scrub floors. So threw the papers away and made a white muslin dress for myself. H. amused himself for an hour by going down in the cellar and shooting with his revolver at a tin. Of course every ten minutes I had to go and call out to him, to make sure he hadn't shot himself by mistake.

7th December:

'Forget what did'.

18th December:

Alice ruined my blue blouse. Likewise my temper. I went to town to shop and recover. In afternoon went to the High School breaking up since I had promised Mrs Garvin to do so and felt like a schoolgirl at the sight of all the familiar things. They introduced me to a crowd of people and I came away with a headache from the clapping. Night read Great Expectations — *it is magnificent.*

21st December:

Shopped busily all day — such lots of little presents I had to get. Then H. and I went round to buy me a Xmas present, we both enjoyed it so much, going from shop to shop to find the very nicest thing for the money, I nearly decided on a little brass afternoon tea kettle that would have swallowed all the money, then I thought it would be nicer to get a lot of little things for the house.

25th December:

Mr and Mrs Soderberg came. H. and I, Rosie and Harold went to church though the heat was simply frightful. Such a merry time we all had afterwards and Mrs Soderberg has made me a beautiful over-mantle. Mother gave H. and me a hen and four chickens.

31st December:

I did a good day's sewing and in afternoon Children's Page. At night H. and I went to the Thompson's for an hour or two — we sat out on the verandah when we returned home and watched the new year in and wondered if ever such a perfect year's happiness could ever come to us again.

In the book *White Roof Tree*, there is a short story by E.T. called 'Marriage Morn' — the similarities between Ethel's and Ellice's wedding day are touching and delightful:

> She had looked for the sun hour after hour during the wakeful night, but now, when he came flooding magnificently into the room, her head was well down among the pillows and she was far away from all thought or care of him.
>
> Such a happy day! A sun, shining-eyed and yet gentle, though here were the days of midsummer. He let the dew tumble on the grass, and the rose leaves, and the spiders' magic silver that swung between the shrubs for more than an hour beyond the short grace he usually allowed it!
>
> How trim were the flowerbeds! How closely cropped the lawns!
>
> They looked unfamiliar to Ellice's eyes, for this was no house of wealth; she was used to standing early at her window and being nodded to by long-haired, poetic lawns and careless wealths of flowers and weeds.
>
> Last night — was it only last night she had stood at this same window and cried and cried and cried? She was tired, of course, tired to death, with helping with all the preparations, and packing her clothes, and writing hurried letters of thanks for wedding presents just come, and soothing Maude, and keeping her father good-humoured.
>
> She had sobbed that she wouldn't be married, that she couldn't be married — that it was all no use; she would slip away quietly in the morning and go and stay somewhere all by herself, and people could laugh and wonder till they died. She couldn't dress up in those strange white clothes and be stared at by crowds of people that she cared nothing for and kissed by forty girl-friends and forty aunts and friends of her mother.

Family outings were happy and simple occasions, and one of my favourite pictures is this one taken one Sunday when they went by rowing boat up Middle Harbour. Left to Right: Mr Curlewis (Herbert's father), Ethel Turner, Adrian, Jean. Mr Alfred Curlewis (Herbert's uncle).

1897

Dreamed Sweet Dreams

Ethel is absorbed with her new life and being a house-wife and she sets to work in earnest to create her own home. Servants are a constant problem and she seems to have a never-ending stream of new ones to break in — some only lasting several days.

Throughout her books and her life, 'sunshine', 'sunbeams' and the varying effects of 'sunrise' and 'sunset' play a prominent part. She uses the sun to let light and happiness into homes where there are happy families, and for contrast, her description tells of a house whose grey walls were saturated with damp, while mists descend and all is overshadowed by huge, stiff, depressing pine trees.

This could be accounted for by her early childhood in England. One has the feeling that her memory of those days was of a dull and misty land where sad memories of losing her own father and step-father must have left a deep impression. Therefore her appreciation and awareness of the effect of sunshine on her life is very apparent in many of her books.

1st January:
Alice had the day out so I was kitchen queen. In preparation for tomorrow I made tarts and custard tarts, sponge roll and scones. Such a long time it took me and I was so tired. I had got nearly every utensil in the kitchen in use and was trying to screw up courage to attack them when H. whisked me into the dining room to lie down, and washed up everything himself. Then we had a cosy little tea and a cosy evening.

5th January:
We had the loveliest of days. Packed a picnic basket and tramped off to Pearl Bay. Were fortunate enough to find no one there at all, so were able to have the baths. And had our first swim together, H. swims splendidly, and he says I swim very well though I get breathless after a time. We jumped off the springboard several times and I also dived. It was simply glorious. Then we had lunch in a little summerhouse, and afterwards I read for a time and H. smoked. And then he read to me and I knitted.

7th January:
Went to Gordon for the day to help Mother with sewing. Said goodbye to Harold — poor little Rosie is feeling it very much for they won't see each other for a year and then only for three weeks. He starts for New Zealand on Saturday to study at the Agricultural College at Christchurch.

14th January:
H. worked at the bush house and I trimmed a black lace hat — made my old one look quite new and charming with a little fresh ribbon and pink chiffon. Then I made from beginning to end, a bedspread for our room, very pretty and dainty it looks, salmon pink under drawn-thread muslin. Then we sat out in the moonlight and after had a game of bezique. This is going to be my last idle week, next Monday H. is going back to Chambers and I shall start writing again.

17th January:
Sunday. H. was wicked enough to paint the front of the bush house. I objected on the grounds that it would offend the eyes of the Sunday-school-going population, but he could not be dissuaded. But when the Goulding force passed I made him hide. Only the steps were left to tell tales.

21st January:
Had the blues in morning, I think I overtired myself at Balmoral baths. Couldn't look at a pen, so I did a lot of neglected darning — H. gets such big holes, the wicked boy — and other odd bits of sewing. At night I got the book out to make a frantic attempt at the Little Maids, *and H. lying smoking on the sofa, said, do a short story. 'I haven't an idea', I said. He smoked a little longer and I laboured at a sentence or two. Then 'How would this do' he said — 'have a nurse tell some kids ghost stories, and let them not be frightened but set to work to trap a ghost'. I saw possibilities in it and turned it over, got a sheaf of fresh paper and began. It worked itself out splendidly — and at 10.30 pm I was still scribbling hard, but had to leave off as it was bedtime.*

22nd January:
Got up early, had breakfast and sat down to my Ghost story by 10 — my pen flew along without a break. Finished it at 4, so redeemed the week a little, it's 5,400 words — ten guineas at the least*.

2nd February:
Nell and I went to town — first to Dr Brady since they tell me I am becoming deafer. He says I am no worse with bad ear but slightly so with the good which sounds unpleasant. I am to get a Politzer bag and use daily for a time. We lunched at Quong Tarts and came home very tired.

8th March:
Morning finished proofs of Miss Bobbie *— I wish I could afford to stuff it all in the kitchen fire and never let it come out. Afternoon went to town, shopped and saw Dr Brady. I asked him to tell me frankly if I was threatened with complete deafness, but he*

---

*This story was to be named 'A New Lenore' and is to be found in the collection *Betty and Co.*

says no, though I may get worse than I am. Consoling. He ran two horrible long instruments along Eustachean tubes and hurt me a good deal. Night we went to the Arthurs, I didn't care for it for I was stuck down with a lot of middle-aged women to play whist. I'd far rather have played chess with the men.

26th March:
Morning made a jar of lemon cheese, and boiled up my quince jelly again with a second lot of gelatine. And I forgot it and it boiled all over the stove — I don't think I'll try jelly making again. Afternoon wrote at 'Doll's Dressmaker*, it is a hateful, hateful story. I'll never never again write to the order of 'a story with a distinctly moral tone', it cramps and ruins one, this is about the poorest stuff I've done and if I could afford to refuse the £50 for it I would. The only comfort is, it is only for a weekly paper, not book form.

8th April:
Went to town to H's chambers, he has removed to 93 Elizabeth St, up two flights, but a much bigger, nicer room. His linoleum made only a ridiculous little patch in the middle and the place looked forlorn altogether. At last H. said he would spend a pound on the floor and I undertook to scour Sydney for the shop where I could get a chaste, legal, strong covering for that very modest sum. Linoleum was out of the question but at last I lighted on some tiled, rather pretty oilcloth. It will only last about 18 months or two years but by then he will be able to afford something better. I got some serge for a curtain for the bottom of his book shelves and on Saturday afternoon we will come and make the place look magnificent between us. Lunched at Fresh Food then to Dr Brady again to have his skewers stuck into me.

12th April:
Went to Chatswood and spent morning with Louie at last. Read some chapters of Teens *— some of it is good, some seems to trickle in rather a thin stream of schoolgirl talk. On the whole I think not nearly as good as* World is Round. *Talked royalties and publishing and housekeeping. Louie says she hates the latter, that it cramps and cripples her, etc. I'm afraid she is growing inclined to think everything an author does but write is infradig to the author. The house-keeping both of us have won't hurt us; with our dear new little homes and a good servant each we haven't much to grumble at. I wouldn't give up the reins of my little house for anything. She says she shall and is even talking vaguely of lodgings; leaving the Chatswood greenery and going to smoky horrid Darlinghurst.*

---

*This title later changes to *Betty and Co.*

14th April:
Left our little cottage to go to Kurrajong for a week, reached Richmond at 11 am, then took the coach, H. and I had the box seat so we had a glorious view and any amount of dust all the way up. Made acquaintance with a Mr Scott in the coach, his father used to be Warden at Paul's College and he had been to the University so H. and he were soon friendly. Reached Dunstan's at 2 pm very hungry. After dinner, which we thoroughly enjoyed, we went down a gully nearby, for schoolboy H. was dying to have a good practice with his revolver. Then tea at which a mixture of boarders turned up — none to our liking — and we went outside and paced the beautiful verandah. At which the boarders were a little hurt I'm afraid. They had asked us to 'come and have a little music, they were sure we were musical'. But we said we weren't at all and fled to the safety of the verandah, while a school girl performed conscientiously, the whole evening, and they all sat stiffly round the room.

22nd April:
Just a year. I wonder if any other couple ever had so ideally perfect a first year. There has not been a shadow of a cloud on our sunshine. We have both been splendidly well and full of spirits all the time. The year could not have been so lovely if I had been perpetually ailing and in the doctors' hands like Lola and several girls I know. We have been such friends as well as lovers, and husband and wife — done everything together and gone everywhere together. Not a single Saturday or Sunday or night apart. I wonder what I shall have to write this day next year, it hardly seems possible we could be allowed another year of such happiness . . .

> *And yet there might be even greater happiness . . . I am often thinking so now. And H. will not mind now we have had one year alone.*

25th April:
It rained too heavily for us to go to Gordon so we played games and sang songs and amused ourselves and were as ridiculous as two children. I think Alice must occasionally think we are bereft of our senses; she comes in to set the table and finds me being carried round the room or chased round, or her master climbing in the window because I have locked him out of the room. And we've been married a year and should be growing sedate. *

8th May:
Alice left at 9 am so I had plenty to do in morning. Afternoon read on the verandah while H. gardened. The new girl Lottie R. came at 5 pm, such a nice bright little thing she seems, pretty too; I hope she will prove as good as she looks.

11th May:
Lottie can't make puddings! A sad discovery. Servant hunting all morning and went to registry and engaged a girl Emma who seems likely but had no reference.

---

*Next Door a short story in *Betty and Co.* uses this entry as copy material.

19th May:

Morning the spirit seemed to move me to a new book, I couldn't touch the short stories. I went off and bought an exercise book at the little library and came home on light feet. The weather is so fresh and bright it makes one feel equal to anything. Wrote nearly a chapter: A Sydney Suburb *I think I shall call it, it is a kind of mixed sequel both to the* Larrikin *and* Misrule, *both families are introduced and will divide the pages of the book among them*. Afternoon returned Mrs Cullen's call — I do like her more than anyone else here. Night read more of* Vanity Fair. *I couldn't put it down and never fully appreciated it before. I think it's the finest novel without a doubt in the language.*

5th June:

The new servant Mabel came — I am sure she will not do. Letter from Mr A. B. Paterson asking me to write something for the Antipodean. *Can't, I'm too busy.*

11th June:

Went to town and did some shopping — to registry and engaged yet another servant, Maggie, I don't think I shall ever be settled again. Then to Jean's to lunch with Mr Paterson. He asked me to reconsider my decision — says they want to show what Australian writers can do, so I shall be 'patriotic' and write something though I can't afford to when I get so much bigger prices in England.

26th June:

At night there came Dr and Mrs Arthur, Mr and Mrs Meillon, Mr and Mrs Prideham, Mr Shaw, Mr Nicholls, Mr Bassett. Made drawing-room pretty with flowers and had two tables with whist, and three sets of chess in dining room.

28th June:

In evening Mr Dolman and Mr A. B. Paterson came to dinner and we all had a pleasant 'shop' gossip over the drawing-room fire. I do like Mr Paterson — he is a 'real good fellow'.

5th July:

Engaged a new girl Ellen — I wonder if I shall ever be out of deep domestic waters again. Afternoon Mrs Soderberg came and found me sewing muslin and lace and had to be told my secret.

9th July:

Felt queer all the morning and had to lie down. Should have gone to dinner at the Trocadero and afterwards to the theatre but for two or three reasons didn't go. H. went however to take Mr Dolman and I had my first dinner and evening alone since we have been married. Sat by drawing room fire and sewed and dreamed sweet dreams over the tiny garment.

---

*This book, a *Sydney Suburb* did not quite eventuate because of an agreement with Ward Lock about their right to publish any book containing the characters of *Seven Little Australians*.

14th July:

Idled all morning. Afternoon the new girl Harriet came. I shall be glad to see the last of Ellen but she had nowhere to go so I let her stay the night. H. and I went to the Arthur's. I beat Mrs Hamlet easily and then played two games with Mr Britton, very long games, but I just lost each time. He told Dr Arthur I was the best lady chess player he had ever played with — I feel quite elated.

24th July:

Little Lil came this morning — I'm afraid I rather neglected Mrs O'Brien we had so much to talk of. They are to be married very likely in September. And to live at Gordon — Bukyangi! It takes a great weight from my mind, for I am frightened at the thought of them living on so little. Lil is not strong. They would pay something to Mother of course, but there would be no furniture to get and no big expenses. The study will be their own sitting room. It is Mr Cope who is so eager for them to do so. He can't bear the thought of losing Lil, and poor little Mother with her two big girls gone — she and Rosie never pull together well — would be miserable. At night Fred came and we had a fire in the drawing room.

30th July:

Went to town to meet little Lil. Dr Hinder says she is in a complete state of collapse and wants entire rest. She is to go to Moss Vale on Tuesday with Parnell's. She and Fred won't be married now in Sept. — not until April — it is very hard for them.

6th August:

Went to town and engaged another — yet another servant. Afternoon paid some long overdue calls and at night enjoyed myself vastly with Shorter's Charlotte Bronte and her Circle. *The life of those three sisters has a strange and intense fascination for me. How in earnest they were — they worked with their very heartblood. What a trifler I seem beside them, nearly everything is made smooth for me, I've health and happiness and enough money to keep me from the necessity of pot-boiling, and I waste my time and work half-heartedly and grudge trouble very often — I'm not fit to be trusted with a pen.*

7th August:

Morning got out 3 Little Maids and faced it sternly. It's the poorest, weakest, most unconvincing twaddle ever penned, I don't know how I could do 12 chapters of it without being seriously ill. Well, its fate has come upon it — I won't use one word of it, though someday I may start and write the same tale of our little lives again.

10th August:

Morning did more copying out and wrote the end of Second Nature.* I detest the story, and it has *given me so much trouble. Dr Arthur came in to say he was sending a nurse in to see me — it seems to bring February very close.*

---

*This story is the last in the collection *The Camp at Wandinong.*

26th August:

Our servant Florrie left yesterday and at 2 in the afternoon came Mrs Rolin with her nurse and two babies, Mrs Shaw and her infant, Mrs Cullen and hers; I had arranged for them all to meet here as they are old friends, but it made rather a hard day of it for me — getting afternoon tea and everything alone. I do like Mrs Rolin. Then I got dinner ready and was fairly wrecked. So then H. turned to — first of all put me to bed and turned my gas down and bade me go to sleep — which I did. And then the dear old laddie set to and washed up: breakfast things, lunch, afternoon tea (10 cups) and dinner. He did it all thoroughly too and left a neat kithcen so I should have no trouble the next day. But it took him till 10 pm.

27th August:

Morning very busy with housework. Despite the trouble servants are I wouldn't be without for worlds permanently — it is such shocking waste of time doing all the thousand and one details of work in a house. Nellie to start tomorrow.

6th September:

Children's Page. And paced and paced about the house, bitten with a longing to write a magnificent book, and crumbling to nothingness the minute I touched the pen. Night paced again, I really think I can do something good as a sequel to Larrikin *— or rather it will be a tale of Meg Woolcot married; Alan has been dismissed from hospital under a cloud and they struggle and struggle. If I could write it as I think, I could make a fine story of it.*

20th September:

Wrote letters — Steele — Mr Lock to ask to be released from the clause in an agreement that stipulated I should give them all books in which 7 Little A characters were introduced, at same rate as 7 L A. It would be iniquitous. But I had wanted to bring Meg into the sequel of the Larrikin.

24th September:

Lil stayed till 12 noon and we sewed together. Then, stimulated by a talk we had had about the funny things we used to do when we were little I got a brand new exercise book and started a brand new version of Three Little Maids *— I feel sure I can do something with the subject but the last attempt of 12 chapters is certainly worthless and wishy-washy. Only wrote ten lines but it has started me. Night had a wretched feeling of oppression and depression so H. had to cheer me up. The post brought an early copy of* Miss Bobbie. *It is very well bound and looks nicer than any of the books. But the matter is miserable — I am ashamed of it.*

1st October:

Finished off my green cape. And made my heliotrope tea-gown elegant with a new front and ribbons. Afternoon went to town to see Dr Oram about my ear. He says he does not think I shall ever hear quite well but he thinks he can improve me. But will not do anything in the way of an operation until after 1st February. Wore my new cape and felt horribly self-conscious and shrinking. Unless I can possibly help it I won't go to town again, there are only four months more. Mr Cope came for dinner and evening — a high honour — and a real pleasure. I am very fond of the dear old fellow despite all his crotchets.

1st November:

A hard day's writing at Little Maids. *There are XI chapters done now. Night felt tired out, brain like a sponge. It has been a dreadful day, a hot westerly blowing.*

22nd November:

Went to town by 9.30 am boat and Mother was waiting for me to take me to Dr Worrell's according to Dr Arthur's wish. He says I am very well. Thank goodness that visit is over. Went shopping and bought an ice chest which will be a great boon, and a number of 'small items'.

8th December:

Nellie not back yet, I am getting desperate. It is too wet to go and seek any help — even a washerwoman, and the clothes have all been soaking for three days. Such a silent house it is with only the cat for company.

10th December:

Children's Page all morning. And most of afternoon. I want to get a number done in advance. A letter from Mother conveying the startling news that Dr Hinder is going home to marry — not dear old Ella as I had hoped, she has been so good to me and Doodie. Not even Flo. But Enid! Enid who went away with her hair down her back and in short frocks. Harold (who got back after his year in New Zealand, much to Rosie's happiness) says they are to be married next month. I can't believe it; for one thing he last saw Enid about four months after he buried poor Ethel. When could he have learnt to love little Enid? It must be from her photographs since and her letters.

17th December:

A telegram came summoning Nellie to her father who is dying. I hurried her off as quickly as I could and was dreadfully sorry. But oh my little me, I'm sorry for myself too; it's dreadfully hot, I'm not too well and get tired very easily, and I don't much like being alone in the house just at present. Mrs Shaw and Mrs Cullen came in afternoon, the former is going to try and send me an old servant of hers, of course so close to Xmas it is worse than useless to try advertising or registries.

Sarah Jane Cope, Ethel's mother. Though her baptismal name was Sarah Jane, she was always known by family and friends as Jean.

January 1906. On left: *Rex Cope and Rosie.* Three children: *Rob Pockley, Dick Thompson, Marcia Pockley.* Back row: *Herbert, Fred Thompson, Mr Cope, Jean.* Front row: *Mrs Cope, Ethel, Lilian, Adrian.*

Adrian and Jean with their young friends at the Blue Mountains.

Avenel about 1906. This home had a beautiful view across Middle Harbour. It was demolished in 1970 and Town House home units have been built on the site.

Ethel Curlewis 1907, the year she wrote her book That Girl.

Adrian, birthday photo aged 8, 1909.

At Professor David's home in the Blue Mountains, Ethel, centre.

December 1908. Jean's class at Killarney School.

R.M.S. Orvieto, *the ship on which the Curlewis family sailed to Naples from Sydney 22 January*

Jean and Adrian on donkeys, Port Said 1910.
Miss Stevens, Ethel Curlewis, Adrian and Jean at the ruins of Pompeii 1910.

18th December:

A truly-drefful day. Fiercely hot and oh so little done. My jellies wouldn't jell for the children this afternoon till I had boiled them three times. The three little Brooks and the Arthurs came, the Pockleys couldn't. All afternoon we dressed dolls and got the toys ready for the City Mission. By night I was half dead so H. washed up everything and made me lie on the lounge.

19th December:

Morning packed Mission Box and did various things. At 4 pm in afternoon Mr Prideham came in, most excited and upset to announce the birth of a son, half an hour before. He stayed with us to tea and evening with occasional trips to see how the little mother was doing, for of course he was of less importance in the house than the family cat; and the nurse and doctor and mother-in-law kept 'shooing' him out of every room.

20th December:

Very busy in morning and almost in despair for 12 noon came and no Maggie. But in afternoon she came and I lay down and folded my hands in thankfulness. H. came hurrying home at 3 pm to help and was quite pathetically relieved to find we could be tidy and that there was a prospect of a dinner other than eggs and pink and yellow jelly on which we have been subsisting. And no washing up! Is is sad she can't stay past Thursday.

31st December:

Mother showed Kate the ways of the house and I lazied.

Although Ethel says she will 'never, never again write a story with a distinctly moral tone', quite a number of her short stories do exactly this. In most instances however, it is characters with a conscience that win through and they seem to become stronger for having had to battle through difficult situations.

'Poppet had a little dead chicken in her hand.'
Family at Misrule

1898

That Strange
Little Urgent Cry

The anxieties of her new role as that of a mother are felt at first, but after the frightening experience of finding herself alone, without nurse or mother to lean on, Ethel then settled down to the joys and fulfillment of motherhood and a very close relationship with her own child. For many years she had written about this bond in her imaginary families.

3rd January:
Hardly slept a bit last night, I must *stop seeing people, my brain seems to get excited with so much talk and I do get so tired. Mother went servant hunting but no success. The race wants exterminating.*

10th January:
Morning did Children's Page. Mrs Shaw came and brought a servant on approval but she had such horrid hands and teeth I couldn't *have taken her. Rosie ran in for an hour, Harold goes to New Zealand on Saturday, and Rosie to Sutton Forest for a holiday. Rose says everything at Gordon is as peaceful as a mill-pond again and Mr C's efforts to be good are quite pathetic. He and Mother are the best of friends again.*

14th January:
The new girl Lizzie tells me she thinks it will be too lonely for her and that there isn't enough work to fill her time. A very new complaint this last. Read Little Journeys to Homes of Famous Women *— very interestingly written. Evening read* A Daughter of Today. *A very good study. Elfrida might have been sketched straight from Louie. And I believe, such is Louie's present state of soulfulness and revolt and modernism that if I told her of the resemblance she would be flattered.*

20th January:
Yet another servant Maud started today, she is pretty and seems anxious to please, rather slow and not very efficient but I daresay will improve. The post brought a wild little love letter from some little 13-year-old girl — unsigned. Says she loves me with all her heart, that she is thinking of me all day and would gladly die for me — would give all the world to know me, etc. etc. It is a dear little letter but so extravagant — I can hardly think it genuine. Except that I know what queer mortals little girls of 13 are.

24th January:
Mine birthday — I have arrived at the respectable age of 26. I am to go with H. and choose something for his present when I am well again. For the meantime, just to mark the day, he brought me a copy of Le Gallienne's translation of Omar Khayyam. *We had a lovely evening on the sofa reading it together, and comparing passages with Fitzgerald's version, which is comparably finer; still it's nice to have both versions.*

27th January:
Morning sewed a little, idled a much. Then Mother came and there was nothing but talk. Lil is to be married the first week in March and now I wish, wish to-morrow was my time — the question is will I be well enough to be there.

2nd February:
Spent a profitless, dull day. I can't settle to anything. Dr Arthur came for a chat and we talked Shakespeare and the musical glasses.

7th February:
My little girl was born at 20 minutes past 7. I was seventeen hours ill; the last eight being exquisite agony. Pain will always be a matter of comparison now; I believe I should be able to smile over a trifling matter like having a limb sawn slowly off. They used a 2 oz. bottle of chloroform on me but it scarcely had any effect, I was never quite unconscious a moment, and knew all the time what they were doing. They owned that I had a very bad time, being so small. But the moment I heard that strange little urgent cry! 'Is that my little baby' I said and fell to crying myself. Later Laddie came in — just one moment to kiss me and I cried again at his face. And yet he had put his head under the shower-bath and dipped his face in water and drunk half a tumbler of brandy to try and get it under his control again so that he might not hurt me. My poor old Laddie. It was bad for me but forty times worse for him those dreadful hours. About 12 o'clock I have a memory of waking from a doze and seeing little Lil kneeling by baby. I meant to speak to her in a minute but fell asleep again. Oh the moment when I held my little, little babe in my arms against my breast. Laddie came and sat by me and *held my hand many times, my poor Laddie.*

19th February:
Felt rather low-spirited most of the day and at tea suddenly dissolved in tears. Then they began to take my temperature again and found it had run up suddenly to 104°. The next thing I knew the doctor was in the room. Such a hot troubled day it seemed. I was in a burning fever, my head ached maddeningly and I had pains in every limb.

21st February:
The third dreadful day of fever and headache — ice bags on my head and in the evening came a specialist Dr Worrell. I began to wonder dull-ly [sic] *if I was going down to the great shadow.*

22nd February:

Lil's Wedding Day. Much better, fever abated rapidly, headache almost gone. No need for Dr Worrell and his horrid black bag. They think it was a sharp attack of influenza that I have had. Darling Lil's wedding day and I away! When it was 2 pm I was thinking and thinking of the darling and I couldn't help having a cry to think I was not there. I shall never forgive the Thompsons for their 'No-wedding-in-Lent insistence'. Little Mother came flying to me the second the wedding guests began to go — but they couldn't let her see me, I was in such a nervous strung-up state and crying and crying till Mother said I nearly broke her heart.

23rd February:

Almost well again. Twas influenza for a morality. Mother came again in afternoon and this time was allowed to see me.

26th February:

H. carried me into the drawing room which was a lovely change for me. After three weeks of the blue walls of my bedroom the garden, grass and the scarlet cannas and the gum trees opposite looked things of exquisite beauty.

4th March:

Packed up and did several straightening jobs about the house. I have never seen a place in such a dreadful state, my pretty little home is half-ruined, quantities of china and glass broken, grease dropped on carpets and matting, mildew and iron mould on linen — everything possible spoiled — the result of an incapable servant at such a time. I feel so dispirited about it all I hardly seem to want to see it again and am longing to get away from it all.

5th March:

Nurse Stolz, Babe and I set off at 10 am for Gordon. I felt very tottery walking up to the tram but the little journey was quite intoxicatingly lovely for me. Got a cab from Chatswood to Gordon to the lovingest of welcomes home. She was acknowledged on all hands of course to be the most wonderful baby ever seen. The household cheerfully upset itself from end to end to make room for the small queen and her train.

19th March:

Came down with Mother and Babe on the 12 noon train, all luggage having gone on before. It is lovely to be in the dear little house again. Nellie has been such a good girl and got every place into perfect order again and cleanliness reigns supreme. Mother and Mr C. went home at 3 pm. Now H. and I faced the frightful responsibility of managing 'her' unaided, nurse gone, Mother gone. It is a marvel to me that we neither rose up white-headed after the first night alone with her; we were afraid to close our eyes lest something should happen and even when we did snatch a few minutes slumber we woke up, hot and nervous, lest she should have smothered herself in the cradle at my side. Once or twice when she screwed up her face we were assured she threatened convulsions and we longed to be able to keep the doctor chained on the premises. The morning broke however and nothing had happened so we were confident that we would settle down to a more peaceful dominion of her.

25th March:
Baby restless and not very well. Her Mother ditto. The girlie loves her bath but the minute I take her out she screams and screams till by the time I have her dressed she has me reduced almost to tears also. Then she smiles complacently as if that were her sole object and falls off into a lovely sleep. She and I both had an afternoon sleep and woke much restored. Dr A. came and said Baby looked well. Examined my ears — he wants to try hypnotizing me for my deafness.

27th March:
We have bought a pocket Kodak that we may lose none of the Babe's expressions and attitudes, sweet and otherwise. She is a good baby at night, gets herself to sleep — no rocking allowed; we are thoroughly up to date parents and think too much of her digestion to allow her to be 'jigged'.

18th April:
In afternoon we went to look at a piece of land I like on Military Road. Night Dr Arthur came for chess and I beat him two out of three games. And I had not played for quite five months. But as I grow stronger there is a delightful feeling of mental vigour coming to me, I believe if I could only get the time I could write a really good book.

22nd April:
Our wedding day. H. took a half holiday to celebrate this day of days and we made our pilgrimage to Rothesay. Well whatever the future brings we have had two of the most perfect years possible in this world. I think every month we grow more deeply happy and grow more dear and necessary to each other. That is because we are playmates and chums, as well as lovers, as well as husband and wife, as well as mother and father.

26th April:
Morning actually dipped my pen in the ink and made a fresh start at Three Little Maids. *But oh so many interruptions. Hardly wrote 1,000 words. Rose Bishop, my new nursegirl came.*

13th May:
Night H. and I both read. We had a long fierce struggle with the little Babe; she resisted most vigorously any attempt to put her in her cradle and shrieked wildly. Once or twice I gave in and lifted her thinking she might be in pain. And she immediately looked round in her interested fashion at everything and bobbed her little head and laughed. Then down she went again, and again the evening air was pierced with her yells. I had to go away and leave her to H. finally, for the yells began to give way to sobs of sorrowful and woeful little hiccoughs of vanquishment. Even H's stony heart was touched. Finally she fell off to sleep with her dear little hand spread on the pillow and a tear on her cheek and her lip drooped. Heigho I hope the battle will not last very long, but the victory must *be to us, I couldn't bear the little girl to be one of the spoilt, tyrannous children one is always meeting.*

15th June:

The Patersons are lending us their Manly house for a few days and all from Gordon, and H., Babe and I are going. Lil and Fred can't leave as they have had a burglar scare and are afraid.

21st July:

Morning Lil and Rex came for lunch. Then I went off, taking Babe to meet Rosie. Went with her to have our photo taken at Falk's. Then on to the Darlinghurst Rink for our first essay on skates since the last skating fever some seven or eight years ago. We both got on very well, not a single fall, and we even attempted the Dutch roll and crossing our feet, before we left.

24th July:

Took H. to see The Neuk again — he too likes the position and the lovely view so much that he too is willing to shut his eyes to the many inconveniences of the house which is chiefly built to look quaint and mad. We have decided to take it if rent is reasonable.

25th July:

Went to town to see the agent. The Neuk was £72 but he is letting us have it for £66, taking it for a year. I am so glad we have got it*.

26th July:

I went to the new house and measured floors and otherwise arranged the place according to my eye. It is the dearest, loveliest little place and oh so mad. We can't even think what we shall do with the second wardrobe and linen press and lots of things as the upstairs rooms slope so. But the view and quaintness compensate for everything. The drawing room and dining room too are very pleasant — with the end of each given up to windows looking out on the view of dancing blue water and beaches and the red winding hill. H. came home with Election results, Reid in — Carruthers by an overwhelming majority. Dugald Thompson for Mosman.

4th August:

Removing. The exodus took place. At 11 I left the little old cottage to Nellie and went to the new with Rose and Babe. Well, we can hardly be happier than we have been for these two and a half years in Yanalla. Our first little home and the home where little Babe first opened her eyes to the world. We felt very melancholy about going though the Neuk is twice as pretty, and has such a glorious situation. A most tiring day — I was quite broken up by the time H. came home — he couldn't take a holiday.

---

*The Neuk was demolished in about 1938 and a new home was built on the site. It is now No. 4 Moruben Road, Mosman.

23rd August:

Town. Met Louie and we went about together. Lunched at Schneider's, Louie introduced me to Mr Lambert the artist and Mr Longstaff. Went to Bulletin *and saw Mr Stephen and Mr Archibald. At night H. and I went to the* Yeoman of the Guard. *We had front row of reserved stalls and yet I did not hear well. It is a very poor company, Dorothy Vane is rather pretty and very dainty, but no actress or singer. H. lost the tickets and had to buy fresh ones so the seats cost £1.*

17th September:

Tried desperately to write in morning but everyone interrupted me — the needlewoman, Rose, Nellie — I feel in despair, can't *collect my thoughts and settle down. Night we went to Society of Artists' Ball. I enjoyed the dancing exceedingly, just the sheer pleasure of the movement, danced every dance till we left — 11 pm. Did not care particularly for any of the men. Marmee came to mind Babe.*

19th September:

A really good writing day. Shut myself up in my tiny upstairs room and refused to be interrupted by anyone. Afternoon made up parcel of Part 1, Little Maids *and sent off by registered post.*

22nd September:

The record day's heat for September 90° in the shade. Afternoon I returned the call on my next door neighbours the Corbetts — such lonely shut up lives those poor girls seem to lead, they know no one at all here, never go out, do all their own work, they play not neither do they draw.

28th September:

My day at home — Mrs Fort, Mrs Ralston, Mrs Attenbury, Clara Windeyer and Nina Church came.

4th October:

Morning wrote a little at chapter 26 of Three Little Maids. *Afternoon to Old High School Committee meeting — oh dear, what unbusinesslike creatures women are — we wasted long enough before anything was started and then half of us had to go before anything was done. H. came home very late, he and Kelynack are defending Lisson in this dreadful case.*

11th October:

Mrs Corbett from next door came in in the morning and wasted me an hour or two, pouring what is surely a wild, mad story into my ears, a story about a husband who is a bad lot it seems and George Reid the Premier who is her cousin, and is keeping her out of money, and about a man who throws stones on her roof and drops kittens down the chimney. I think the poor old lady must suffer from melancholia and it is all a delusion; but what a dreadful life in any case for those two girls who are shut up as it were in a nunnery. I must try and brighten things for them a little, they know absolutely no one.

15th October:

Morning wrote for half an hour. Afternoon gardened. At night we challenged each other to write a Child Song each. H. wrote 'As Baby Sees' I, 'A Trembling Star'. I liked his best.

This poem was later published in *The Bulletin*, but it seems a good opportunity to include it here.

A Trembling Star

'There is my little trembling star,' she said
    I looked: once more
The tender sea had put the sun to bed,
    And heaven's floor
    Was grey.

And nowhere else in all that young night-sky
    Was any star,
But one that hung above the sea, not high,
    Nor very far
    Away.

'I watch it every night,' she said, and crept
    Within my arm.
'Soft little star, I wish the angels kept
    It safe from harm
    Alway.'

'I know it is afraid,' she said, her eyes
    Held a sweet tear.
They send it all alone into the skies,
    No big stars near
    To play.

They push it out before the sweet, kind moon
    Lights up the sea.
They laugh because it fears the dark. 'Soon, soon,
    You'll braver be,'
    They say.

'One night I climbed far up that high white tree
    Beside the beach,
And tried to stretch my hand across the sea,
    And tried to reach
    The grey.

'For something made me feel my heart would break
Unless that night
I in my hand my trembling star could take,
And kiss its fright
Away.

'There only blew a strange wind, chillily,
And clouds were swept;
The angels would not let my own star see
That someone wept.
I pray.

'To Christ, Who hears my little prayers each night,
that He will seek
Through all His skies for that sweet, frightened light;
And stoop His cheek
And say:

'My angels must not send so frail a thing
To light the west.
Lift up the little trembling star to cling
About My breast
Alway.'

20th October:

Finished Little Maids. *Wrote all morning and then by afternoon wrote the last words of* Three Little Maids. *Oh the exquisite relief and joy of finishing a book, there's nothing like it. And this has been such a torment and worry to me, and I've torn up so much, and written it again and again — half a dozen times have almost consigned it to the fire. And perhaps that would have been the best place — though I think the end is an improvement on the beginning which is most tame I am afraid.*

24th October:

As H. displayed a rash I sent for Dr Arthur who pronounced him ill of German Measles. He says it is too late to send Babe away, that she has been exposed to the infection too long; that H. must be kept away from her for a fortnight. So I have to be very careful, I put a wrapper over my dress when I go into him and afterwards take it off and disinfect my hands before going to Babe. My packet of 16 copies of Wandinong *arrived, prettily got up.* Telegraph *and* Herald *gave it a favourable review.*

25th November:

Went to town early and did a good deal of my Xmas shopping; a large number of toys for poor children. I never saw toys so cheap — when you can get a toy stable with animals and cart for 4½d, a set of furniture for 9d, little brooms and dustpans for 3d and other things as cheap, there ought not to be many forgotten by Santa Claus. For 11/- I got quite a large box of things.

7th December:

Went to town all day. To Dr Oram's, and got hurt rather badly; he pushed the instrument further than ever yet, for I told him I was deafer than ever. When I got to H. I was quite upset, so he set to work to make me better; took me out for a particularly nice lunch and then round to buy an unbirthday present, anything I liked — I got a white little teapot. I tell him I shall be badly hurt again now every week.

13th December:

At 2 pm went to Speech Day at the High School. Mr Hogue presented the prizes amongst them, with flattering words, mine, which fell to a girl named Edith Fry for her essay on Anthony and Cleopatra *— a really good story, good style and humorous; a marvellous commodity, humour for a schoolgirl. Talked to Miss Garvin, Miss Bruce — Mrs Walker rather, Mr Holmes, Mr Crompton, etc. Rosie and her friend Miss Anderson came to dinner and for evening after bathe.*

25th December:

Very happy Xmas day, all together — all but Harold so poor Rosie was a little desolate. Lil and Fred, H. and I — and Babe, Mr and Mrs Soderberg, Mother and Mr Cope, Rex and Rosie. Present-giving all done quietly this year as none of us would allow Lil and Fred to give in their present circumstances.

After many fruitless attempts to re-construct and rewrite *Three Little Maids*, Ethel finally sent it off to a publisher, and one can nearly feel the sigh of relief as she parcelled it up — it was over two years before, that she had first tried to write the story. The first part of the book tells of the style of life the three little girls remembered in England. There is quite a deal of baby-talk at the beginning and this is inclined to slow down the reader's progress. In fact, in many of the E.T. books a child is depicted with a speech impediment or a childish voice such as substituting 'w' for 'r'. In her adults too she occasionally gives them an accent or an uncultured voice to gain effect for her characters. In spite of her deafness she had a remarkably perceptive ear for hearing these impediments and ungrammatical phrases, and some she would mentally note and others she would jot down on paper. We have come across a variety of memo books that she kept — one containing quotations, another lines of poetry, yet another comments and phrases — these she would record at the time and draw upon at a later date when the need arose.

As mentioned in the foreword of these diaries, *Three Little Maids* is not altogether historically accurate. The authoress has no hesitation whatsoever in blending together fact and fantasy, and she leaves it to her reader to determine where one ends and the other begins.

Ethel, taken in London, 1910. Ethel was obliged to wear black when she first arrived in London, as the whole country was in mourning after the death of King Edward VII.

1899

Flying Down the Tram Line Tracks

Bicycles were a real novelty to Ethel during this year and one can sense the exhilarating feeling of freedom and speed that she experienced once she mastered the art. Naturally it had to be incorporated in her writing and in *Little Mother Meg*, Pip, Bunty and Poppet all purchase bicycles and have similar reactions and sentiments with their new machines, as she has with hers.

In this book also there is a remarkable similarity between the preparations for Nell's dance at Misrule and the ones described in the diaries with the Japanese lanterns, programmes with their tasselled pencils attached, and the supper menu which included jellies and ices, cream-cakes and trifles. Major Woolcott has faded into the back-ground and has mellowed with the passing years, as indeed had Mr Cope in Ethel's life, after her marriage to Herbert.

18th January:
Morning finished off some Child Verses — 'A Trembling Star' and 'Leila Watering' and sent to Bulletin. *Afternoon started a short story, 'Early Morning at Browns'.**

25th January:
A letter from Henry Lawson saying he was 'both surprised and delighted at my invitation and that it came just as he was suffering from a reaction after his bitter outburst in Bulletin'. *He evidently takes it for granted he is to bring his wife and infant son — well, I am sure they will be welcome.*

27th January:
Went to town, saw Oram and told him I was as deaf as ever. He told me to leave off the inhaler and gave me some menthol ointment instead. Shopped. Then met H. and we went to look at bicycles — hired one, a Rover, at Bennett and Woods for me to learn on. H. rode it home from the ferry and we gave about five minutes to dinner and then went off to try it. Went to a flat place on Spit Road and H. held the saddle while I made attempts. Went back at 8 pm as we had promised to go to the Arthur's. Played chess with the Doctor and talked bikes.

---

*'Early Morning at Browns' appears in *The Camp at Wandinong.*

28th January:

Got up at 6 am and found a piece of grass to try on. H. says I have lots of pluck — I could see I should never get on without confidence so I did not mind how often I fell. I bruised myself fifty times at least, but before we went to breakfast I could keep on for a little time. Tried again on grass about 3 pm. Rosie and Harold Pockley came to tea and afterwards H. said I was far too good for the grass so I went on the road and rode up and down in style.

29th January:

6 am again. Am quite steady in my saddle and fast gaining control of the machine. Tried mounting — very hard — H. got a stone at last and I went off each time from that; I can't spring up yet. Tried again at 11 am — met Dr Arthur who said I have got on surprisingly. I came down the road swiftly and steadily, but feel the incline going back.

31st January:

Before breakfast again. H. is a most patient and enthusiastic teacher — he has really taught me splendidly. Practised mounting. Also tried at riding and picking up pedal.

In afternoon came Henry Lawson, his wife and Baby — about Little Girl's age but small and delicate. Mrs Lawson told me — we grew friendly quickly over our babies — all the troubles they have had, and quite broke down, poor thing, when she told me the Doctor said her husband is in a consumption and must not go to England. And so poor they are — he is depending entirely on his pen and has to keep it going ceaselessly to pay boarding house dues. I like him muchly, he said the afternoon had done him worlds of good, it had taken him out of himself.

4th February:

Up at 6 am for a spin. H. had Dr A's bike and so it was quite the best time. We went about two miles and I enjoyed it 'menjously'. It is lovely to come flying down the tram line tracks.

6th February:

To town by 1 pm boat — shopped. Met H. who had both bikes waiting and we got out at the Point and rode them home, big pull for me up the hill. Fell off — sheer stupidity more than deafness — in front of a horse and a cart and horse. They pulled up and looked scared and H. a good way behind, was in a great state but I survived and got on again and rode home.

7th February:

Little Babe's birthday — sweet little girl, what a sunshiny year she has made for us. Letters from everyone by the post and plenty of presents she has had. Then Mother came to pay her respects.

21st February:

Settled down in real earnest to work at my new book — The Common Problem *I think I shall call it.* I feel very eager to get to the heart of it and am thinking of it continually.*

5th March:

Rosie and I went to church at Gordon. I sat in the old pew but could not hear sermon — worse than I was two years back. When I got back there was H., he had come up on his bicycle.

30th March:

Worked splendidly at play most of the day. Had an hour's ride — my first quite alone. Night H. was kept late over the Berghofer Divorce case and I worked at play again. Have done some 3–4,000 words today.

10th April:

A splendid day's work. Wrote some 3,500 words of a short story 'Runaway Engine'.** Now I want to go to a station — learn more about engines.

11th April:

Wrote to Mrs A. Morley. The unfortunate woman has been refused yet and yet again. She sent me another story — full of spelling faults (I told her of them). I corrected it and sent it to Bulletin, *asking Mr Archibald to take it. To appointment with Mr McMillan and Mr Souter about my Annual,* Gum Leaves. *They are willing to take it and we are to go shares in the profits.*

13th April:

Mrs Cullen's little Baby is dead. Went to town to Searl's for flowers for it — a tiny wreath of pale rosebuds, violets and maidenhair and took it to Tregoyd.

16th April:

H. rode to Narrabeen with John Meillon. I stayed at home — have been out too much and things are neglected.

20th April:

Off to Eveleigh to Lil's. We had a very happy evening together — Lil is very bright and well. But Fred's ill luck is dreadful. I don't like to think it but I am afraid he is a bit lethargic — I don't believe he is trying much to find work. And rather than do nothing and run into debt I must say I should admire him more if he took the work that Mr Curlewis offers him at the Brick Works. It is £2. 15. 0 a week which is better than absolutely nothing. It is ruining Lil's style, grinding out short stories, just to pay butchers, etc.

**The Common Problem* eventually is published as *The Wonder Child.*

**'Runaway Engine' changed its name to 'A Rogue Locomotive' and is to be found in *Betty and Co.*

24th April:

Rosie came, bag and baggage. She and mother have had a quarrel and she has come out of the house. Of course I must give the child a home even though she may be wrong. I tell them both I am going to be as neutral as possible.

29th April:

Worked hard at play — the love scene between Basil and Bertha in 1st Act. Afternoon H., Mrs Arthur and I rode out to Narrabeen, had tea there and reached home about 11, 21 miles, and one of the pleasantest rides we have had. Rosie was at home with Baby so I felt comfortable.

17th May:

Afternoon little Theo Meillon came to play with Babe, and I gave up everything for the pleasure of watching the two together. Theo was a little shy at first but Baby was most eager. I peeped through the window and found little Girlie kissing him constantly. He stood passively, barely enduring it.

24th May:

H., the Dr and I went off on our bikes, rode to St Leonards, then train to Turramurra where Rosie and Harold met us, then we all rode to the top of Cowan Creek, hid our bicycles in the bush and went down to the water. Got a boat and rowed about, then made a fire and boiled our billy. Rode home again in the moonlight — about 20 miles in all; quite the pleasantest trip we have had.

3rd June:

Afternoon a great event, our piano came. I have wanted one badly all this time — at least not very badly for I have so little time for practice, but it is very nice to have it. And Babe is delighted, sits and plays and plays, and even sings. Night I tried to pick up my forgotten music — I can't play two pages without 40 mistakes.

10th June:

Night Marmee came to dinner and looked after Babe while H. and I went to theatre. Got front seat reserved stalls and yet heard nothing — unless I put up Alice's ear-trumpet when the lights were down, then I got on pretty well, but it was a great strain. Yet for ordinary conversation and daily life I get on very well — many do not know I am deaf at all.

14th June:

Started sequel to Misrule *and wrote nearly a chapter. No visitors for it was pouring with rain.*

16th June:

Went for a long day's shopping, got a dining room carpet for Lil, toys for Little Girl, lace to do up my white silk for the University Ball, etc. etc. Mrs Cullen and her boys came at 4 pm much to Babe's delight.

Jean and Adrian at the Tower of London, 1910.

At the site of the Bastille, Paris.

Feeding pigeons in St Mark's Square, Venice 1910.

A pilgrimage to Attleborough Quarry House, Nuneaton, England, where Ethel lived when she was a young child.

Aldworth, Haslemere, where Ethel and Jean stayed with Lord Tennyson, son of the famous poet, and his wife.

Another photograph taken during Ethel's stay in London. Ethel writes on leaving that city: 'Goodbye to London — the last glimpse of Westminster Abbey and the dear grey streets made my throat swell. It has begun to grip me very hard, this London.'

Jean, left, Adrian, seated with ship's doctor, Dr Muir on the return voyage from England on R.M.S. Osterley.

Back home again to Avenel, the house and garden that Ethel loved so dearly.

26th June:
Wrote most of day at an extra special Children's Page — a Mock Trial at Court. Mr Jeffrey has 'raised my wages' to 30/- a week for the page.

29th June:
Ran across to town for gloves, etc. Night went to Ball — a tremendous crush because the Governor and Lady Mary Lygon were there. I wonder what they think of colonial manners — for the Viceregal Lancers there was a rush to that end of the room to watch every step and look of the Viceregalities. Danced with Mr Lloyd, Gilchrist, Dr Sawkins, H., etc. etc. Left at 11.15 pm to catch 12 boat and managed to get a cabby out of bed to drive us from Steele's — otherwise must have walked.

15th July:
Gossiped with Mother all morning. To dinner came Mr Cope and Rex — the latter had a long confidence for me, the story of his first love affair, with Mother's last lady help, Miss Knight. She encouraged the poor laddie and let him kiss her continually and then laughed at him. He is well again — her ridicule cured him but he is a bit sore.

20th July:
Mrs Kearney arrived, having come from Orange a couple of days ago to discuss our joint effort. We went through the play, and agreed and disagreed over various points. I asked her to come here till Saturday to stay to save the difficulties of travelling.

22nd July:
Mrs Kearney went early — a sense of relief came over us all. Thank goodness Lil and I are only literary as far as our pens are concerned. I couldn't live with anyone like Mrs K. She is untidy — horribly so, and always in a confusion of some sort. Yet I am very sorry for her, for her life has been full of disappointments. I hope (if it is only for her sake) the play succeeds.

27th July:
Henry Lawson came early to say the Baby was ill and they could not come tonight. Went down to Macquarie St to Mrs Kearney; finished off the play, correcting type-written sheets, red inking, etc. Made it in a parcel and carried it to Theatre Royal, delivering it into stage manager's hands with a note for Mr Brough. And now to await the news of it.

1st August:
A note from Mr Brough, an icy shower bath. He finds nothing good to say for the play — radically wrong — wishes he could say something pleasanter but must be candid. Alack a day. The disappointment will nearly kill poor Mrs Kearney; it will be far more to her than to me, her heart is so set on it. Wrote to her to try to cheer her up, saying someone else may find it good, but I fear she will refuse to be comforted. She has gone back to Orange I think.

12th August:

At 2 pm went to Consumptive Home Bazaar. It was very interesting, squandered about a £1 on souvenir books and other things and had pleasant little chats at the different stalls with Mr Quinn, the Curnows, Henry Lawson and Louie (who jumped off the North Shore boat last night into the harbour and was rescued by a man).

19th August:

Rosie and I went off in the rain and mud to the opening of the Society of Artists; looked at pictures as much as we could for having to stop and chat with various people we knew. Mr George Lambert has a magnificent piece of work — ten plough horses — Blacksoil Country. And I liked Howard Ashton's Dawn.

21st August:

To town to Dr Pockley about my eyes. He examined them and condemned me to wear glasses but only for working or for fine sewing. Went to registry and engaged a very pleasant-looking Nurse in place of Emily who goes — alas — next Wednesday.

27th August:

Afternoon went to beach with H. and Babe to build castles. Mr Lister Lister was down there.

28th August:

Morning did Children's Page. Afternoon went to the Arts Society. Mrs Julian Ashton, the Curnows and Mrs Teece were hostesses. Night opened competitions and wrote letters.

4th September:

Went to town, shopped — spring things. Saw Mr Souter about Gum Leaves. He gave me a copy of Bubbles, his Book which he has illustrated really splendidly.

8th September:

H. went to the Old Newingtonians' dinner so I should have had a lonely evening only the Doctor came round, chess board under his arm and we had some very good games, won one each, and drew the last.

15th September:

Morning trimmed a hat and made Babe a bathing gown! And told her stories — she knows such a number and keeps them all distinct. When I begin the Three Bears and say 'so Goldilocks went to the front door and . . .' (and before I can get further, she knocks on the chair) and I say yes, she knocked at the door and what else did she do? Then she imitates the pulling of the bell — and so on all through the story. In afternoon took her with Annie to see the Punch and Judy show at bazaar. Also bought a number of useless trifles. Of course.

19th September:

Went to town, had a little lunch festival with H. with strawberries and cream and a present of an inkstand — a peace offering because we had quarrelled this morning over the question of 'smacking' little girl. Sometimes when she kicks and screams I acknowledge there is nothing like a bit of pain on her arm or leg for bringing her to her senses — but last night it seemed unnecessary to me. I returned the compliment with cigars and we both bought Tiny a present home.

29th September:

Afternoon did not feel up to going to the Book Tea so stayed at home. Night went to the Mack's concert, which went off very well. Florrie was in very good voice, Gert looked a very sweet young debutante and played well. Louie recited her 'Evening with the Bushies' and 'On the Wharf'. But it seems to me a bit cool to get up on a platform and say your own things. Dickens did — but he was Dickens.

2nd October:

The more I have to do the more I do. Nellie had the day out and I had no nurse, so managed Babe and cooked dinner, dressed and went out with H. and Babe to the Prideham's for afternoon, and into the bargain did Children's Page and wrote a long poem for Town and Country *Christmas number — 'Johnnie and I Are Out'.*

Johnnie and I are Out

We've shut the door of the playhouse, there sounds no call or shout,
For things are running crossways, and Johnnie and I are out.
We who have played together through summer and winter days,
In future are always going upon our separate ways.

We quarrelled about the Indians. Johnnie is always chief.
He sent me for Bridget's feathers, and she caught me and called me a thief.
Truly we wouldn't have hurt them, she need not have scolded so,
But I had to go back to Johnnie with never a feather to show.

Well, of course he called me a ninny, but I smiled and that went past,
And I helped him to chase the turkey, and he got his feathers at last;
And I lent him my drawing crayons, and he used all the red and green
For stripes on his face, till truly he was a horrible thing to be seen.

And he took off his boots and stockings, and striped his legs all blue,
And turned his jacket inside out as it seems all Indians do.
And I fetched him the axe, and he chopped some boughs, and made a
  wigwam snug,
But I was only his squaw, he said, and must sit outside on a rug.

I've never said so to Johnnie, but I don't like being a squaw;
He says they can't wear feathers or march away to war.
He even won't let me blue my face, 'that's only for chiefs,' says he,
But while he's off shouting and fighting, it's dull at the wigwam for me.

So just for once in a while today I brought sweet May-bell down,
In her pink kid boots, and her Paris hat, and her lovely green silk gown.
And Johnnie went off to get some scalps, but I didn't care a scrap,
For I couldn't be dull if I tried, you see, with May-bell on my lap.

Then suddenly Johnnie shouted out that I must go up to cook
For bread and jam for a feast day. I never thought he would look
Into the hollow gum tree, so I made May-bell a nest,
And kissed her good-bye, and told her to have a few minutes' rest.

And then — ah, I can't help crying, though I thought I could cry no
    more —
My sweet little, dear little, May-bell! Johnnie was home from war.
And what do you think he was doing? I shudder with anguish yet!
My poor little frightened May-bell, my sweet little tender pet!

All her gold hair — he had pulled it off — it was hanging over his belt;
Her dress was here and her hat was there, and in front of a fire, he knelt;
And there in a billy that hung on sticks my darling's body I saw,
And I shrieked and shrieked — but he only said, 'We hardly can eat her
    raw.'

So now you can understand me — nothing could be more plain —
Never as long as the world goes round can we play together again.
Down in the bush, all by himself, he can hunt for the red man's trail —
I shall stay up in the house and sew, or read my new fairy tale.

Yes, I shall take to threading beads, and using my proper toys —
Johnnie must build his wigwams alone, or play with the next-door boys —
Only I don't believe that he ever will like their ways —
The knack that I had in matting floors he always used to praise.

He must play alone, and I, yes, I shall practise scales and sew.
Perhaps I shall get consumption, and thinner, and thinner grow,
Till at last I die, and they bury me. I wonder would Johnnie cry,
And think of the days when we Indians played — no one but he and I?

Who is this coming? Johnnie himself. I'll shut my eyes at him so;
But what's he got held fast in his arms, that makes him walk so slow?
His cricket bat, and the ball, and stumps — even his football brown!
But why is he coming up to me, and why does he put them down?

'You haven't got anything else to give!' I don't know what you mean.
'All of these are for me to keep!' and a sob the words between!
Dear little John, you didn't mean to hurt, yes, yes, I know,
And perhaps May-bell will mend again, perhaps the joins won't show.

Let's run off out and play again — beads are such stupid things —
Let's build the wigwam up again, and make some spears and slings.
And may I really paint my face, and be a fighting squaw?
Why, Johnnie, dear, this Indian game's the best I ever saw.

23rd October:

A letter from Mother to say Lil has begun to be ill. I was trying to do Children's Page all day but the constant thinking about her and her faring brought about a curious thing. I had pains of the same character and almost as severe as the day before Babe was born — pains experienced never before nor since till to-day. So bad I had to lie down. The odd part too is that Lil said the night before Babe was born she suffered dreadfully. Well, two people could hardly be in greater sympathy.

27th October:

Was asleep on the sofa beside Baby when in came Nellie with two telegrams — one bearing the words 'Son arrived, both doing well'. F. L. Thompson. What a Red Letter Day. I was so excited I could hardly dress myself and Nellie helped me off. I ran hard but just missed a train so telephoned to H. while waiting for next. Went over on boat with Dr Arthur, a sympathetic companion at such a time. He got a cab for me and I just caught the train and got to Burwood at 3.40 pm. All was calm and quiet — Mother had missed being there after all through a bungling of the telephone message. Lil asked for me so the nurse let me in just for one minute: the dear, dear little mother was very bright though it was only four hours after. I just kissed her, and devoured the babe with my eyes — very like Lil he looked, dear little laddie, then out I went. She did not suffer as much as I from all accounts — the chloroform took effect better.

2nd November:

Very warm over my new book; wrote with a vigour and ease, delicious after such a spell of inability. Wrote nearly all day with the exception of a little walk with Babe to buy a toy. About 4,000 words. The book is going to be good, I can feel it. I can think Maud Macarthy for the idea — girl of genius.

3rd November:

Morning did not write. Head felt like a squeezed sponge so used my hands. Mended the hose and did other mending. Afternoon H. came home early — a half holiday to see the second lot of the Contingent off the Transvaal. I know several in this lot, Capt. Jack Antill, A. B. Paterson — War Correspondent, H. Spooner, ditto.

13th November:

A very busy day — household, Babe and Children's Page. For the latter too I wrote an article, 'War! War! War!' in which the Court Jester makes the whole court volunteer.

22nd November:

Morning interrupted. Too often to write, engaged a new nurse, I have been without for two months but cannot manage — there are so many trifling things to waste time over, and such a lot of sewing and mending accumulates.

2nd December:
Morning I did nothing in particular and did it very well. Afternoon Nellie Hague Smith came. At night a phenomenal heat wave arrived — temperature went up 17 degrees after tea. Sat out on grass with Nellie and H. till nearly 2 o'clock.

18th December:
Went to town — saw Mr Brookes about Gum Leaves. *He proposes to pay £45 early next year on ac. royalties. Lunched with H. Shopped after.*

23rd December:
Went for a sail with Mr Gilchrist — H., Dolly and I — and a Mr Maxted. A very rough day, we were tossed about like a cork and drenched a dozen times but that only added to the fun.

25th December:
Finished present-giving — Babe got a very nice cradle, three dolls, three picture books, two other toys and a box of blocks. She was everyone's darling and was very winning and sweet.

Mother had a very dainty dinner, shorn of 'heaviness' and the Soderbergs came also. Then a lazy afternoon.

27th December:
Night H. and I went to Maud Macarthy's last concert, enjoyed it very much, but a stifling concert hall is no place to hear music like hers.

30th December:
Year's Pen Work.
Playthings of Fate *(play with Mrs Kearney)*
5 short stories for magazines
2 chapters of a projected novel, The Common Problem *— never be more than projected.*
4 chapters of a sequel to Misrule.
8 chapters of new book — Challis *— Selection story*
52 Children's Pages
Compiled Gum Leaves

The Blue Mountains were recognized as an excellent place for restoring health to children who were looking frail or convalescing after an illness, and in numerous books E.T. sends her families off to the Mountains to receive the benefits of its invigorating climate, as she did in this year's book, *Little Mother Meg*. It seemed to her that an opportunity to get to the Mountains gave the patient some divine healing that could cure any illness, though years later this faith of hers was shattered.

1900

The Land is Ours

The views around Mosman persuaded Herbert and Ethel that the only place they wanted to build would be somewhere in that vicinity. Finally they discovered a beautiful block of land overlooking Middle Harbour, and they made an immediate offer which was accepted.

4th January:
Mother and Rex ran up for half an hour on their way to Manly. Then in afternoon arrived Lil and the Boy, got a large bedroom comfortably ready and found a cradle and made a nest of it.

9th January:
Night H. and I went for dinner and evening to the Soderberg's and discussed heaven and earth and the musical glasses and war. More especially war. Yesterday the Boers made a strong attempt on Ladysmith but were repulsed. The British temper could not have brooked another defeat.

13th January:
Morning rode to Gordon. Afternoon Lil and Fred and little Boy left us to return to Gordon. Night we went for a lovely moonlight ride, and for the first time revisited all the nooks and places at Lindfield made sacred during our engagement. It seemed full of ghosts but it is a very sweet thing to feel that neither of us have lost our illusions yet, or found each other wanting. We are happier now a thousand times than ever in those sweet days.

14th January:
Morning H. and I went to church at Gordon and married ourselves over again in memory during the service. Afternoon we went, taking Babe, to the Windeyer's and had a pleasant afternoon tea out of doors in the bush. They have five children — all under seven — who keep their hands busy and purses light. Dick Windeyer is not much further on than H. at the Bar.

23rd January:
Got into a splendid mood for writing — wrote from 10 am to 3 pm with a break of half an hour for lunch. Chapter X Mortimer telling his love. Think I shall call this book The Common Problem *instead of the one I began before.*

26th January:
A very pleasant day for our sail. Mr Gilchrist, Mr Gerber, Claude and Dolly, Miss McCulloch, Rex, H. and I. Had an exciting adventure — went to the rescue of a capsized crew and took them all into our boat, four men and a little boy; they had been ten minutes in the water but were not much the worse for it. Later, after we had towed their boat in, we went to Middle Harbour — it was very rough which we all liked!

2nd February:
Odd things in morning and Children's Page. Afternoon went to town and took Babe with me — she was a little villain and cried dreadfully when I took her out of the toy department — first time she has disgraced me.

7th February:
Busy with Little Girl's Birthday Party, her first — two years old today. Bruce, Gwen and Baby Arthur, Sylvia and Miriam Morris, Theo and Girlie Meillon, Birdie Wallace, Nancy and Wilfred Browne were her guests. We played games with them, then they were given a mask each and made a lot of fun out of them. Then tea on a low table, they sitting on the ground, jellies and chocolates and sponge cakes and such infantile harmless things. Then upstairs to the tiny bedroom to see what the fairy had brought — they believe implicitly in her. Out came a bran pie with a little present for each. Babe was very demure and quiet and found it rather a bore to kiss all the children both coming and going.

19th February:
A hard morning at Gum Leaves *getting it into shape and improving. Afternoon went to the Shore to see Mrs Lawson — her baby is eight days old. 'Henry' was out; I only stayed three or four minutes for fear of exciting her. Took her a pretty bonnet for the babe and a toy for him.*

20th February:
Morning thought hard but wrote little. Afternoon bathing — Babe let me take her out in the deep and dip her right to her neck. Night I went to the Patriotic Concert here with the Arthurs — and during it — just as they were reciting 'Absent Minded Beggar' someone brought in news that the Victorian troops had been entrapped and slaughtered to a man.

21st February:
Wrote splendidly — a very long chapter — War chapter, Mortimer Stevenson at a Boer farm house.

26th February:
Children's Page and some more letters for Gum Leaves. *At night H. and I worked at a column we are going to suggest* Daily Telegraph *has each week, 'The Family Dinner Table'; running commentary on every day events, both of us writing it.*

Sir William Cullen, Lieutenant-Governor and Chief Justice of New South Wales, lifelong friend of Ethel and garden adviser.
By kind permission of the National Library, Canberra.

Jean and Adrian in the middle of a picnic group with the Miller family at Blackheath in the Blue Mountains in 1911.

A favourite spot in the garden showing Ethel standing at the sundial. Jean chose its motto: 'Come what may, Time and the hour runs through the roughest day.'

Lord Tennyson commented on Jean's remarkable knowledge and appreciation of literature.

Adrian, aged 13.

28th February:
Bush Contingent. H. stayed at home all day, being a public holiday. Then we went down to Dr Pockley's, Macquarie St to watch the procession. A splendid sight to see all those fine Bushmen and their splendid horses; the enthusiasm was immense — contagious — it brought a lump to my throat. Harry Pockley and William Cope have gone — the former as 2nd, the latter 1st lieutenant. This morning's cables brought news of Cronje's surrender so there may not be much work for them to do.

4th March:
Morning read. Afternoon Henry Lawson came bringing his little boy Jim and we talked shop and such interesting matter. Rex also ran in and Mr Gilchrist at 5 pm to take us for a sail. As it was calm I took Babe too — she enjoyed it exceedingly — her first sail.

7th March:
Town shopping till 2 pm. Afternoon Babe and I went to the Lawsons — they go to England by the Medic in a month, I must see what I can do, her hands are so full with the 2 babies, none of her sewing done and the baby only three weeks old.

26th March:
Morning wrote. Afternoon Babe and I went to spend afternoon with Mrs Cullen. And when I got home H. had very pleasant news. He has been given a Crown Prosecutorship for Deniliquin. Will go on Good Friday — it will be a very pleasant trip for him apart from the money.

5th April:
Corrected typed sheets most of the day. Ida Wilshire came in afternoon for advice on 'how to be an author'. It is lovely to think I have the book finished as early in the year as this — eight chapters the month or two before Xmas and the 14 since. The Common Problem *I am* sure *is my best work yet and I have loved writing it.*

12th April:
Today was Day of Humiliation for the Plague. Also opening of Show. And the Bishop and Show promoters are at daggers drawn in consequence.

2nd May:
Wrote three verses for dedication page of Three Little Maids

To My Tiny Daughter

Here is a chain for you, sweet,
   Hold up your soft hands to catch it;
Pansy and white marguerite,
   You will think nothing can match it.

But you will say, Are they true?
   All of the flowers in the chain, dear?
Did they all grow up with you,
   Or some of them just in your brain dear?

Count true the white marguerite,
   Pansies — as false I must own them.
Life, it may well be my sweet,
   Had not so fair to you grown them.
               E.S.C.

3rd May:
Idled all morning. Felt inclined for nothing of greater tax then Children's Page so got next Monday's ready. H. came home at 7 pm. He got his cheque for Crown Prosecuting — £50. 8. 0, eight guineas expenses and the £42 clear for doing nothing at all. We wish a few more would come his way.

18th May:
Babe and I went to Stanmore to 'Grandma C'lewis' for the day. Greatest excitement — guns, flags, everywhere — it is reported (unofficially) that Mafeking is relieved at last — Baden Powell had held out seven whole months.

19th May:
Morning read Pendennis. *Afternoon took Babe to Theo Meillon's fourth birthday party which she enjoyed with quiet dignity as usual. No absolute confirmation about Mafeking yet.*

23rd May:
Public Holiday for the Relief of Mafeking.

13th June:
Dolly came in suddenly — she has been away in the country over three months. They are going to do Hermsley up thoroughly and want me to undertake the choice of wall papers, paint, carpets, etc. etc. I shall enjoy it.

22nd June:

A stay-at-home-day at last after the busy week. But the running about has done me good. Afternoon Rosie and I went to ask after Mrs Bartholomew — Babe and I were asked into the bedroom for a few minutes and Babe gazed with rapture at the fortnight-old baby. Then she said 'I love that Baby, Mover, you must buy me one'. First copy of Gum Leaves *came — very nicely produced.*

Gum Leaves was a light-hearted book of nonsense and fun, delightfully illustrated by D.H. Souter. This poem gives an idea of the humour of the work.

Concerning Cables

I once knew a shark who one morning in May
    Was swimming about the Atlantic,
He'd had nothing to eat for three weeks and a day
    With hunger he almost was frantic.

When he found at the bottom of ocean's deep bed
    A thing that a huge eel resembled;
And for pleasure the fish fairly stood on his head,
    While his tail with beatitude trembled.

Said he, 'Of the things I've devoured in my time,
    If I told you, you'd say "Did you ever!"
But a submarine cable! I tell you it's prime,
    And I thought I should taste of it never.'

Now, just when he thought he'd attained his desire,
    And was going to tackle it gaily,
To Sydney was being transmitted a wire
    To appear in a great morning 'daily'.

The shark took a bite with delight on his face,
    But quickly the morsel rejected,
And with many a shudder and horrid grimace,
    Said, 'To eat that I can't be expected'.

The toughest of morsels I do not despise
    And to swallow most things I am able;
But I'm shot if I'm going to swallow the lies
    That they put in a newspaper cable'.

12th July:

Felt ill and lay on ottoman on verandah most of the day. The journey and jolting seem to have been too much for me. Night H. grew anxious and called Dr Arthur, then came Nurse Scott to mind me lest I moved at all.

27th July:

Morning nothing. Afternoon went with Mrs Arthur to Rose of Persia. *But I did not hear at all well — indeed it was chiefly spectacular for me, for we were up in D.C. and I can only hear in Orchestral Stalls. Then after I met H. and we went out to Edgecliff to the Raine's. Such a beautiful new house they have built — we went to talk the advisability or otherwise of building and as they had been twice through the mill, they were ready to give advice. Not that we could attempt their style — they must have spent £3,000 on theirs. Had a very pleasant evening.*

4th August:

Morning anysing. Afternoon gardened. Night came Mr Steele to dinner — Mr Steele of Ward Lock with whom I have been at enmity ever since I put my affairs into Watt's hands! At least he has been at enmity with me — I didn't feel so particularly but of course he was hurt! But the axe is buried now and we are the best of friends again.

5th August:

H., Babe and I to Hermsley for the day. And we hardly knew where we were! Poor old Hermsley spick and span everywhere with paint and artistic wallpapers, new carpets and curtains, a cook in the kitchen and a neat housemaid in cap and apron waiting at table.

7th August:

Actually got my play out and attacked it — Keeping Up Appearances *I think will be its name. Night Mr Steele invited us to go to hear Donald McDonald on 'The Siege of Ladysmith'. Enjoyed the lecture immensely — the man in khaki was such an unaffected graphic speaker it was a pleasure to hear him. Afterwards Mr Steele took us behind and introduced us to the lion. He was very nice — said he had all my books and would like to send me his war book when it is out and his book of Natural History which he published some years ago.*

21st August:

Babe and I had a day in town — lunched with H. too at Fresh Food; then he took her small ladyship up to Chambers with him and put her to sleep under his table on a contribution of legal gowns from several in the office. Meantime I finished shopping.

29th August:

Tried to get in Sequel to Misrule mood but it wouldn't go. Instead copied down this story told by Babe — almost verbatim — the other night:

'Well an' so was once a little girl an' had lovely golden hair yight down her back, — all this long, an' her Mama said not go up steps an' get lost for Anysing. An' her Mama went to town, an' little girl went up steps an' she walked an' she walked an' she walked sroo the bush an' sud'nly zere came a drefful monstrous noise an' ' (finger up, voice fallen to a sepulchral whisper) 'an' what you does fink it was? It was ze Plague'.

She has heard Nurse and Nellie talking of the Plague and imagines it, I suppose, like some Ogre. Looks across to Manly and says 'Nuvver case of Plague, zere goes a ship in korryntine' And the other morning said 'Ony one case of Plague, isn't it a shame, Daddie.'

1st September:
Went off to look at a piece of land — found a piece I hadn't come to look for and its owner Mr Rohde on the spot; I like it better than any piece I have seen yet.

2nd September:
Took H. off to view land and met Mr Rohde there. Even H. likes it muchly — such a glorious view.

3rd September:
Too excited to settle to anything — rang up Mr Peddle, the architect and got him to come out and view the land for practical purposes. And he too thinks it is an excellent piece. So Herbert actually sat down and made an offer in writing to Mr Rohde, who told us we could have it for £150. H. in a business spirit offered £130— chiefly lest he should say oh £160 or £180 when he knows we like it so much. Night H. had to go back to town, and I wrote answers to a heap of letters — girls — aspiring authoresses chiefly. It takes a lot of time but one can't leave them unanswered.

4th September:
Morning glued myself to my chair and wrote part II of sequel. Mr Rohde wrote that they could not take less than £150, so H. went up and accepted the offer. Mr Rohde says he will see to title and H. is to take till Monday to decide he says — we don't want to, however.

6th September:
Morning sternly went to study — how I longed to sit and draw plans! But they have to be paid for. Couldn't get in Misrule *mood so attacked little play again,* Keeping Up Appearances. *At lunch in walked Lil. Fred has another position, a clerical one under Dr at Parramatta Asylum. They have now the joy of moving again from Chatswood. And a very serious thing is ahead: She is in my state of health again — and Dick only ten months old where Jean is two and a half.*

7th September:
At night Dr Arthur came and brought me a surprising and agreeable present — an unobtrusive ear arrangement. Just a tube and mouthpiece and I can sit at theatre or anywhere and hear without being seen to put anything up. Nothing so horrid as an ear trumpet. The exciting part is I hear very well all over the dining room, no one raising their voice in the least, even a semitone.

14th September:
Morning sewed, and went to sleep with Babe. Afternoon paid off three calls — Mrs Lister Lister, Mrs Coloquhuon and Mrs Hedley.

29th October:
Children's Page all morning. Babe and I went down to the Spit Beach by the new tram, only opened on Saturday.

10th November:
Letter from Mother saying Lil's little boy is very ill, Dr Reid said hydrocephalus, Dr Traill says a tendency to rickets! And such a healthy, chubby boy he looked, nothing ever ailing him; I simply wouldn't believe it. At night H. took me to Chatswood to see for myself.

22nd November:
A Do-nothing day. And yet it is such a cool, pleasant week I ought to feel brighter. I want to lie on the lounge and go to sleep all the time. We are hoping very much H. will get post of Lecturer in Pleading and Procedure, Law School — he is trying very hard for it but so many men of longer standing are in for it. It is £200 a year and wouldn't interfere with his Bar work.

23rd November:
Dick still very bad, but doctor said it is not hydrocephalus; they can only give him concentrated chicken, peptonized milk and brandy. And the chicken is 3/6 a day so it is ruinous for them, and Fred still has no position. I don't know what will happen — all this doctoring and trouble — Lil unable to write a word and expenses going on daily.

25th November:
Mother and Charlie came in for lunch. Charlie had just escaped a bad accident — he had been knocked down by an electric train but fortunately only had a few cuts and bruises. At night went up to get the Doctor to witness my signature for money to be drawn from Bank for the Land — I can't go to town of course.

18th December:
A day of trifles, lying down a good deal. Very cool and delightful however. Wrote to Louie and sent her 3 Little Maids and a big photo of Babe. Poor little thing the clouds are black on her sky at present. Went next door to Mrs Mapleson to leave first cards, she seems very nice.

24th December:
H. took Babe to Gordon to wish them merry Xmas and she came home with a beautiful doll that she has already named Larkspur. And I was lying on the sofa when the door opened and in came . . . Lil!!! The Doctor had told them to take Dick to Moss Vale or Bowral tomorrow, and she said she couldn't go without paying me a flying visit; she left Dick with the trained nurse. He is no worse but makes so little improvement that the country is the only thing left. Fresh expense of course as the Burwood house is taken for 6 months; but health first of all. Fred has gone up today to find accommodation and she will take Emily to help her. Such a two hours' talk we had!!

25th December:
Boy and I and Little Girl had a very happy little Xmas day after all — the first we have had alone. I kept thinking of little Lil in the train with her boy.

Jean at the completion of her school career at S.C.E.G.G.S. Darlinghurst.

Adrian, top right of photo, diving from the top level of the tower at the Lavender Bay baths.

Ethel Curlewis, taken in London 1910. This photograph appeared as frontispiece to The Ethel Turner Birthday Book.

Dorothea Mackellar published a number of books of verse including The Closed Door, The Witch Maid *and* Dream Harbour, *as well as several novels. One of her poems,* My Country, *is very widely known.*

By kind permission of the Mitchell Library.

Ginger Meggs: this Christmas day edition of 'Us Fellers' was the first appearance of Ginger. Several weeks before this, Ethel had written to the Managing Director of The Sun *newspaper saying that she wanted 'something in the shape of a small boy, half imp, half angel, who did mischievous and funny things every week from the top of the page to the bottom.'*

By kind permission of J.C. Bancks Estate

Adrian (centre) at a garden party with Miss Ailsa Cullen, daughter of the Chief Justice of New South Wales, Sir William Cullen (left).

Ethel and Adrian in the family car.

Jean after she had returned from England. At this time she wrote articles for the Home *magazine and* Australia Beautiful.

26th December:

Felt more energetic and did quite a lot of mending of Babe's things and tidying of her toys and putting some away for the future or she will have toy-indigestion.

31st December:

The land is ours and paid for — now to get the plans out and the first stones laid. I am afraid it will be August before we are living in the house. Have decided to have Ern. Thompson to be our architect.

' "I watch it every night," she said.'
A Trembling Star

1901-1909

There are Too Many 'Departments' in Life

1901

With the added responsibilities, and demands on her time, the diaries change rather dramatically at this stage. They become more a record of daily events, rather than the personal reactions, frustrations, ambitions and emotions that have previously been so fascinating to read. In fact she frequently neglected to make entries in her diaries which, for so many years, had been a necessary part of daily routine, and I feel certain they had been like a 'confidante' or a sympathetic friend to her.

This poem to Jean , written in 1901, was found among Ethel's papers. Its tenderness shows the great love she felt for her baby daughter.

> *A boat on the sea. My boat*
> *Eager and frail*
> *Sweet Skies smile as you look*
> *On that fairy sail.*
>
> *Waves, great waves — many years*
> *You have worked your will.*
> *Just while she passes through,*
> *Kind waves, be still.*
>
> *Winds — ah, I may not ask*
> *That you never blow.*
> *But spare her the moaning note,*
> *That the old boats know.*

2nd January:
Again a do-nothing sort of day. Felt very oppressed and tired of everything by evening — I am afraid this is going to be a dreary month. I can get about very little and the time goes so slowly.

4th January:
Idled, read while nurse went shopping for me. Night H., Babe and I went to foot of Harbour St to see the Illuminations and Fireworks for Commonwealth Day. It was quite cold. We had a splendid view, couldn't have found a better place and Little Girl was delighted. My longest walk for a long time.

11th January:
Energetic again, did all manner of things which included painting some kitchen tins red. I am weary to death of reading and sewing and quiet things. At night I worked off several business letters — Lil's business with Steele and others. I felt I had better get them done.

12th and 13th January:
A busy day changing furniture — or at least directing H. Writing table moved out of bedroom, etc. Life as usual till dinner bell rang at 6 pm. Then I knew suddenly the time was short. H. rushed for Dr Arthur — only to find he had gone to Bowral. For Dr Doak — away on a holiday. For Nurse Scott — gone to town. Finally brought Dr Van Someren down who ordered me to bed but said 'not just yet' and then went off with H. to scour the place for a nurse. At last came Nurse Single about 11 pm and she and the Doctor said to me 'try to sleep a little'. Just as well tell the passengers on a burning ship to 'have a little doze!' Still I didn't suffer at all till 12 or 1 am and not badly till 3 am. After that a bad hour. Then the Dr AND chloroform. Oh the blessed thing that is. I was completely under for three hours, I woke up to hear the Dr say 'A very fine little boy' but didn't believe it till they laid him beside me, naked and rosy and kicking vigorously, my little son. Soon after H. to kiss me. And my girlie to kiss me. I felt so well. So different from after Jean's birth — the chloroform did me hardly any good then and Dr Arthur wouldn't use enough. Very well all day I felt.

After this entry there are many weeks of blanks, and we can imagine that Ethel's days were filled caring for her family.

However, many more books were written and many interesting events occurred which influenced her stories, and therefore if you yet have patience to bear with the ramblings of one who struggles with the written word, I shall give a brief summary of the following years, occasionally interspersed with her own entries, so that the final picture will be more complete.

Her two children Jean and Adrian were a great joy to her and she divided her time between her husband, her children and her writing. The never-ending stream of unsatisfactory servants and nurses 'vexed' her greatly and hampered her at every turn. This was one of many:

Waited and waited for Bertha to come and relieve me of Baby. At last ran up to her room and found she had 'folded her tent like the Arab and as silently stolen away'. Bertha whom I thought was going to be the prop of my old age! I shall be white-haired if this continues much longer.

She farewelled her schoolgirl friend Louie Mack (now Creed) who was to leave for England.

11th April:

Went across to a hastily convened meeting in Mr Sid Long's studio to get up a souvenir to give to Louie, she goes to Melbourne on Sunday to catch the Omrah *there for London. Julian Ashton, Mrs Aronson, Mr Charles Arnold, etc. there. Decided on a purse of sovereigns, each of us giving a guinea.*

Rushed back home for lunch and to do justice by little Boy. Marmee had come for the day. Then back to town to meet Rosie and Jean and go to The Australia with Mr Gilchrist to tea. To meet the lady of his most romantic story. Liked her very well but it is a difficult position for me — he is just ready to fall headlong in love with her, and yet afraid as she is rich and delicate and he fears there would be no happiness. And he practically leaves the onus of deciding to me — says he can trust my judgement so well and so on. Rosie for dinner and evening.

Rosie was married to Harold Pockley in June and Jean was a flower-girl:

18th June:

. . . in her tiny white silk frock and lace, a wreath of violets on her curly gold mop and a muff of violets hanging from her neck. She kept jumping up and down the step to the altar to while away the tedium of the homilies, but knelt decorously at each prayer.

Well, and there is the last of us gone — Phyl, Dolly and now Weenie*. I am sure she will be happy too though it is a long, long way to go. I quite loved Harold — he is a dear old fellow, so thoroughly genuine. A great crush of guests — heaps of Pockleys and Antils, etc. etc. and many I didn't know.

The building of their own home, which Ethel and Herbert called Avenel, was very time-consuming, builders to see, decisions to make, rooms to decorate and making her 'castles in the air' a reality.

1902

This entry on 10th January must surely reflect the feelings of many overtaxed mothers of young children, who wonder how they can possibly fulfill such a demanding role:

10th January:

A day at the Spit, Dolly, Jean, Adrian, Emily and I. Had a lovely swim — a thing I seldom find time for now. I don't think 48 hours to the day would see all my work finished — there are too many 'departments' in life to be head of — probably it is I am a bad manager. But there is the roll-top desk department and the garden (a big matter at present) and the nursery, which mustn't be neglected and Society — which is neglected — I've 100 calls at least owing I believe — and the Clothes department and the House linen and the Pantries and the Orders and the Servants. I have Miss Price again for

---

*These are the names she gives Lil, herself and Rosie in the story *Three Little Maids.*

sewing but there is still much I must do and H. does get his buttons off dreadfully. And then there is Shopping. And the calls of one's family — and the rights of a husband to have me at leisure in an evening, and letters, and accounts, and, and, and, and, and, and, . . . I suppose it is the removal and the summer and disturbed nights with the boy — when I feel alright again I'll steer my boat better.

In a thin Writing Album with pastel coloured pages Ethel recorded the progress of her daughter Jean, from babyhood, through the miraculous stages of the first smile, first tooth, age of crawling and walking, etc, to kindergarten and early school days. Some very early entries kept details, which may otherwise have been forgotten, of quaint sayings such as flow-by (blow-fly) hop-grasser (grass-hopper) flutterby (butterfly), Little Bee Pope. Then on 21st July (when Jean was four and a half) she wrote:

21st July:
She had been at the beach all the afternoon and so happy about the sparkling sea. Then she began to sing odd lines and again when going to bed at night. So I took a pencil and she sang it line by line just like this with absolutely no word on my part. Even the name she called it was entirely her own — 'The Book of Water Tides'.

> *Water lilies and water leaves*
> *Gold and silver tide are flowing*
> *Under the boughs and bushes*
> *Under the willows and green trees.*
> *Water droops upon thy head*
> *Green trees are flowing and slowly away*
> *The green leaves are drooping from bough to bough*
> *The water slowly flows away.*
> *And up the river and down the river*
> *And slowly flows away.*
> *Gold and silver tide is low*
> *Dabble children as it flow*
> *Sing a happy song*
> *As you dabble as it flows*
> *The white snow is falling down below*
> *Side by side they keep and lie there*
> *The water lilies and water leaves*
> *Around thy be-guided*
> *White swans adorning*
> *They swim from pool to pool*

She has a very good memory and a good store of miscellaneous information. Her chief delight though is stories. Stories, stories all the day. Grimm, Alice in Wonderland, The Water Babies *are her chiefest friends. I am also introducing her to Tennyson and her appreciation is great of 'The Lady of Shallot', the 'Revenge', etc.*

At times of crisis or national disasters E.T. became very involved; and reacted by forming committees, launching appeals, or writing to newspapers or magazines in support of the newest 'worthy cause'. As with the Marcus Clarke widow in 1895 she now felt concern for the devastating drought and the Bush Sufferers.

28th November:
Wrote a long 'Appeal for Bush Sufferers' in the hope of getting the Daily Telegraph *to publish it. The distress in the bush is frightful just now — for myself I can't get away from the thought of it. They say many are living on bran and treacle. I think my Bush Box scheme would work well — thought it out most of the day.*

During this year, Rosie's first baby was born — a son whom she called Robert.

1903

E.T. was delighted to discover that the new Editor of the *Evening News* was her friend Banjo Paterson, and one evening when he came to dinner he presented her with a copy of the *Man from Snowy River* and *Rio Grand*.

The first copy of her book of short stories *Betty and Co* arrived on the same day as Lil's *Australian Lassie*:

It was so nice them coming together and in the same kind of binding. I like Australian Lassie *far better than my* Betty *which is poor stuff.*

In October she purchased a block of land at Leura on the Blue Mountains in Balmoral Road. She paid £60 for a hundred-foot frontage and wasted no time in employing a builder and erecting a small cottage which she called Yanalla after their first home in Harbour St, Mosman. The method of transport from Mosman to Leura was rather a challenge in those days — first to Spit Junction by tram, then another tram down to Mosman's Bay wharf, across in the ferry, tram from Circular Quay to Central, steam train to Leura, then waggonette or cart from the railway station to the little cottage. Luggage, children, nurses etc. all added up to making each trip quite a major exercise. The cottage at Leura proved to be a great success and the family often managed to find time to leave Sydney and enjoy the mountain air. However, other members of the family also found it inviting and enjoyable, and they would arrive at the same time with luggage, babies and nurses and all squeeze into the little cottage until its seams were nearly fit to burst.

Of course I am glad to have them all and for all to have a change, but it has been the least restful holiday I, personally, have ever had and I have wished more than once that I had never built the place. Well the moral is, I'll lend it to them all sometimes but I'll never have a houseful like this again. 5 tiny children in a cottage on a wet day is no light joke. I am longing for the quiet and comfort of Avenel again.

She started a new book called *The Child That was Lost* but later renamed it *Gift Impossible.*

1904

She felt keenly the trouble and difficulties of the other members of the family:

Worried over the O'Brien's troubles and Lil's troubles and H's brothers troubles till I could only see one solution — I must write a play that will bring at least £10,000. Book writing only produces a quiet, unsensational income. Sketched out a plot that I have had 'simmering' for some time.

During the year Herbert had frequent attacks which the doctors attributed to acute dyspepsia — he suffered from these attacks for fourteen years until 1918 when they changed the diagnosis and decided to operate for gallstones.

Ethel finished her book *Gift Impossible* and sent the manuscript to Ward Lock in Melbourne.

A letter from Steele saying they (the English Firm) had altered my title The Gift Impossible *to* Mother's Little Girl. *I never felt so angry — so wildly angry in all my life. Went over to H. and wrote a letter demanding that the book be kept back and the title altered to my own. The first copy of the book came and I positively could not look at it under so vulgar and namby-pamby a title.*

1905

Recording Jean's progress, Ethel says:

Hair a cloudy tangle of gold, growing nearly to her waist. Eyes clear hazel very long lashed, and skin so clear and smooth. She climbs and jumps like a boy, can swim though not very well. Her chief progress is in her reading, she devours everything now — two or three books a week and dips into anything with covers on. At this age has read Swiss Family Robinson, *one of her chief favourites, Grimm and a dozen other fairy books. All my books,* Nell Hawthorne's Wonder Book, *and* Tanglewood Tales, Alice in Wonderland *and* Looking Glass, Little Women, What Katy Did, Coral Island, *etc. etc. She has a surprising amount of general information picked up from kindergarten and her reading, and stored away in that safe little granary. In temperament the sunniest, sweetest, most loving little nature it is possible to conceive.*

Moved by devastating bush fires raging all over the colony, she organised a meeting for the Bush Fire sufferers and they determined the best means of offering assistance.

She had a passion for writing poems and after completing this one called 'The Rainbow' she said:

. . . it gave me extreme pleasure in the making; a curious fountain of delight seems to spring up in me after the creation of verse, mediocre tho' mine is. It gives me far more delight than prose.

The Rainbow

Oh, if that rainbow up there,
    Spanning the sky past the hill,
Slenderly, tenderly fair,
    Shining with colours that thrill;
Oh, if that rainbow up there
    Just for a moment could reach
Through the wet slope of the air,
    Here where I stand on the beach.

Here where the waves wash the strand,
    Swing itself lovingly low,
Let me catch fast with one hand,
    Climb its frail rigging and go.
Climb its frail rigging and go!
    Where is its haven of rest?
Out in the gleam and the glow
    Of the blood-red waves of the West?

Or where the isles of the dawn
    Lie on an amethyst sea,
Does it drift, pale and forlorn,
    Ghost of the glory I see?
Is there, ah, is there a land
    Such as the Icelanders say,
Or past the West's ruddy strand
    Or on the edge of the day?

Some undiscovered clime
    Seen through a cloud's sudden rift,
Where all the rainbows of Time
    Slowly and silently drift?
Some happy port of a sea
    Never a world's sail has made,
Where till the earth's shadows flee
    Never a rainbow may fade?

Oh, if that rainbow up there,
    Just for a moment would reach
Through the wet slope of the air,
    Here where I stand on the beach.
Here where the waves wash the strand,
    Swing itself lovingly low,
Let me catch fast with one hand,
    Climb its frail rigging and go!

Herbert's first article for the 'Mirror of Justice' appeared in the *Daily Telegraph* and he received three guineas a week for the series. These articles were an interpretation into lay language of the otherwise perplexing reports of current law suits.

On completing her book *In the Mist of the Mountains*, Ethel said:

. . . it has come easier than any book I have done — just rippled off the end of my pen.

In this story Hugh Kinross a celebrated author displays the same sentiments as Ethel — a dislike of interviews, a desire for peaceful and quiet surroundings to inspire him, and occasions when one can look critically at one's own work and then determine whether to destroy it and start afresh, or whether to persevere and re-write. With several of her stories, we can feel that Ethel would like the courage to burn some of her attempts but cannot quite bring herself to the deed.

Immediately after finishing this book she set to work on another *The Stolen Voyage*. This is the story of two young boys conspiring to change places for a time and the adventures that befall them. The method by which they engineered the plot shows E.T's sense of fun and ingenuity. She has an amazing capacity for inventing incredible situations and throughout her books she shows a delightful sense of humour. As *The Stolen Voyage* was not long enough to be published as a book, she gathered together a number of short stories that had previously been submitted to or published in magazines or newspapers. This she also did with four others books namely *The Little Duchess, The Camp at Wandinong, Betty and Co., and A White Roof Tree.*

In August Jean started at Killarney School under the headmistress, Miss Carter:

Well, this starts a new era in the little girl's life — new interests and so on. I expect I shall come to occupy a less important place now in her estimate of things.

Ethel worked feverishly towards the end of this year but realised that working late into the night, and often till the early hours of the morning, was not good and she determined to lock her pen away for a while as she felt on the verge of a nervous breakdown.

1906

On New Year's Day Ethel notes:

To Gordon for the gathering of the clans. Lil with Dick and Eric, Ro with Rob and Marcia, I with Jean and Adrian, Fred and Herbert (Harold had to go back) Rex, Mother and Charlie.

The family had numerous trips to Leura during the year. She had put aside enough pen money to do additions to Yanalla and put in a tennis court. My father (Adrian) remembers the excitement and anticipation of arriving at the mountain home each visit, for somehow there was always a small treasure beneath the 'fairy tree' for himself and Jean. It still remains a mystery to him how his mother could have 'planted' the small gift so mysteriously just in the brief time that they took to unload a box or two from the waggonette.

Ethel found her trips to Leura acted as a tonic for her:

I am going to take up golf and let the brassy be mightier than the pen for a time. I am really going to try to do without writing for about six months and grow able-bodied and able-nerved again.

1907

For some years she had been trying to write a play called *The Sundowners* but had suffered numerous rejections or suggested alterations:

Wrote a little at Act III Scene IV which entirely finishes the play. At Last. At Last. Did a war-dance with the chickens, they are as glad and as excited as I am at finishing. Well, this will be my sixth attempt, and if Mr Williamson thinks it is no good, it will be my last.

Adrian started at Killarney School with Jean and one evening he told his mother of his frightening experiences which prompted her to write:

Walking to School

Now I am five, my father says
* (And what he says you've got to mind)*
That mother's not to hold my hand
* Or even follow me behind.*

To see I'm safe. But down the road
* And all the way up the next street*
I am to walk now quite alone,
* No matter what the things I meet.*

Though horrid horses rear and plunge
* And cows come trampling, big and bold,*
And fighting boys are strutting out,
* I shall have no one's hand to hold.*

Still, five is really very old;
* It's pretty close to being a man.*
Since I a soldier wish to be,
* I s'pose it's time that I began.*

I'll swell my chest right out, like this,
* And swing my books behind, just so,*
And wear my hat stuck sideways on,
* And whistle all the way I go.*

There is a little boy I pass,
  He's always swinging on the gate,
He'll think that I am very old —
  Perhaps he'll think I'm seven or eight.

There is a little girl I see,
  She's always standing at her door.
When I come whistling boldly past,
  She'll wish that she were more than four.

What I mind most of all are dogs;
  My sister says dogs seldom bite,
But how can I be sure of this?
  Your sisters are not always right.

There is an awful dog I hear;
  It barks and barks as I go by.
I know some day it will get loose,
  And fiercely at my throat will fly.

And other dogs come round and sniff,
  (I've sandals, and my legs are bare);
Perhaps it's true they will not bite,
  Perhaps some day I shall not care.

When you were five and walked to school,
  And you met things to tremble at,
Were you as brave as great big men,
  Or did your heart go pit-a-pat?

In the book *That Girl* which she wrote in 1907 Ethel gave her imagination full rein when describing the history and background of her characters. These graphic details give the reader a very personal involvement and sympathy as the personalities develop. It is amazing, as one reads through the books, that E.T. can draw upon an inexhaustible number of complex situations, such as in this book the sequence of events that resulted in Marie living with Mr and Mrs Henderson. In this story, as with many others that she wrote, the loss of one or both parents bring out in the child a fierce sense of pride and honesty making them independent, fun-loving, forthright and with a refusal to be pitied.

1908

This diary only consists of a few pages clipped together and with very few entries. The only note-worthy entry seems to be that Rex announced his engagement to Marie Steber.

Ethel received her first copies of a book called *Happy Hearts* — which contained a collection of children's stories and verse. The following poem appeared in this book:

After the Battle

I can hear them call, but I cannot go,
    For my eyes are red. I will creep
Down here, where the wattle is hanging low,
    And hide me safe while I weep.

Spread out your skirts for me, Wattle dear,
    Shake all your gold veil round,
Or the other children will wander here,
    And I red-eyed shall be found.

Oh, Wattle, Wattle! My heart will break!
    Let me rest my head on your knee —
On your gentle knee my shamed head take,
    Shed one golden tear on me.

We were soldiers, Wattle, the boys and I,
    And we marched in the garden there;
And we shouted and sang, for our hearts were high
    With our victories everywhere.

Oh, we were as glad and gay as you,
    Dear Wattle, are, when you fling
Your yellow head backwards, and shake the dew
    From your hair, and sway and sing.

And we crashed and dashed as we won the heights
    Of every bank on the lawn,
And we panted for fiercer and fiercer fights,
    That should see our flag upborne.

And a sortie we made through a break in the fence
    To the paddock that slopes away,
Half-hidden in grass, to the trees, and thence
    To the sun, where he dies each day.

Half-hidden in grass, ah, in poppies too!
    The poppies flame thick and wild,
And they dance and they laugh and they nod at you,
    And kiss you — if you're a child.

'The foe! The foe!' cried the boys. 'The foe!'
    And into the midst we plunged,
And here and there, at each startled row,
    With our wooden swords we lunged.

And with shouts and cheers and our flag awave
    We cut them down where they stood;
The white a-tremble, the pink more brave,
    And the red dyed deep in blood.

Then the battle ebbed, and it died away,
Like a wave on a worn sea-shore;
And the boys rushed off to a further fray,
And I was alone once more.

Alone, with the fire gone out of my heart —
I am only a girl you know —
And something was making me slow to start
From the field of the fallen foe.

And I wandered back to the golden grass,
Where the wind hung sad and still,
And it mournfully parted to let me pass,
And I stood with my heart a-thrill.

So still they lay, so still at my feet,
That had danced and laughed like mad,
That had touched my cheeks with their mouths so sweet
So still, so meek, so sad!

Dead at my feet — at my feet quite dead!
And I — I helped to slay,
The piteous pink ones, the startled red,
And the white that had been at play.

Spread out your skirts for me, Wattle dear,
Shake all your gold veil round,
Or the other children will wander here,
And I red-eyed shall be found.

Oh, Wattle, Wattle! My heart will break!
Let me rest my head on your knee —
On my gentle knee my shamed head take,
Shed one golden tear on me.

Of Jean she writes:

. . . up to this year I allowed few or no home lessons and when the others had afternoon school I kept her at home so she might play or go to the beach, but she more than holds her own. Out of 10 weeks in a quarter she is top quite 8 or 9 times — the youngest in the class too.

1909

13th January:
Gave Adrian a happy birthday. I had a model boatshed made to hold his 19 little boats, and made life-buoys and sailors and fishing nets, etc. for it. It gave him the greatest delight.

Under doctor's orders Herbert was advised to go overseas and forget his legal practice for a time, in order to restore his health. So there was a big economy drive and a determined effort to write with all her heart and soul to help save enough to take the whole family to Europe the following year. Twice during the year Ethel decided to leave the many interruptions of the home situation, and she banished herself to a boarding house at Merrylands for a week of intensive writing. She finished a story which she had started the previous year and called it *Fugitives from Fortune*. Immediately it was finished she started the next one, *Fair Ines*. This is the first time she had written a book entirely about adults. The characters are life-like and well-defined, but it lacks the humorous observations of childhood behaviour that characterise her earlier books.

She completed this book in four months and in June she writes:

10th June:
Worked at Fair Ines — *and finished it! Twenty-eight chapters. Thanks be. But another one stares me in the face if we are to go to England in January. Can I do another this year?*

A closed door into his mother's study meant to Adrian as a young boy that writing was in progress, and therefore he 'must not disturb unless absolutely necessary'. However on the completion of a book the study door would fly open and with great joy his mother would press into his and Jean's hand a newly minted half-crown.

Ethel started to write the *Apple of Happiness* and wrote with great fervour until chapter XIX after which there are many weeks of blanks in the diaries. Quite possibly time was her enemy, and preparations for the overseas trip demanded too much of her to be able to complete it before departure. In this story the Gillespie family are tempted away from their simple country life to try one of sophistication in the town. However after a time they all realise that their happiness is back at their modest apple orchard where they had very few luxuries but a wealth of joy and freedom.

Without consciously meaning to, this, and many of her other books do have a moral, and the predominant theme running through them all is that the poorer middle classes are basically very much happier than their rich relations.

She took elocution lessons from Miss Dumolo — Jean's teacher — to see if a few lessons would take away her nervousness of speaking at meetings. Of course the Children's Page still had to be prepared each week and so she made arrangements for Lil to do it for the coming year. In November she received her first copies of the *Ethel Turner Birthday Book*, one in pale green padded morocco, the other in white calf. It had a photo of her in the front and a flattering foreword by Coulson Kernahan.

On 19 June 1917 Herbert Raine Curlewis was appointed a Judge of the Industrial Arbitration Court. He was later made a Judge of the District Court.

Jean's wedding day, 23 October, 1923. The bridesmaids were Miss Ailsa Cullen, Miss Amy Hungerford, Miss Hylda Holdship and Miss Lucille Stewart. Ethel commented 'My darling girl made the sweetest of brides'.

The Law School rowing champions of 1921 from left: cox: J. F. Mant, stroke: A. H. Curlewis, H. T. E. Holt,
A. F. Mansfield, R. Burns, F. Berne, H. A. Hunter, L. F. Herron, bow: D. B. Hunter, standing at rear the coach: R. Maclean.

The second clubhouse at Palm Beach was in Horden Park.

Adrian riding his surfboard in an unconventional manner at Palm Beach, Christmas 1925.

Adrian and Betty engaged.

Adrian was admitted to the Bar in 1927 and later became His Honour Judge Sir Adrian Curlewis C.V.O., C.B.E.

1910

Ports and Happy Havens

The family sailed from Sydney in the *Orvieto* in January calling at Colombo and Aden, and disembarking at Naples. A tiny black note-book crowded with memories, later served as a guide for recounting her impressions and adventures as they unfolded. E.T. wrote a series of weekly articles for the *Daily Telegraph* after her return and in 1911 these were compiled into book form and called *Ports and Happy Havens*. So many travel books have been written, with descriptions by countless people, that it would be untimely just now to take you on yet another guided tour. Suffice it to say that the wonder of it all coming to life, after so many years of acquaintance through books, was like a miracle to Ethel. Though I will not attempt a comprehensive coverage of the trip, a few quotations from the book and some entries in the diaries will give you an idea of the countries they visited and also the delightful humour that she found in everyday and commonplace situations.
In Port Said:

A promising young Arab spied children in our party, and instantly clattered down the main street to us, riding one donkey and leading another.

'Hello Winston Churchill', he said to us by way of greeting. 'Hello Washington! Hello Mr Roosevelt!' Then he dismounted, and, his stock of English being entirely exhausted, conveyed the fact to us, mainly by signs, that the donkeys, having been expressly made for the children to ride, at the absolutely ruinous reduction of fifty paras a piece (a para is about equal to a farthing) no time should be lost in closing with the bargain.

The young Australians at once closed with it.

In Naples she notes:

I have seen reckless driving, plenty of it, but never anything to approach the absolute abandonment of it to these Neopolitans — a Naples coachman would have no appetite for his evening polenta and chianti unless he had thirteen times at least during the day forced his clients to the conclusion that they were about to be hurled into eternity, and thirteen times a day made them realise that he had saved their lives by the flick of an eyelash.

Who could not be affected by this description of the ruins of Pompeii in her book *Ports and Happy Havens*.

Imagine one's own city laughing in the sunshine today, full of eager plans for years and years ahead — imagine there bursting out, in the middle of a summer day, from a peacefully sleeping mountain at her side, a great column of black, black smoke.

It is true, Pompeii knew that the giant Vesuvius brooding over it was not dead, but sleeping. Sixteen years before had not that giant moved its great knees and stretched out its cramped arms a little, and down had gone all the city's proud buildings just as down topple the card-houses raised by a child.

But she built them up again, Pompeii, just as trustfully as does your child — she built them up more lovingly than ever.

And then one day — looking up and seeing that frightful column of inky smoke rising to the sky. Imagine that smoke descending, not as descends the harmless smoke we know, but as a ceaseless shower of thick, fine ashes. Imagine that city wading in it, with terrified eyes — ankle deep at first, then waist-deep, shoulder-deep, lost to sight — one's own city with the laugh still on her lips, the love-light in her eyes, drowned on the dry shores of her own waters, all in a summer day.

In Rome:
Morning we all went to the Coliseum. Got a guide who told us all the cheerful details tourists evidently expect about the precise spots where the Christian martyrs were eaten, and where they languished in their dens waiting to be eaten, and where the lovely ladies sat waiting to see them be eaten. The effect of the mammoth place reared up against the sky — empty — useless and the gay life of Rome, ebbing and flowing almost to its door yet, is impressive.

Then to Florence where she describes the Ponte Vecchio across the River Arno as a quaint and artistic spot with its houses *'clinging to the bridge-walls like periwinkles'.* And during a train trip she says *'Adrian busy collecting tunnels — 49 between Florence and Venice'.*

She was initially very disappointed with her first impression of Venice — but gradually she awakened to its charm, beauty and uniqueness. I shall quote several verses from her poem 'Interlude' which convey this transformation of her feeling.

Coming to the City

Dead painters, why did all your brushes lie?
Dead poets — ah, the false and cruel throats!
For I had towered my Venice to the sky,
Yea, raised her all of tints and trilling notes.
And see, my world lies round me in grey heaps.

Then Venice stared at me, a cold spring morn
Venice as grey as grief — Death's not as grey.
A great grey swan by sullen seas upborne.
I could not look but turned my eyes away,
My eyes wide-gazing for that gold and gleam.

Leaving Her

Venice, thou holdest firm thy grasp of me,
Venice, that is my heart there in thy clutch,
*   I am in thrall to thee,*
*   Wedded, as is this sea,*
And all a-tremble at thy magic touch.

And now no more with garish hues I play,
Where'er I shut my eyes and dream my dream,
I dream my Venice grey,
Grey on a cold spring day,
And just beneath the wide, grey folds, the gleam.

Next on to Milan where she says, in *Port and Happy Havens:*

Here it is at last, my dream Cathedral.

Here it rises, soft as an exhalation. That marble — that white mountain in front of us! It is a thing of mist, unsubstantial as mist, exquisite as mist that the sunlight is fretting into lovely shapes and wraiths.

The great noble body of it rising superbly, serenely to the sky; and then all over it, as if to conceal — and to reveal — the massive strength, a veil of lacy loveliness, an exquisite fretwork of lovely statues and carvings. There are thousands of these statues — in actual figures, six thousand of them — hiding in niches, clustering round pinnacles, clinging round doorways, holding pillars aloft, crouching round basements, leaning out from gutterings, flying straight heavenward with the spires.

With the spires! The forest of spires! Spires that make you think of prayers crystallized into tangible form in their passage upward. Spires, pierced through and through to catch the sun and the sky, and the glory at every point.

15th March:

Milan to Lucerne: To train at 12.30 pm. Best journey we have had yet — a cosy, comfortable clean *(first time) carriage to ourselves. Outside the most glorious scenery — the country green and with primroses in patches everywhere. The Alps right up against the windows, so to speak — slopes of glittering snow, valleys with green farms and toy villages, chalets perched on hillsides, toy carved animals (I know they weren't real) dotted here and there. I am sure the men and women and trees had bits of wood glued under their feet and had just come out of toy boxes and been stood about to make things just as they should be for the tourist.*

While still in Switzerland, Ethel makes further observations recorded in *Ports and Happy Havens:*

Pine trees that rise up the peaks and fall down into the gullies, stretching white feathery uplifted skirts around them. Sometimes so heavy is the snow burden that they cannot lift these skirts at all, but trail them to earth like birds with broken wings.

Here and there the woodcutters' little houses, struggling to keep their necks above the drifts, just a high door and a chimney, and a line of smoke visible, all else buried until the summer. They look like so many little white rabbits with just an eye and an ear and a warm breath apiece peeping from their hiding-places.

In the same book she gives a whimsical and exuberant account of their first attempts at skiing under the heading 'A Recipe for Growing Young'.

You start the day at — well at your own age, which is no longer a figure you care to write down in black and white. And they strap preposterous lengths of wood beneath your feet, and give you a stick with an iron spike at the end, and you go gingerly forth into a white freezingly cold world; your stick flies up in the air, and down you go headlong into the thick powdery snow. In most other cases of distress you have found your husband rushing with concern to your side and helping you through. But when you turn aggrieved eyes to discover why he renders you no aid, you find he is also on his back waving one leg frantically in the air, according to his interpretation of the guide's instruction.

Ethel travels on through picturesque scenery and awe-inspiring cities in Germany to the waters of the Rhine:

Our steam-boat, the Parsifal, *makes very pleasant travelling. For lunch, there is a comfortable saloon meal, for afternoon tea (I should say afternoon coffee, for once only do we have a cup of tea in Germany, and the one occasion quite suffices), the stewards bring tables on deck and we partake of castles, cakes, confectionery and coffee at one and the same time.*

Ethel was impressed by the cleanliness and neatness of Holland:

It is my private belief that there is a committee of lynx-eyed Dutch vrows who spend their lives travelling up and down to report at headquarters 'How Holland Looks from the Train'. It is my belief that when these ladies see anything in the landscape to offend their searchlight vision — anything like a dustbin or an untidy backyard or a broken fence — they immediately haul away the house-holder and administer such a punishment that the offence is never repeated.

Then on to Brussels with a pilgrimage to the battlefield of Waterloo:

Is it conceivable that once a June sun rose over it, and saw it covered with angry seas of armies, that dashed in terrific waves against each other, and recoiled and gathered together and dashed again, until all the fair green was hidden with frightful human wreckage?

Is it conceivable that once a June wind passed over these same quiet fields and was forced to bear on its trembling wings such a clash of arms, such a roar of cannon, such a hideous neighing, such an anguish of dying shrieks and groans, as the very hosts of hell itself at conflict could not have outpassed?

Is it conceivable that there, on that rising ground, and there, near that little château sleeping in this grove of trees, there paced and strode and sat and rode and reined up and had his heartstrings loosened and tightened a thousand times in the day, the most memorable man the world has ever known, at the most memorable moment of his life?

Finally the family arrived at their long-awaited destination — England!

8th April:

Reached white-cliffed Dover about 2.30 pm. Found a big boarding house on the seafront and put Adrian to bed as his temperature was up.

9th April:

Called Dr in as Boy had a rash and he pronounced it — Measles! Fortunately not a bad case but no joke when travelling, for delay and the difficulties of boarding house illness. No use kicking against it though, so we were making the best of things.

So the sojourn in Dover, instead of lasting one day, lasted 5 weeks, as a fortnight later Jean had the same complaint, and both children suffered secondary infections. This necessitated brief visits to London individually by Herbert or Ethel to fulfill previously arranged engagements. One such function was a most gala occasion for Ethel at the Whitefriars Banquet:

The room very brilliant with all the bright dresses, and rows of glittering tables. A printed plan for everyone with each guest's name printed at his or her place so that it was easy to find who was who — Sir Gilbert Parker presided. At the end of the evening, news — not quite certain, was brought to the Banquet that the King had died.

9th May:

Nothing spoken but the King's death — all England is transfixed by the thunderbolt. Fortunately for Jean, who was able to be up at the window, the Proclamation Ceremony for George V was just under these windows. A big platform was erected with a flag staff. Then troops came along from Dover Castle, and marines and blue jackets and formed a square. And the hail and rain came down like fury. 'Hail King George, Reign King George!' said Jean, which was not bad for her age. The Mayor and Councillors, in robes of state, The Town Crier, Town Clerk and other dignitaries walked up on the platform, the proclamation was read, and Dover Castle blinked down on it all with its furrowed grey face and its narrow grey eyes, just as it had blinked on all the other scenes in its history.

10th May:

London. Packed swiftly, paid my dues and shook the dust of Dover off our feet. Express took us to Charing Cross and then taxi to Bayswater. Such a black, black London that had looked so gay a week ago. Positively every woman but myself is in the inkiest garb — I must buy some black things or be arrested for high treason. Went for a walk in Kensington Gardens than which in their earliest spring green I can imagine nothing more lovely. The grass slopes, the lovely distances and haze among the trees, the trees themselves — oh these English trees — I shall never forget this first glimpse of Kensington Gardens.

12th May:

H. to his tailor. I to rush about and try to buy some mourning — they say it is quite phenomenal — abnormal — anything, this wild rush of the entire nation to buy black. It is highly unpleasant I can vouch for that. No one will promise anything for a fortnight, prices of black have gone up and to get near a counter at all costs strategy. And just after I had already wasted several days buying coloured clothes.

20th May:

King's Funeral. Up at 5.30 am and away before 7 am. Hundreds and hundreds of thousands — no millions and millions to see it. I hardly slept last night fearing the dangers for the chicks, but thanks to Sir George Reid our place was so good there was no crowding or danger at all. We went to it along Bird Cage Walk which was not overcrowded. Had to wait 2 or 3 hours of course — everyone had, but we got a seat. Later stood on them and saw magnificently — no one in London better I'm sure. Saw the gun carriage with the King's body; King George V, Emperor William of Germany, Duke of Connaught, Kings of Spain, Norway, Greece, Denmark, Portugal, etc. — nine Kings in all. Princes and many other potentates. Lord Roberts, Kitchener — eight state carriages, red with splendidly trapped horses, and magnificent coachmen. Queen Alexandra we saw very plainly, her veil very thin, heavy one thrown back. Very white, very sweet — altogether the Queen of the photographs we have always known. The immense crowd absolutely silent — the stillest crowd I suppose the world had ever seen. In next carriage Queen Mary, Princess Mary, etc, Riderless horse, little dog. The still crowd and then the roll of the funeral music sent a wave of emotion it was impossible to avoid being swept along with. Many throats swelled I am sure. Back in great comfort and ease by 11.30 am. At night we heard there were a thousand casualties.

27th May:

An invitation from Sir George Reid to meet Mr and Mrs Roosevelt. Also a very cordial letter from Lady Tennyson who said she had seen a paragraph in The Times, *saying we were in London, and asking us to go down to Aldworth Saturday, Sunday and return Monday. There is nothing in the wide world I should like better.*

28th May:

H. is not coming with me — he wants Jean to come instead. Arrived at Haselmere, there was Lady Tennyson herself come to meet us, driving a pair of black ponies, one of which she had brought from Australia. She drove us through a dear old village, then country roads, then the loveliest of English lanes, right into Sussex. On the moor below the garden, there had come to meet us, with the two dogs, Lord Tennyson — the 'Hallam' of recollections. It is the sweetest house in the world — no one but a poet could possibly have conceived it. Then to our rooms with great old-fashioned beds and oak tables — a maid unpacked and laid out our evening clothes and wanted to help us dress — but what should I do with a maid. Dinner with three footmen behind us and a round table with silver candles, and shaded lights and old silver and many courses, but it was all very pleasant and not a bit stiff, there were so many things we were mutually interested in — travels and books we had all read and so on. Lord Tennyson drew Jean out and she chatted away back to him in a way he seemed to like very much. He told me afterwards she had quite a wonderful knowledge of books. Coffee in the drawing room and more talk — then to bed — but not to sleep — hardly shut my eyes till 3 am.

29th May:

Lord Tennyson took me to his study and showed me various things he keeps there — the pall worked by the North Country women with the last verse of 'Crossing the Bar' on it. The laurel wreath presented by Queen Victoria — books, etc. It was his father's study too. Then Lady Tennyson showed me her bedroom — her bed is the one the poet died in and her room the same. She told me how on the night he died the moon was so bright they had no other light and it came through the great window flooding the bed. She sat on the edge holding his hand till he died.

Then we went to church driving in a landau — Lady Tennyson, Jean, I and four of the servants. Church is an old, old Norman church. With a typical English rector and a typical English verger to take up the freepenny bits. In afternoon a scramble up and down gully and moor — Lord and Lady T, J and I. After dinner Lord T. read aloud at my request, 'The Revenge', 'Passing of Arthur' and a lyric or two. Lady T says he reads just as his father did. Then Jean to bed, Lord T. to his study and Lady T. and I for a long talk — she told me all about her boys and family — all sorts of confidences, talked for hours together and made me tell her all about home and the chicks, etc.

30th May:

Lord T. got up and saw us off after breakfast. Gave Jean an inscribed copy of the Ballads *and he's going to send me his* Life of his father. *A long drive through 'Tennyson's Lane', the old village and the visit was over. To Charing Cross Station and back to lunch with H. and Boy. Just time to dress and get off again. At 4 pm to the reception at the Ritz given by Sir George Reid to Mr and Mrs Roosevelt. Sir George introduced me as 'Our most famous Australian authoress, Ethel Turner' and Mr Roosevelt was very cordial and said he had the books.*

9th June:

To Whiteleys in afternoon to look over a Model £200 furn. house that Jean had fallen in love with and made me come to see. Quite a delightful place with its oak panelled walls and square hall with pewter and blue china and its latticed windows. Jean's account of it and pleasure in it gave me a notion for a short story — a woman — saleswoman, middle-aged, unmarried, has been entrusted by head of firm with the arrangement of the little house. She throws herself into the task with pathetic ardour, all the details, books on table, flowers, red geraniums in kitchen window — it is all like a poem to her.

Weather very very sultry and thunderous — earthquakes below Naples yesterday. The wearing o' the black is a burden that is to be lightened however on 17th when we are to be graciously allowed a touch of white and violet.

12th June:

When we got back yesterday a lot of letters — Australian mail in. Especially interesting one from Lil — Yanalla is sold, dear little mountain cottage we built with such pleasure. It cost a pang or two but we are very glad, for after a trip like this we need the money. It sold for £400 and they are to have an auction of the furniture. Lil is going up to arrange things — yes, we are very glad. And sorry.

18th June:

Coming back from Grosvenor St we watched the great Women's Suffrage Procession — tens of thousands watching, and thousands in the procession — 500 of the Prisoners marching with silver arrows held aloft and bands playing and banners flying. They are certainly in earnest.

22nd June:

At night went for first time to see Louie Creed who had written to ask me several times. It is nine years since she came from Australia, fifteen since we were such pen and school friends — yet it all might have been yesterday. She has grown stout, and developed a marked accent — says it is her five years in Italy. She kept the room almost dark for hours for some occult reason, so did not see her too plainly. She has changed in many respects immensely. She spoke of Creed — asked after him, etc. Showed me her last 2 books, Theodora's Husband *and* In a White Palace. *A very curious evening altogether — and a sad — though she seems happy enough and says she is making £1,000 a year. Home very late and very tired.*

For the next two and a half months she attended numerous receptions, writers' club luncheons and dinners, and acquainted herself with her three publishers Ward Lock, Hodder and Stoughton, and Fisher Unwin. The family travelled around England for a time and the thrill of being in the literary and historic town of Stratford Upon Avon, for Ethel was a highlight. Whilst in that area she made a pilgrimage to the Attleborough Quarry House near Nuneaton.

6th July:

Took a carriage and drove through the very lovely Warwickshire country. Oh very, very lovely — the most satisfying country, if one wanted to end one's days in peace, that could be found. On by train to Nuneaton. Alighted here to go on a quest I have meant to go ever since reaching England, to find the old Attleborough Quarry House where we used to live. Took a carriage whose coachman said he knew it and drove some mile or more out. Here a doubt met us, there were three old houses, and driver thought that two had been called the Quarry House. Asked at the first, the very one Miss Evan's had photographed for me on her visit — and the one that Mother said was wrong — but they said no, the real 'Quarry House' was further. We drove on to that and I could not but go and knock at door and ask inside about it. The owners are the Brock Harrises, he a solicitor, and they were most nice and hospitable — insisted on taking us all over to see if I could recollect — the house was bigger than I remembered it — they said they had added a wing. I remembered a monkey tree and an apricot vine on a wall, and it

The sanctum beyond the Avenel dining room. Many of Ethel Turner's books were written here.

This photograph of the entrance to Avenel appeared in The Australian Home Beautiful, *2 July, 1928.*

Ethel in the drawing room at 'Avenel'

seemed, many things in the beautiful old garden. But not a tower place built at the end of the garden and in which they said George Eliot had written one of her books. Which makes me doubt a little, for a child would keep a memory of a quaint little place like that. They insist that theirs is the original 'Quarry House' — had been so called since 1760 when it was built. It is a lovely old English home with such a garden as is seldom seen — I hope that it is the right one. They are going to inquire. The other one does not seem right, though it too is a very pleasant home with a lovely garden. One of the two is the place. Mrs Brock Harris insisted on us staying for tea, and we took a photo or two, and she gave me a postcard of it to show Mother. A most interesting visit.

26th July:

Final packing and off at 9 am to Victoria for the train to Newhaven. Goodbye to London — the last glimpse of Westminster Abbey and the dear grey streets made my throat swell. It had begun to grip me very hard, this London. Then through Kent — all the buttercups and primroses gone but wheatfields and poppies in their place. Haystacks — fern waggons — the lambs turned sheep — the summer almost gone, like ourselves. Boat at Newhaven waiting, only just time to go on board. We ran straight into the wildest weather — waves mountains high, the Brighton a cork plaything. Nearly everyone on board ill — except H. and the babes whom it only exhilarated. They are horribly superior people at sea, these same Curlewises. It comes of being coarse-fibred folks, I tell them. A lady travelling in their company, of a higher organisation and spiritual temperament went under badly — leaned back with a delicate greyish green shade of countenance and though not actually ill, felt deadly from time to time. H. and the chicks had the indecency to be wildly hungry too and were the only people to go down to lunch, which they ate with avidity while the crockery flew and smashed in all directions.

But even four hours came to an end and we reached Dieppe at last. I felt exasperated to think that all the way from Australia — all the rough trip on the Zuyder Zee, and crossing from Ostend, I was superior too and then succumbed with a bit of a trip like this.

In the chapter on Paris in *Ports and Happy Havens* she describes their attempts to cross the vast square of the Place de la Concorde:

It is easier to write 'cross the square' than to do so.

Nothing will convince me that it is not the highest ambition of a French taxi-driver to run people down, or that he sleeps with any degree of happiness on the nights that he has not killed at least an old man, a child or a dog.

The moment he sees you leave the pavement and attempt to negotiate a great square, his eye lights up, and he rushes directly at you full speed, from at least five radiating streets at one and the same instant.

The policeman in London is a god; in Paris, merely a worm, and the driver no more thinks of heeding his upraised hand than of heeding the wing of a flying bird; this fact has bestowed on Paris the distinction of having the worst managed traffic in the world.

I am convinced that this much talked about shrinking population of France is solely due to these assassinations — by the taxis. The only way to be safe in Paris is to be inside one.

From Paris, they went to Lyon, then through the Valley of the Rhone to Marseilles.

There lies the ship; there, poised, waiting a little moment on the dancing waters of the Mediterranean, lies the ship that soon will be ploughing its way with us over the great ocean, back to

'The long wash of Australasian seas'

back to the land of Blue Skies that has no historied towers, no crumbling Roman remains, no ancient battlefields, and yet a greater magic than all of these, the magic of Home.

The holiday is ended, and the dream is dreamed, but, like the pilgrims when they came from Lourdes, we, too, have round our neck rosaries that have been dipped in miraculous waters, beads that we can tell over and over to ourselves and never tire.

'Aren't you going to stop and see Clem off?'
The Little Larrikin

1911-1918

Oh, Boys in Brown

1911

This year the Spit to Manly tram was opened and E.T. noted that it would be a 'great boon' for people who depended on public transport. The mountain cottage Yanalla had been sold and for the following years, the family rented various cottages when the mountain air beckoned them.

During this year Ethel was made a vice-president of the Girls Realm Guild – an organisation that she actively supported. Their aims were briefly that 'those who have received the gifts of education, refinement, and religious training are bound to pass them on.' They strived to give Service and Good Fellowship and worked strenuously under their president Lady Chelmsford.

Sir William Cullen, Chief Justice of N.S.W. was appointed Acting Governor of the state in April and a close friendship developed between the two families. They had a love of gardening, amongst other things, in common and there are numerous entries recording Sir William bringing new shrubs or giving advice about the landscaping of the new section of garden which Ethel and Herbert acquired later in the year.

9th May:

To meet Mrs Baynton who came to help me choose H's wedding present to me, a lovely diamond ring – she is quite a gem expert and I am not. Looked at her magnificent opals, tiara and necklet – fit for some gorgeous Eastern queen. Got a really lovely ring, one large and seven small diamonds in a cluster – it is my engagement ring, H. says, because in the days of long ago he was not satisfied with the plain little ring which was all he could afford then. But I was. Still it is a lovely dazzling thing this new one and the best of all is that this day, 9th May, was the real engagement day.

Ethel acquired, at an Art show, a Lister Lister painting for five guineas and enjoyed talking to the artist about the scene – a watercolour of a long beach and a roll of wave.

In October she writes:

Land Sale. The half acre of precipice in front of our garden at Avenel was put up to auction – Clive went to bid for us and had to give £60 more than our limit for it. Still we are very glad to have it – I am greatly excited at the thought of getting and laying our half-acre of new garden. All our present piece which began with precipices and stumps, I have tamed till it is very pretty and restful and running over with flowers. The other will have to be wilder.

The lower part of this land was levelled to build a tennis court and gradually lantana and weeds were replaced by native shrubs.

During the year she gathered together some poems, limericks, children's stories and other material and formed them into a book which she called an *Ogre Up to Date*.

This limerick from the book was written for Adrian:

Two Doors

There was a young boy at North Shore
Who always left open the door,
He used to say, 'Hang it;
The wind will soon bang it.
To shut it with hands is a bore.'

Now this very same boy at North Shore
Had two pigeons on which he set store,
When he came home one day,
They had both flown away —
Wide open was flung the cage door.

Then 'alack' and 'heyday', he wept sore,
'Oh, mother, just look at that door!'
She simply said, 'Hang it;
The wind will soon bang it,
To shut it with hands is a bore.'

She records that she received suede-covered editions of her two miniature books of poems — they were called *A Tiny House* and *Fifteen and Fair*.

1912

This diary entry on 18th April obviously affected Ethel very deeply.

Most harrowing accounts of this frightful wreck of the Titanic *— they seem so realistic one suffers as if one were undergoing the horrors of it personally.*

And then five days later:

Started a new book and think its name will be Secret of the Sea *— the germ of the idea being one of the* Titanic *cablegrams '7 infants have lost their parents and no means exist by which to identify them'. Wrote part of a chapter. To town in afternoon at 12 — David Jones asked me to allow them to use my name to advertise something! Just as John Strange Winter did! I told him not for £10,000 a year.*

The story of *Secret of the Sea* focuses on four of the babies — two sets of twins. They all enjoy great companionship and a happy childhood with Lord and Lady Brenchley, until finally David, as a teenager, goes on a quest to discover his true identity.

1913

It may be interesting for some readers to learn that until the early 1900s it was illegal to swim between sunrise and sunset in any area exposed to the public view. Costume regulations until after 1934 required that 'all persons over the age of four years must be clad in a bathing costume covering the body from the neck to the knee'. Even in public baths mixed bathing was prohibited.

13th January:
Adrian and I went down to Manly for a swim in the men's bath, which are kept for women until 1 pm. I have much more breath now and can do about 150 yards quite comfortably. Adrian did all manner of tricks off the toboggan and dived off first tier of diving tower.

Later the same month Adrian started at Sydney Church of England School, later to be known as Shore.

During the year Rosie had her third child, a son Grahame*, brother to Robert and Marcia and Theo.

(An interesting letter, written by Sarah Jane to Rose about her father Henry Turner, is included in Appendix V. It is a revealing insight into the life of the Turner family in England.)

Ethel and Herbert purchased a block of land from the Doaks at Leura which was on the road to Sublime Point, however they had no immediate plans for building and they continued to rent cottages for the school holidays for a number of years.

Playing tennis she tore a ligament in her leg and after several days of being immobilized she records:

Came down for dinner — H. carried me down. Lay on sofa and we had the French conversation as usual with Mademoiselle Amourin. Finished chapter 26 of Flower O' the Pine. *And Last! Last! Last! The book has given me less care than any yet — I have been so fond of Flower I don't like to lose her —*

The child Flower was based on her neice Marcia whom she often had to stay. Flower becomes a real and lovable personality in the book and it is easy to understand how her creator could become attached to the child. The setting of the book was Manly where Ethel was staying for several weeks during midsummer, and the book communicates her delight in the comparatively new sensation of surfing.

This is the dedication in the book *Flower O'the Pine.*

> *Dear Lord and Lady Tennyson — you gave me many flowers of England*
> *— the white flowers of sleeping under his roof — the fragrant flowers of your*
> *own friendship — the blue flowers of your woods — I have few keener*
> *memories of England than the first moment when we came on those magic*
> *carpets of bluebells in your woods.*
>
> *Will you take in return this rough little Flower of the Australia that you,*
> *too, know and love so well?*   *Sincerely*
>   *'Ethel Curlewis'.*
>   *E.T.*

---

*Grahame: Later became a famous airman and in World War II was awarded the D.F.C. and Bar – he was lost when his plane was shot down over Borneo in 1945.

1914

Ethel, from her earliest days as an authoress battled with her publishers for the best terms possible. In 1909 she had deserted Ward Lock as the royalties that they offered were, she thought, unsatisfactory, and so she sent her next five books to Hodder and Stoughton. Mr Steele, her discoverer, friend and promoter over many years, was greatly disappointed and on numerous occasions corresponded with her trying to entice her back to Wark Lock. On one occasion in 1913 she replied:

When you bring not only one author out in that series but half a dozen until they all look as much alike as tins of jam, well frankly the prospect is not sufficiently alluring. So I will continue another year with my new publishers. I hate, as you know, writing these letters and not doing as you ask, but you will understand that I must be a good businesswoman just as you are a good businessman.

13th January:
Adrian's birthday — 13, dear lad. His father gave him a very good flute and I money as oh alas! nearly all his wants are supplied — camera, electricity*, bike, etc. etc.

8th May:
To Government House Garden Party with H. Most noteworthy thing was seeing the first hydro-aeroplane in Australia, Guillaux on board, flying over Rose Bay — a glorious sight. Talked to various and different people — Judge Docker, who told me about his trip, Judge and Mrs Ferguson, Sir William Cullen, Mrs Raine, etc. etc.

19th May:
To town in afternoon, Women's Club, to listen to papers on Dorothea Mackellar and F. Bedford — a solemn and ridiculous waste of time that it is amazing such scores of women sit through every Tuesday afternoon — why can't people read the books — hardly any had done that it seems — and have done with it. But to take your literature in public, in silly little doses at Women's Clubs — heaven preserve me from such a repetition!
 Still frightfully restless. Unable to concentrate or do anything.

As E.T. gradually tamed the wilderness of the lower garden, she developed an area that was always a favourite spot with her — it was rather like a lookout and one could stand and survey the wild and native shrubs that grew in abundance down in the valley. In the middle of this area she erected a sundial which I believe is still there to-day. On 23rd May she writes:

My sundial pedestal arrived and two masons to put it into place. We copied Sir Walter Scott's, only changed the motto from 'For the Night Cometh' (which isn't a cheerful reminder in a sunny garden) to 'Come what may, Time and the hour runs through the roughest day' — Jean's choice.

---

*Adrian had set up on the back verandah a series of battery-operated electric bells and lights, as well as a train system.

Wedding photograph of Adrian and Betty Carr who were married on 12 December 1928.

Garth, a cottage at Leura in the Blue Mountains, built at the end of 1928 in order to have a home to go to whilst visiting Jean in hospital.

Avenel, taken in 1928.

Ethel Turner looking out her study window.

A photo taken with my grandmother in the drawing room at Avenel. This appeared, together with an interview, in the Woman *newspaper in 1934.*
By kind permission of *The Sun* newspaper.

Two months later War was formally declared. A week afterwards she and Lady Cullen set to work to organize ambulance and first aid classes. They also arranged for groups of women to do sewing for the hospital — pyjamas, hospital requirements and bandages.

She felt the situation so keenly that she started a series of articles which appeared in the *Sydney Morning Herald* called 'Wartime and Women' — these were aimed at being a guide for women in the part they could play to help the war effort, and in it she included a plea to many Australian families to adopt a Belgian war orphan.

12th September:
A frightful shock in afternoon. Someone — an officer from the Barracks, rang up to say Capt Brian Pockley (who went with the Army Medical Corps), has been killed in action at Samoa and would H. go and break it to Dr Pockley before it got into Evening News. And Ellie with heart disease! Someone from E. News however had rung up to warn him, so there was no need.

The finest, bravest lad I knew — it is heart-breaking.

21st September:
Started The Cub *again with new ideas and did half a chapter!*

14th October:
My article, 'War Orphans' in Herald *in a very good place, just after the leaders, so it may attract attention and offer some more homes. We are beginning here to look at dolls and books still about and say they will do for* our *orphan when it arrives. Papers say Louie Mack was in Antwerp at bombardment.*

The Cub was completed in a record time of five weeks and the above entries all come to life in the book — including the groups of women who met in Mrs Calthrop's sitting room to play an active and worthwhile part, just as they were doing at the same time at Avenel.

1915

12th February:
In afternoon to the Fete for the Belgian War Orphans given at the Girls' Grammar School. I had to open it and make a speech. Making speeches makes me sick with fright, I turned base coward and read it. Jean helped at Fancy Stall and has worked hard for it.

6th May:
Typed an article, 'Follow the King'. Wrote letters, etc. Among wounded at Dardenelles Lieut. Curlewis (George), Western Australia. Marie very anxious about her brother Jack, also at Dardenelles, some of his officers killed. Colonel McLauren, a friend of H's has fallen.

8th May:
Tried to write a short story, 'His Wonders to Perform' but couldn't. Lusitania *sunk.*
1500 souls lost. The horrors deepen.

Many of her close friends were farewelling sons to go to the front and a number of
Jean's contemporaries were taking their last leave. This prompted Ethel to write
such poems as 'Bayonets' and 'Boys in Brown'. A verse from the latter follows.

> *'Oh, boys in brown,' we cried to you, 'go save the world for us,' we cried.*
> *' 'Tis youth, 'tis youth, must save us all; the old must wistful stand aside.'*
> *There came the sound of your hurrying feet,*
> *Your eager tramplings in the street;*
> *The roll of a drum, the flag going by,*
> *A transport's smoke dying down the sky.*
> *That was the way of your swift consent.*
> *You cheered, and you waved, and you laughed — and went.*
>   *Oh, boys in brown, light brown.*

There are numerous entries at this stage that show how depressed, unsettled and
dispirited she was — trying to write and having to abandon many attempts, until
finally she writes:

Spent day lying in the sun trying to think out — and succeeding — new book, a story of
a small boy. And to be a jolly one!! At night did a few pages of it — call it A Man's
House *at present.*

This title was eventually changed to *John of Daunt*.

17th June:
In afternoon to Miss Badham's breaking up. Lady Cullen presented the prizes. Jean did
excellently — Dux of the School Prize, Italian, General Knowledge, Essay — four.
Adrian's football team, he is captain, won match and he had his trophy presented.

During this year F. Beaumont Smith produced a play called *Seven Little Australians*
which successfully toured New Zealand. It was not an accurate presentation at all
and in fact combined *7 L As* with *Miss Bobbie* and numerous unrelated incidents,
resulting in a literary 'hash'. The child actress Cecil Haines who played 'Suds' was
highly applauded by newspaper critics and in July the company presented the play
at the Palace Theatre in Sydney.

25th August:
Wrote free, fast and furiously the entire day. And finished my book John of Daunt *at*
chapter 22!!

A noticeable attribute in most of her books is that she introduces her characters
sparingly at first and then lets you become intimately acquainted before presenting
the next players. In this way the personalities remain clearly defined and one is not
overburdened with too many names to digest.

In *John of Daunt* she returns to the subject matter that she excels at — the pranks and thoughts and ways of childhood. Ian is a lovable lad who is full of mischief and the telling of his exploits is masterful. There was obviously a feeling of uneasiness for German citizens residing in Australia at the outbreak of war and the references in the book to the cook Gertrud are taken directly from the diaries.

My dear little German cook Marie is very unhappy — she says she will go back to her Fatherland (her father was in the Franco Prussian War and she says they know what War can be in Germany) — I have plenty to do to preserve the balance of power in the kitchen just now.

With all these tragedies and problems she became fired with the desire to do something dramatic towards the war effort. She had read that twenty thousand pounds a day was the amount spent on drink in N.S.W. alone. This money, to her, seemed a criminal waste when it was needed urgently for arms and equipment. She took up a cause for 'Total Abstinence during the War' and wrote a powerful article called 'Twenty Thousand a Day' which she forwarded to the *Herald*. A reply came immediately from the *Herald* saying they dare not and would not touch it because of its impracticability and in loyalty to the whiskey advertisers. She then sent it off to the *Telegraph* with similar results, but eventually she writes:

25th September:
Both S.M. Herald *and* Telegraph *published my 'Alcohol and the War' letter — both on main page and with headlines — the subject is growing too serious for them any longer to refuse it a place.*

9th October:
Full of eager zeal for an article on Hotel Closing — 'The Gallant Risk'. Worked at it the entire day and typed three copies — sort of appeal to the Government to do the right thing in wartime and close the hotels.

12th October:
Article 'Gallant Risk', not in papers. I went to town to see if they were too strong and might be a little mitigated. Saw Mr Brahan, new editor of the Daily Telegraph *for first time. He says he will publish it when Cabinet has decided. Then on to* Herald, *Mr Heney would publish it but not if I let* Telegraph *have it too.*

15th October:
'Gallant Risk' published in Daily Telegraph *on the leader page. Now it may do some good.*

As a result of the publishing of the letter, she received many herself from ministers of religion and others supporting her, to temperance and crank letters — she records:

... it's enough to make a woman take to drink herself.

She continued to write many articles, most of them with a wartime theme and this entry on 29th November added a touch of humour:

Night to a dinner given by Institute of Journalists, of which I am a brand new member, to the Prime Minister Hughes. Mr Heney as president welcomed me very nicely and did me the honour to escort me to a high place and put the Vice-president McMillan beside me, before he seated the chief guests, Hughes and Carmichael. Mr Fitzgerald whom I had thrust at in the article on Saturday was magnanimous and came up bringing people to introduce — Hughes himself who was very nice and others. At dinner Mr Brahan of the Telegraph *and Mr Fitzgerald both lifted their glasses to me and signalled 'Water', which I was greatly pleased with and drank back in lemonade. Introduced also to Mr Adam McKay whose work on the* Sun *I like so well. Enjoyed myself immensely.*

1916

9th March:
To lunch at Civil Service with Mr Bertram Stevens to talk over the proposed Gift Book *for Funds of Voluntary workers — they asked Mr Bertram Stevens and myself to edit it*.*

During this year she completed, *Captain Cub*, which is the continuing story of John Calthrop on active service at Gallipoli and tells of the Lindsay family's move to Yanco in the Irrigation Area.

She wrote numerous short stories for newspapers and magazines and each week sent off her Children's Page competitions, etc.

Having done what she could in the Abstinence cause, Ethel now felt moved to work towards conscription and with this in mind, sent an article 'The Other Woman's Son' to the *Herald* — she was pleased when it was given position of honour on the leader page.

1917

Still possessed by the waste and needlessness of excessive drinking she started a new book.

Wrote all morning at my new book — my story that is to make at least an effort to help kill drink. Am going at it heart and soul — St Tom and the Dragon *or* Letters of Flame *or some such title*

---

*This book was published later in the year and contained an interesting selection of poems, short stories and paintings by well-known personalities. The Voluntary Workers were a group of men dedicated to the task of building cottages for disabled servicemen, and war widows and their families.

This is a true satire and obviously written with great conviction and pathos. The devastating effect of excessive alcohol is seen in a frightening way when Mr Goodwin's personality completely alters under the influence of drink. Ethel captures and dwells on the inequality of the upper and working classes when she describes the differences between upper and lower Rockton. There is an interlude at the Rockton boys' school when Tom and the Barkley boy are challenging for first place in the Diving Championships. This was, in fact, prompted by an actual event that happened to Adrian at his own school sports. The two finalists in the diving championships, Adrian and Harold Lewarne had thus far an equal score and in order to determine the winner, the two boys were asked to do one final fancy dive. Harold did his first and then it was Adrian's turn. He climbed to the first stage, then the second and recklessly on to the top stage of the tower where he had never ventured before. He looked down to the water below with a sinking heart and would have given the world to retrace his steps and climb down again, however with the whole school watching this was out of the question. With a supreme effort, the shaking was controlled and the dive performed amidst cheers and clapping.

25th April:
Anzac Day. To Town Hall with Jean to help with the War Widows' Entertainment — tea, flowers and speeches. Tragic sight — about four hundred of the black-robed figures. A Mrs Lysaght, after Dr Arthur's speech, offered a hundred pounds and a block of land for a Widow's Cottage.

19th June:
At night came the great news that has been throbbing in the air of uncertainty for last day or two — H. has been appointed to a Judgeship in Judge Pickburn's place. After hours of suspense the telephone went and Nina came with a puzzled face — Mr Curlewis to speak to you and he says I am to say the Judge wants to speak to you. I was planting a row of artichokes in the garden.

27th July:
To Police Court — Central — in the interests of St Tom and Dragon. Dr A. had arranged with missionary (Creagh) to take me. A really severe experience — shall never forget it.

11th August:
Adrian volunteered — without his father's permission, as a locomotive cleaner; a number of school boys took strikers' places at Eveleigh. He had a long, long day; up at 4.30 am walked to boat, walked from Quay, worked all day, walked back, from Lavender Bay. To a dance at Dr Retallack's at night — and walked home! H. will not let him go again — must remain neutral.

1918

3rd April:

Light Horse Ball; to town all day. Dressed and off to ball at 6.45 pm. Adrian came too — his first appearance. Jean looked delightful — frock very pretty and simple — pale yellow and a gold chaplet of flowers in her hair — never saw her look better. Could have filled her programme several times. I did not dance — couldn't with war news what it is — talked to Judge and Mrs Ferguson, the Rolins, Vero Read and wife, etc. etc.

7th June:

Went to Italian Red Cross Fete at the High School to please Mrs Garvin. Home about 11 pm. Adrian came home with the heart-breaking news that Stickie Forbes has been killed.

19th July:

In the evening news came of the best advance yet — the Americans at the Marne — and for practically the first time whistles were blown and flags flown. We have got out of the way of expecting good news.

Gradually war news started improving and spirits revived — writing became easier and one night she was so inspired she had an all-night sitting at *Brigid and the Cub*, eventually going to bed at 6 am. Her long-standing friend Mr William Steele (Ward Lock in Australia) died during the year.

8th November:

1st Peace: To town — the wildest scene, entire town turned out — night proved news not authenticated but still the celebrations continued.

13th November:

Peace Day, real verification — armistice is signed. The shock of delight is over with the false alarm — but still. Wrote chapter 24 — had to — it must leave next week so there is not time to celebrate. It is going to be money towards War Chest and Children's (Fallen Soldiers) Xmas Committee — we've got to remember they are not feeling too full of rejoicing whatever we are.

16th November:

Finished Book: finished ch. 27. At last the book has three parts, killed me since chapter 18 — up to there did not feel it. Last two months have been like a nightmare with it.

After many years of discomfort and numerous 'attacks' the doctors decided to operate on Herbert for gallstones.

At the close of the year, though the war was over, there came yet another trial with the outbreak of a very severe epidemic of influenza.

1919-1929
Catching Sunbeams

1919

The first case of Spanish 'flu in Sydney was confirmed on 28th January and people were advised to be inoculated against it — then shortly afterwards there was an edict to say all must wear masks. Newspapers reported daily on the number of new cases and the number of deaths. People became fearful of leaving the safety of their own homes. In April came an urgent plea for volunteer workers to relieve the nurses in the hospitals who were dropping from exhaustion. Jean volunteered immediately and was sent to the Walker Hospital on Parramatta River. The tremendous tension, fear and anxiety of the next five months' entries are dramatic reading in the diaries. Ethel offered her own services for nursing but was rejected owing to her deafness. There was nothing left but to work ceaselessly in order to keep up her own morale, but she found she was writing her next book *Laughing Water* with a very heavy heart. Many balls, receptions and official functions were cancelled during this period. As one would expect one of the main characters in the book *Laughing Water* was taken ill with influenza. The isolation, disinfection, notification of the authorities, and other precautions taken, give an interesting flashback of those worrying days. By May the epidemic was over and life in Sydney returned to normal once more. However the toll taken on Jean's health was very severe as she was run down and depressed from the tiring months of VAD work. Years later it was thought that her illness could have had its beginnings at this time.

In June E.T. received a letter to say that the *Town and Country Journal* was giving up publication. So her Children's Page was at an end and Dame Durden (Ethel's pseudonym in this paper) was to retire after 27 years! As the profits for the past two years had been handed over to Lil for her boys, Ethel now racked her brain to think of something that would be a substitute for it.

She had always hoped that one day children would have a special paper of their own and with this in mind she sent this letter to the Sydney Sun.

18th July

Gentlemen,

Just before the war I had been planning to bring out an Australian penny weekly for young people, for which I had thought a circulation of 50,000 copies or even more could be attained, with the ideas I had for it, which included a somewhat unique idea by which the advertisement part might be made unusually successful and a plan by which it might be circulated in all the state schools in N.S.W.

I think in time it could be made a very valuable property and be as distinct a paper as *St Nicholas* is in America and *The Scout* in England.

Young people want specialising for in their sports, their school matters and their leisure, and are omniverous readers — and very faithful ones — of matter that really has an appeal and interest for them.

I planned the paper for three reasons —

1. I think the rising generation here has need of higher and broader ideals; perhaps such a paper might, without any preachiness, help to spread such.

2. Money. I do not need more than bread and butter to eat myself, but I see so much of the seamy side of life that I am ambitious for a gold mine into which I may dip.

3. It is the kind of work I can do tolerably well, and into which I could throw myself with pleasure.

Now that the war is over I again see the chances for real success for the paper, but I doubt whether I could carry the thing alone — the business part would be too much. I therefore lay the matter before your company. You have a *Daily Sun* and a *Sunday Sun* — do you feel inclined to begin *The Rising Run?* I would suggest a form similar to *The Scout,* which I send with this.

My proposition is that in such a paper I be given a certain number of shares and the editorship — the latter at all events for a year or two, when, having put it well on its feet, I might be glad to give up the very active part of it and just help with ideas for it and some contributions.

Faithfully Yours,

Ethel Curlewis

(Ethel Turner)

I may add that the expense for copy for such a paper would be comparatively small, after more than 20 years of editing a children's page in the *Town and Country Journal,* I have found that young people prefer their own and contemporaries' efforts in print to the best professional matter: several pages of these would be advisable — stories, skits, snap-shots, etc; I used to deal with a mass of manuscripts each week — competitive work for prizes — some of it very good, enough in quantity to have filled a paper, instead of a corner of one.

May I add that the matter of this letter is a confidential one.

Mr Campbell Jones, Managing Director of the *Sun,* asked her to come for an interview to talk over the proposed Children's Newspaper. He said his board of directors were sympathic to the scheme and thought it should be a paper for all Australia, not just N.S.W., however nothing could be finalised until they had investigated costs, etc.

Her social engagements and other commitments kept her occupied for the next month and no more contact, by interview or correspondence with the *Sun,* is recorded.

10th September:
Wrote most of the day and evening too. And finished Laughing Water — *28 chapters there are. I am so happy to hear the news about Adrian, who has won the Brian Pockley Memorial Prize for the year — the best and most honourable of all the S.C.E.G.S. prizes.*

1920

1920

There is not a great deal to record for this year. The location of her new book presented quite a problem — she wanted to set the scene in Central Australia and as she had never been there herself, she had to visit different libraries and read extensively about the Centre in order to acquaint herself with the surroundings and the atmosphere. She considered calling it *Desert Born* but it eventually found its title as *King Anne.* Tom (eight years older and now a doctor) from *St Tom and the Dragon* reappears with the King family in this story, and the suburb of Rockton is re-introduced (quite possibly this could be the Rocks area).

1921

1921

Early this year Jean's first book, *The Ship That Never Set Sail* was published and it was a very proud moment for E.T.

In reply to a further letter regarding the proposed Childrens Newspaper, the *Sun* once again postponed any definite decision until the industrial troubles of the time had passed.

22nd April:
Silver Wedding Day! *First verandah dance. Busy with things all day — all looked so pretty: a white moonlight mild night — pretty Japanese lanterns along the verandah and the rooms bright with flowers and shaded lights. It was a wonderful night and we had such a lot of guests. Silver wedding day and we both feel about 30!!*

At the beginning of winter Jean announced her engagement to a medical student Leo Charlton, but they couldn't make any plans for the wedding until he finished his final year exams.

A close friendship had developed during the past few years with Dorothea Mackellar and this July entry shows the warmth of affection the family felt for her.

12th July:
Dorothea Mackellar for lunch and the afternoon — a sincere pleasure. There ought to be more such spirits in the world — I had the feeling of touching fine porcelain after a course of handling pottery.

Ethel finished another book called *Jennifer J* in September this year, and on the front page it says *'Affectionately dedicated to the Girls of the Sydney High School who migrated in 1921 from the old, much complained of, historied buildings known by myself, to the shining new ones.*

Oh, les beaux jours quand nous étions si malheureuses!'

Several days later she heard that she was to be appointed editor of a Children's Page in the *Sunday Sun.*

28th September:
At first I refused — said I wasn't looking for a job at ordinary journalism, it was just the separate paper that I wanted. But in the end accepted — it will teach me a lot as I go. They offer me £350 a year for it and say it will not take me two days a week.

She sent a further letter to Mr Campbell Jones:

> Dear Sir,
> Before putting my hand actually to the plough, I should like the *Sun's* assurance that as soon as the *Rising Sun* comes into being I am to have a fair number of shares and, unless I show myself during this trial run, unfit for such, the offer of the editorship at a fair salary. While I consider £7 a week quite a good payment for the Children's Page you offer me in the *Sydney Sun,* until the other paper appears, I should not have thought of taking it but for the above idea, I have been writing for so many years that it seems — well, a little infra dig to take a children's page again; that and my husband's position.
> > Yours sincerely
> > Ethel Turner

On 4th October she went to the *Sun* office and met

Mr Tonkin, editor, Mr Souter and Mr Campbell Jones. We fixed up illustration ideas a little and decided to call the page Sunbeams *as we want to keep the* Rising Sun *idea. Am starting disappointed though — they say it would be impossible to give me shares in the new paper, so it only means £500 for new editorship with increases as the circulation goes up.*

A little over a month later she says

To town in morning. Quite a little excitement at the Sun *— they are trying to enlarge* Sunbeams *to a four-page coloured supplement by Sunday next. I shall have more room to move and there will be* Weary Willie *and other pages. I like the idea.*

So on 13th November *Sunbeams* was launched and in the first edition she wrote this editor's letter.

> From a Chair in the Sun
> Dear Boys and Girls,
> Let us shake hands with each other and say we hope we find each other quite well, as it leaves us at present. *The Sunday Sun* has sent over a comfortable basket chair for my sunny verandah, and asked me to sit in it and catch sunbeams for you in between planting silver bells and cockle shells in my garden. When first I saw the chair I was quite alarmed. I thought they meant me to write their leaders in it, or their sporting columns, or their fashion or similar serious things. But when I found it was merely a matter of catching sunbeams! And for you, whom I have known so long! Well, I simply laughed and sat straight down in it.
> > Ever Yours,
> > Ethel Turner

When the second edition was published E.T was somewhat alarmed at the unsuitable content and language used in the front and back comic sections of the supplement — her stories, puzzles, competitions, etc. were in the centre. The issue of 20th November offended her greatly with its reference to drink — this is part of the context:

Weary Willie:	The Keg smells good.
Perry:	It's full of British beer. Give me a shilling fur the keg and oi'll take the tram for the money.
Count:	Only too happy.
Weary Willie:	Close wiv 'im Count. (The keg is opened.)
Weary Willie:	Seawater!
Count:	Ouch!
Perry: (disappearing)	Cheerio Chums.

24th November:

A paragraph in Smiths Weekly *about the company of Domain dossers and such figures being on my Children's Page — which precipitates what I have been practically deciding all week to do — resign or have the comics taken away.*

She immediately wrote this letter:

24th November 1921

Dear Mr Campbell Jones,
    For the last fortnight I have been trying hard to tell myself that I am old fashioned to shrink as I have been doing from the subjects on the *Sunbeam* cover and I have been sincerely hoping that, the first rush over, there would be time to consider more soberly a fit diet for healthy and jolly children. I am most reluctant to seem to want to dictate to you and Mr Tonkin about your own paper but indeed you are offending the susceptibilities of a larger number of your readers than you have any idea of, by the connection of children with drink and crime. Lots of people very lax themselves over their reading are still very careful of the reading of their young folks. I am not questioning the merit of the drawings of the Supplement — I thought them very clever — or their suitability for a paper other than a children's paper. I know there is no real harm in them — I am really no prig — and it is not easy to apply to them a word, which would not over-express what I mean. But the paragraph in *Smiths Weekly*, though exaggerated of course, seems really to express the feelings of my husband, young people and friends. Now, what are we going to do about it? You speak in one of the advertisements of showing the world that Australia has a sense of fun and humour all its own. Couldn't we, at least in its children's paper, show that it doesn't depend for that humour on drunkenness, dishonesty and so on? Couldn't we go one better than America instead of one worse? I hate — and distrust — preachiness quite as much as you do yourself and it is little enough of it you will get from me in the new paper, but the more I know of children, the more I realise the almost fearful plasticity of them. Give them clean and beautiful and honourable and jolly things to look at and live with

and they'll get a distaste for things that aren't so. But if we are going to deliberately tell them to laugh at and admire the humour of drunkards and derelicts — well, where are we? It seems to me these are big days we are living in just now, it is almost as if the world is being born afresh, and a big part of it, having cast off the restraints of old religions and conventions, think honesty and work and kindness and such things can be cast off too.

I was rather cherishing the notion that *The Sun* and I realising our responsibilities with a Billion and a Bit of Boys and Girls looking to us were going to do a bit of good as we went along as well as make a bit of light reading.

Now what are we going to do about it? I can't take Weary Willie under my aegis — no, I really can't. And I believe if you think it over you will agree with me I ought not to.

Sincerely Yours,
Ethel Turner

And so, forced into a tight corner, Mr Campbell-Jones had to act quickly. His newly launched children's paper was threatened by the resignation of its editor if he didn't comply with her wishes. Within the next few days he must have wondered if it was a case of Divine intervention, when a young and enthusiastic artist arrived who was to solve all his problems.

This undated letter that I have discovered probably appeared as an editorial in Sunbeams several months or even years later.

I found my Chair in the Sun a very happy place for a few weeks and was intensely interested in discovering a real wealth of pen and ink talent in Australian young folks.

Then I found there was something I did not like at all, *namely* the 12 pictures appearing on our front page, despite the fact that they were drawn by one of our cleverest and most successful draughtsmen.

I obstinately pointed the fact out to the Director. Sunbeams were for children, these pictures were for grown ups and highly sophisticated grown ups at that.

The Director groaned — the paper was making splendid headway, why disturb things? What was it I wanted?

I wanted, I said, something in the shape of a small boy, half imp, half angel, who did mischievous and funny things every week from the top of the page to the bottom; who, even if he purloined the last tart from the pantry with his left hand, with his right hand presented it to his mate or some hungry child; a very small boy — in socks preferably.

The Chief rubbed his chin 'There may be something in what you say', he said. 'Well, I'll see what I can do about it, though it won't be easy to find the right man.' But there, he could always find the right man!

In a few days there came an urgent telephone call. Could I go to town to see the Chief? He had something to show me. All over his desk he had Ginger!

That was a moment of purest happiness. Moments of purest happiness are very rare.

I remember saying later on to the artist who came in — a young man with a shy yet eager manner and eyes with a glint of laughter in them, the young man, the famous 'Jim Bancks'* — 'But how do you know all this about small boys and their haunts and habits!' And I pointed to sketches of Ginger on a billy cart, Ginger falling in a pond, Ginger fighting.

'Well,' he said modestly, 'I rather like boys and in the street where I live I often watch them from my window racing their billy carts down the hill after school. Great fun they are. I used to have a billy cart myself once.'

Ethel Turner
(Ethel Curlewis)

The comic first appeared under the heading 'Us Fellers' but was soon re-named 'Ginger Meggs' and so the little boy Ginger was born. From that day onwards he has lived and flourished and even today he is still thinking out new mischief and new acts of kindness. When J. C. Bancks died in 1952 a new artist was commissioned to continue the story and children nowadays still love this familiar face that greets them each Sunday morning.

Pacified and content, Ethel Turner changed her title to that of Chief Sunbeamer and she continued to edit the children's page of Sunbeams until 1931. Her capacity for inventing new games, puzzles and competitions for children was truly amazing as it was a weekly commitment which spanned a period of about 45 years dating way back to the days of the *Iris* school magazine in 1887.

At the end of the year she says:

Bade my sub-conscious go hunt for new characters for a book for next year among all the impressions roughly gathered. And lo! I woke with the thing shaping amazingly and several characters standing ready — Nicola Silver —Alec — the father — the stone house slipping down a hill. Two days ago had not one notion in all my brain for one. Idled all day.

1922   **1922**

Nicola Silver was shelved for a considerable time and another book the *Ungardeners* (which she dedicated to the Chief Justice of N.S.W. Sir William Cullen K.C.M.G. L.L.D. and Lady Cullen), claimed her attention — this she completed in four months and sent it off to her publisher. She was once again delighted to see Jean's second book in print, with its title *Drowning Maze. Sunbeams* gathered momentum during the year and she found it demanded quite a large part of her time.

---

*James Charles Bancks 1889–1952 was born at Hornsby N.S.W. and was the son of an Irish railway worker. He took drawing lessons from Dattilo Rubbo and Julian Ashton and drew his cartoons for the *Sunday Sun* for 29 years. In 1951 he transferred to the *Sunday Telegraph* until his death.

She was very honoured to be asked to present the prizes on Speech Day at her old school and admitted that she found it necessary to read her speech. The topic she chose was 'Too Much to do, High School Girls'.

This year there was not a great deal to relate — perhaps it could be described as a lull before the storm. The following year was incredibly eventful and great strength of character was required to face so many traumatic situations.

1923

At the beginning of the year, Ethel and Jean compiled many stories and contributions that had appeared in *Sunbeams* and other magazines, put them into book form and sent them off for publication under the title *The Sunshine Family*. Also Jean's book *Beach Beyond* was accepted for publication by the *Sydney Morning Herald*.

Ethel's mother became very ill and she devoted a great deal of time to visiting her and relieving the permanent nurse. Mr Cope appeared to have mellowed and found contentment in playing the pianola — she commented that he would play it for five or six hours each day and had already worn out three pianolas.

Herbert's father died and two months later his mother (Marmee as she was called in the diaries) also died. Of the latter she wrote:

It is better of course for the end to have come, as her condition was hopeless, but the pang of parting is very real. I wish I had been better to her and gone out oftener. She was longing to go. Three parts of her life she has been chiefly concerned with thinking of the after-life. She knows the secrets now.

Her own mother's illness became graver and in July she says:

To Killara in afternoon. Mother very bad, or had been and just had morphia — grew better after a time. Likes to talk of the past. Told me how Tom Turner had offered her £1,000 to let him and his wife have Ethel to bring up instead of letting her come to Australia. Said he would bring her up like a little Queen. He was very wealthy — roll top desks in Coventry. Odd to wonder now if Mother had thought 2 children were enough to bring over the seas.

This is a situation that Ethel must have known about many years before when she wrote *Three Little Maids*. The more one reads the diaries in conjunction with her books, the more one realises and recognizes the characters, events and situations which she draws from in her own personal experiences. In *Three Little Maids* Alf is taken away from his brothers and sent off to be brought up by a rich uncle in Germany — a perfect parallel to the request made by Tom Turner asking to keep Ethel and bring her up like a little Queen.

This year also the family purchased their first car, a Buick. Adrian started as Associate to Sir William Cullen. *Sunbeams* became increasingly demanding and many nights she would write until 1 o'clock in the morning.

Preparations went ahead for Jean's wedding with the reception to be held at Avenel and those who have experienced such an occasion in their own home would appreciate the thousand and one details to be remembered.

On 21st October, Ethel's beloved mother died, on 22nd October the funeral was held and on 23rd October Jean married Dr Leo Charlton at St Luke's, Mosman. Ethel records:

My darling girl made the sweetest of brides.

A fortnight later Jean and Leo sailed for England for Leo to further his studies.

31st December:
This has been the fullest year and the saddest and the happiest I have known. My girl has gone but it is all for her happiness and the future promises very brightly for her. But I shall be glad when she is this side of the world again.

Little Mother is at rest and H's Father and Mother. But the three deaths came in five months.

Lily's troubles affect me deeply — no hope of Fred's recovery.

With that, and with Leo and Jean likely to need lots of help for some years, my pen must not give up.

So am glad I have done next year's book Nicola Silver. *Must keep* Sunbeams *on too.*

Rex and Marie, living so close, must have help and interest — life is very hard for them.

I am thankful for excellent health at present and comfortable circumstances. I made £1550 this year by pen work only without interest or shares. But it is not enough for the calls on me.

1924-25

The next two years seemed endless to Ethel — she worried about Jean, whose health had become a matter for concern and she was impatient for her daughter's return. Both Fred (Lil's husband) and Charlie Cope died during this period and she found herself having to battle with *Sunbeams* as it became increasingly popular. In June 1924 she notes that she received a record number of entries in one week — 3,960.

She wrote a book called *Funny* and though under stress at home, she at no stage let this be apparent in her writing and she was able to maintain her usual vitality and enthusiasm.

Adrian was a great companion for her at this time and many entries refer to the numerous trips and outings they shared together. He frequently drove her to town or to visit relatives — they spent a week touring the south coast and another week at Blackheath. But the place that had a special lure for them was Palm Beach. Here Ethel could find time to do a little verse writing in between her constant sorties down to the surf. Many times Adrian would take her to the beach at 7 am, return himself for breakfast, and find that when he went back to the beach at 10 am she would still be in the water. Adrian was one of the foundation members of the Surf Club and its captain for a number of years, and his love of the surf was to remain a life-long interest for him.

Ethel's tension and despondency lifted when Jean and Leo returned at the end of 1925.

Jean home. All three of us up at 6.15 am, but a long wait at wharf before the Maunganui *got in. And then a long time while they got through Customs and disposed of baggage. But that did not matter as we had them. J. looked as fragile as when she went away — and sad — though gay, which worried me. Leo very well and grown broader. A long day of talking and happiness. Leo to his home, so we had her to ourselves.*

1926

In April Ethel went to New Zealand by the Ship *Maunganui* to visit Rosie who was at that time living in Wellington. The trip was a welcome diversion from the troubles that were mounting up at home and when she returned she wrote several articles including a series called 'Across the Creek'.

The joy and happiness of having Jean and Leo home was not to last for long. In July they learnt the devastating news that Jean had tuberculosis. The diaries for the next four years are heart-breaking to read. The word 'tuberculosis' is never actually written down at any stage, though the distressing symptoms are. She frequently records Jean's weight and one senses that her thoughts are with her daughter all her waking hours. Jean spent months at a time at a private hospital at Katoomba and Ethel visited her and sat with her, and hoped against hope that the mountains would perform their miraculous cure as had always happened in her books.

1927

2nd January:
Letter from Jean. She was well but had lost 2½ lbs after the trip. H. and I gardening — ungardening indeed — a big growth of rubbishy things had spread in my absence. At night left it to my 'sub-conscious' to make a song of Sydney. Sat and walked the verandah and one came singing in my head, the lines very soon, and then made up an air on the piano that seems to fit. I was on the piano stool till about 9 pm when I finished it. But must get a musician to write it out more elaborately.

4th January:
Adrian home. And with a big secret to tell us — he and Betty are engaged but it is not to be given out till he is through. He is nearly 26 so it had to come and I think we shall grow very fond of her — she has plenty of sweetness as well as beauty. A big thing to think about. H. and I to Manly, had a surf with Lil.

9th March:
Oh fabjous day! A. is through his final. I was in town and the news came by H. about 4 pm.

In June E.T. started a book about Judy's schooldays — an admirer had requested it, as she had so loved Judy and wanted to know more about her personality.

After much thinking it over, I wrote positively at first chapter of Judy's schooldays — I think I shall call it Judy and Punch.

This book is rather remarkable in that she had to recapture a character that she had created 35 years beforehand. With the diverse happenings of the intervening years and the transition from girlhood to a mature woman, E.T. was still empowered to expand and develop Judy's life and character. Judy retained her impish sense of humour, her impulsive and uncomplicated personality, her recklessness, her loyalty and her determination. The story is fast moving and abounds with incidents and adventures that endear the lovable Judy even more to her readers.

Even more remarkable is the fact that E.T. was able to write in her usual vital and joyous vein so that her public knew nothing of the depression and tumult that was ever-present in her own heart with worrying about Jean.

1928

Writing became an intolerable burden to her, though she needed the income for family reasons, so she forced herself to persevere.

24th March, 1928:
A cruel day, wet heat. Sunbeams *was like dragging a load of blue metal up a mountain.*

And in May the same year:

A home day, clearing up debris and emptying out cupboards. A book seems to tie one all up in knots for months and it takes long enough to straighten oneself out again.

At the end of this year she built a cottage on their block of land at Leura and called it Garth. It was built in order to have a home to go to whilst visiting Jean in hospital and also for her to use when well enough.

On 12th December, Adrian married Betty Carr and they came to live in Parriwi Road, Mosman. A son born to them at the end of the following year was, for Ethel, a moment of sunshine in a world that had grown dark.

1929

With such an alert and vigorous brain Jean became bored with days of inactivity on the Mountains and in desperation returned to Sydney to a small flat in Macleay Street though it was against the doctor's orders. Here she wrote articles for the *Home* magazine and became absorbed in other literary pursuits. Ethel went to see her nearly daily and helped her with shopping and other domestic matters.

Jean spent some weeks in hospital in March and again in July.

15th July:
To Jean. Her new room at hospital full of lovely flowers from different friends and a beautiful jade water holder and glasses from Ure Smith and Leon Gellert.

17th August:
Sunbeams — the eternal grind of Sunbeams. I get to be a-weary of The Sun.

7th November:
To Jean taking her an armful of almond blossom sent by Mrs Phillip, the pretty bed jacket I have been embroidering, and also a letter from Dorothea Mackellar sent from England. She was wheeled out onto the balcony in the sun for a time. Not a good day though as she was in pain from strain of coughing. Then back to her flat and spent a couple of hours fixing things up.

(See Appendix VI for article by Dorothea Mackellar about Jean.)

'Bunby came in backwards, lugging five or six pieces of board nailed together haphazard.'
Seven Little Australians

1930

When the Sun
Went Down

The pages of the diaries are blank at the beginning of this year and it was during this time that her adored daughter Jean passed away, but she was too moved to record the final days.

Although written in 1893, this chapter heading and the quotations, taken from *Seven Little Australians*, so vividly describes this period that I feel compelled to quote in her own words some of the depth of feeling that she must have experienced.

Such a sunset!

Down at the foot of the grass hill there was a flame-coloured sky, with purple, soft clouds, massed in banks high up where the dying glory met the paling blue. The belt of trees had grown black, and stretched sombre, motionless arms against the orange background. All the wind had died, and the air hung hot and still, freighted with the strange silence of the bush.

And at the top of the hill, just within the doorway of the little brown hut, her wide eyes on the wonderful heavens, Judy lay dying. She was very quiet now, though she had been talking — talking of all sorts of things. She told them she had no pain at all. . .

Greyer grew the shadows round the little hut, the bullocks' outlines had faded, and only an indistinct mass of soft black loomed across the light. Behind the trees the fire was going out, here and there were yellow, vivid streaks yet, but the flaming sun-edge had dipped beyond the world, and the purple, delicate veil was dropping down.

A curlew's note broke the silence, wild, mournful, unearthly. Meg shivered and sat up straight. Judy's brow grew damp, her eyes dilated, her lips trembled.

'Meg!' she said, in a whisper that cut the air; 'oh, Meg, I'm frightened! I'm so frightened! . . .'

Judy grew quiet and still more quiet. She shut her eyes so she could not see the gathering shadows.

Meg's arms were round her, Meg's cheek was on her brow, Nell was holding her hands, Baby her feet, Bunty's lips were on her hair. Like that they went with her right to the Great Valley, where there are no lights even for stumbling childish feet.

The shadows were cold and smote upon their hearts; they could feel the wind from the strange waters on their brows, but only she who was about to cross heard the low lapping of the waves.

Just as her feet touched the water there was a figure in the doorway.

'Judy!' said a wild voice; and Pip brushed them aside and fell down beside her.

'Judy, Judy, Judy!'

The light flickered back in her eyes. She kissed him with pale lips once, twice; she gave him both her hands, and her last smile.

Then the wind blew over them all, and with a little shudder, she slipped away.

The death of Judy
Seven Little Australians

And Last

With Jean's death from such a prolonged illness, so came the end of Ethel Turner's writing career — she never completed another book though she lived for 25 years more.

Therefore, the time has come to put her diaries back on the shelf, not to gather dust, as they have done for countless years, but to become golden treasure to be stored safely for future generations.

As I come to the end of this work, my own words could not possibly express my feelings nearly as adequately as those written by my grandmother.

My pen has been moving heavily, slowly for these last two chapters; it refuses to run lightly, freely again just yet, so I will lay it aside or I will sadden you.

Some day if you would care to hear it, I should like to tell you more of my young Australians again, slipping a little space of years.

Until then, farewell and adieu.

'I'm writing on the dressing-table by the boy's bedside.'
Little Mother Meg

Appendices

I   Contributions to the *Iris* newspaper (Sydney Girls High School)
II   *Parthenon* Libel Action
III   Poems written by Herbert Raine Curlewis to or about Ethel Turner
IV   Letter from Mr William Steele (Ward Lock Australia)
V   Letter from Sarah Jane Cope to her daughter Rose
VI   'Jean Curlewis' by Dorothea Mackellar
VII   Books written by Ethel Turner
VIII   Family Tree

The illustrations at the end of the chapters were taken from the original editions. They were drawn by A. J. Johnson (pp. 12, 24, 170, 240, 266, 268, 269), D. H. Souter (pp. 210), and Harold Copping (pp. 122).

APPENDIX I

SYDNEY GIRLS HIGH SCHOOL, 1887

THE IRIS

Editress:	Ethel Turner
Sub-editresses:	Marcia Cox, Ethel Maynard.
Treasurer:	F. Johnson
Staff:	N. Church, L. Turner, F. Delohery, M. Hollander, W. H. Smith, F. and N. Hague-Smith

Editorial

We have been told that some girls have imagined the *Iris* to be the Tennis Paper. We distinctly refute the statement. The *Iris* is a general school newspaper and may be written for by the whole school. We hope to receive competitions for the new prizes offered from all the school and not merely from the few who are especially interested in the paper, for we wish it to be distinctly understood, once and for all, that we do not want the *Iris* to belong to certain cliques but to be a paper of general interest in the school and composed of contributions from all and not merely confined to the Staff and Upper School.

School Notes
Feb. 1888

The room in which the *Iris* staff and their friends were wont to refresh themselves with 'the cup that cheers' and other delicacies, and in which they discussed the politics of the day after their weary work was done, has been wrested from them. It is now the receptacle for brooms, mops, a dresser and two objects very much resembling mummies. The *Iris* staff naturally feeling themselves outraged carried their grievance to higher quarters and were consoled by the gift of the Reichstag which they intend beautifying with crimson curtains, photographs and other ornaments.

Competitions

The competition for the gold brooch, so kindly offered by Miss Hollander, ran very close. A full meeting of the staff was held to consider the respective merits of the stories and at the close of the meeting the decision lay between the stories of Louie Mack and Sara Caro, the subjects chosen were so different that it was some time before we arrived at the final decision viz: that L. Mack be declared the winner of the brooch and that a second brooch be given to S. Caro by the staff since the contest was so close.

It is a curious coincidence that the competition for Miss Hollander's prize (a gold brooch) in the *Iris* should be won by the editress of the *Gazette* and that Miss Yates' prize (8 volumes of Shakespeare) in the *Gazette* should be won by the editress of the *Iris*.

Puzzles

We were obliged to reject several contributions of considerable merit as they were sent in with *nom-de-plume* only. We cannot in any case infringe the rule.

Letters to the Editor

Dear Miss Editress,

I wish to appeal to the feelings of the girls on behalf of the unfortunate girls who occupy classroom E. It is the only classroom in which the girls are allowed to lunch and I do not think it is fair that we should suffer as we do daily from the unpleasant scraps of lunch, fruit skins, etc. that are left in our room.

The room is excessively hot and close owing to the zinc roof and I do not think our misfortunes need be unnecessarily added to.

Hoping the practice will be discontinued. I remain or rather I hope I shall *not* remain

A Sufferer of Classroom E.

APPENDIX II

"PARTHENON" LIBEL ACTION.
THE PARTHENON.　　　　　　　February 1890

As many of our readers are aware the Parthenon had, on the 24th of last month, an action for libel brought against it, and as, in the estimation of several people, the Editors and Secretaries included, the reports, leaders and mentions in the daily papers have hardly seemed to allow there were two sides to the question, we give below an account of the causes that led to our first and, we hope, last libel case.

We do this more especially because Mr McKinney has thought it advisable to write to the papers on the subject, and because all the evidence was not brought in at the hearing of the case, which would have been had it been brought against us instead of Messrs. Gordon and Gotch.

In the July issue, among the competitions on the Children's Page, a prize was offered for the most words made from "Regulation."

Numerous papers were sent in from all parts, and the time of competition having expired, we sat down to the tedious and somewhat thankless task of deciding who was the winner.

The paper in question came to hand. The rules were most simple, the chief being: "No word must be used that cannot be found in any standard dictionary." For the benefit of our readers we print a complete list of the child's words just as it came into our hands:—

Ragin, ragnit, raine, rea, realito, rega, regan, regart, regoa, reinga, rei, rengo, reno, riet, riga rindu, ringat, ringe, rintoul, rion, ro roa, roag, roan, roe, rona, rouen, rue, runa, runga, ruti, rail, rain, ran, rag, rage, rane, rang, range, rat, rate, ratel, ratio, ration, raton, real, regal, reign, rein, reit, ren, renal, rent, rental, ret, retail, retain, retina, retinal, rial, riant, rie, rig, rigel, riglet, rigol, rile, ring, ringlet, riot, roan, roe, roil, rot, roint, role, rota, reta, rotal, rote, rouet, rouge, rout, route, routine, rue, rug, rugate, rugine, ruin, ruinate, rile, run, rune, rung, runlet, runt, rut, rutile, rutil, eaton, ega, egin, egina, eglon, egripo, eil, elgin, eno, eo, erang, eria, erin, eringa, erlau, erung, etain, etang, eton, eu, eura, eutria, euroa, ean, ear, earl, earn, eat, egriot, engrail, entail, entrail, era, erato, ergo, ergot, earing, eringo, ern, galion, galt, gao, garo, gaurion, gare, garnet, garton, garu, gaue, genil, genoa, gerontia, gir, genua, gela, gera, gerae, gerant, gerona, gien, glane, glen, girnel, giro, giron, giura, glin, glina, goat, golan, gola, gona, gort, gourin, gran, grant, grein, gren, greta, guinea, guta, gael, gain, gainer, gait, gaiter, gale, galiot, galt, ganil, gaol, gaoler, gate, gaul, gault, gaunt, geal, gear, geat, gelt, gilt, gontil, got, giant, gin, girl, girt, git, glair, glare, glean, glen, glint, gloar, gloat, glout, glue, gluer, glut, gluten, glutine, gnar, gnarl, gnat, gnu, go, goal, goar, goat, goel, goen, goer, goiter, goitre, gola, gole, gone, gore, got, gote, gout, grade, gradin, gradine, grail, grain, grane, granite, granitel, grant, grate, great, greit, gride, grin, groan, grot, groat, groin, grout, grunt, guan, guano, gue, guile, guiler, guilt, guitar, gula, gular, gule, gun, gurt, gut, uger, ugie, uige, ula, ulea, unie, ural, urgo, ulong, ulan, ule, ultion, ultra, ultrage, ungear, unget, unio, unit, unite, uniter, unlage, unoil, untie, until, untile, unto, unveil, uranite, urate, ure, urea, urge, urgent, uria, urinal, urinate, urine, urn, urnal, ut, utile, la, lai, lairg, lan, lang, lange, laon, lar, laren, laret, large, largie, largo, larino, larne, lart, legio, lena, lenga, leon, leti, li, lia, liant, liat, lier, liger, ligor, ligua, lina, linaro, ling, line, linger, linge, lion, lira, lo, loa, loar, logan, logen, logie, logta, loir, loire, loiret, loit, lonair, lone, loan, long, longue, loia, loran, lorn, lort, lot, loung, lung, luan, lug, luga, lugano, lugo, luigo, luina, luing, luna, lunga, lune, lure, lurgan, luro, luton, lag, lain, lair, lane, languet, langour, langura, lanier, lant, lare, lar, larin, late, later, latin, lation, laurine, lea, leau, lear, leantao, learn, leg, legal, legation, legato, legator, legion, lent, lentigo, lentil, lento, lentor, leor, let, liar, lie, lien, lier, lieu, lig, ligan, ligature, ligule, ligure, lin, linage, line, linear, ling, lingel, linger, linget, lingo, lingot, lint, lion, lionet, lite, liter, literal, litorn, litre, lo, loan, log, loin, loiter, lone, long, lorate, lore, loring, lorn, lorna, lorne, lot, lote, loture, lounge, lounger, lour, lout, lu, lug, lunar, lunate, lunet, lunge, lunt, lute, luter, luting, aeng, aero, agen, agno, agout, agrio, agua, ai, aigen, angle, ain, aing, aion, aiou, air, aire, ale, alne, alote, alt, alte, alten, alton, alung, angelo, angol, a, an, antler, argel, argo, arno, aron, art, aru, arun, aterno, aulne, aure, auron, aurin, alor, arto, aulon, aeon, aerugo, age, agen, agent, agile, agio, aglet, aiglet, agon, agone, agouti, agre, argue, aigre, aigret, aigulet, ail, airgun, ait, alert, algor, alien, alienor, align, aloe, alone, along, alter, altern, alto, alure, angel, angelot, anger, anigo, angle, angler, angor, anoil, are, argent, argil, argo, argol, argute, aril, arnot, arnut, aroint, atone, at, ate, atelo, auger, auget, augite, augoer, aune, aunt, tagil, tain, tair, tali, taloe, talu, talung, tangier, tanio, tao, taongi, tar, tarin, tarn, tan, te, teano, tegal, tena, teon, ter, tera, tear, terang, tergue, tern, terni, Te Rua, tet, tiel, tien, tiger, tin, tingera, tino, tio, tioge, tione, tiong, tira, tiran, tirano, tiro, tolna, tong, tonga, tongue, tor, tore, tora, torgau, tornea, toul, toula, trae, trang, trani, trau, traun, treig, trial, trigno, tring, trogen, troia, troian, tron, tua, tuela, tuena, tugelo, tuna, tunai, tunga, tura, turang, turano, turin, turina, turna, turon, taron, terina, turia, tag, tail, tailor, tairn, tale, talion, tan, tang, tangle, tanier, tar, tare, targe, taro, taring, taurine, tea, teal, tea-urn, teg, tegular, teil, ten, tergal, terin, turn, tern, tiar, tie, tier, tig, tige, tiger, tile, tiler, tin, tine, tinea, ting, tinge, tinger, tingle, tire, to, toe, toga, toil, toiler, tol, tola, tole, tolu, ton, tone, torn, tour, tourn, trail, train, trainel, tren, trial, triangle, trig, trigon, trigonal, trinal, trine, tringle, trio, triole, triune, trona, tronage, trone, troul, truage, truan, true, tue-iron, tug, tun, tune, tuner, turgent, turio, turn, ial, I, iantu, iaun, iga, iglau, iglo, in, ina, ingote, ingour, ingul, iron, irun, Iona, ituna, ignaro, ignore, ignote, ile, inert, ing, inga, ingate, ingle, ingot, ingrate, inlet, integral, inter, into, inure, io, ion, iota, irate, ire, it, oat, oena, oeta, ogulin, ogun, oil, olean, olenda, oleri, olga, olgeitu, one, onega, oneglia, oran, orang, ore, orel, oren, oreti, orgueil, oria, orien, orient, oring, orne, orta, orte, ortegal, orua, otra, oulart, our, oura, ouri, outer, o, oar, o'er, ogle, ogler, ogre, oiler, oilet, oilnut, oint, olea, on, onager, or, ora, oral, orange, ore, orgal, organ, orgeat, oriel, oriental, orle, orn, ornate, our, out, outer, outing, outrage, nage, nagor, nagore, nagour, nagur, nal, na-le, nao, nariel, narin, negaito, negril, negrita, negro, neguai, nera, neutra, nge, ngoli, nier, nile, nio, niort, noga, noir, noli, nora, nore, norte, nuer, nail, nailer, nar, nare, nargil, nargile, natio, neal, near, neat, neutra, neroli, net, neutral, nit, niter, nitre, no, noel, nog, noie, noier, nor, noria, not, note, noter, nougat, noul, nil, nilur, nut, nutria.

At first glance we could see many of the words were of an unusual character, words at least that had never come under our notice before. We consulted Standard dictionaries most carefully, Ogilvie's Imperial, Webster's Ordinary, and several works of less importance — there was no trace of quite *three hundred* of them.

We examined it more attentively, and found numbers of words were written twice over *and* added on to the total, words also containing letters not occurring in the word "Regulation" were also introduced *and* added on.

Much annoyed, we flung the paper aside and, instead of putting in a notice of 1st prize, which, had we looked at the figure of the total only, we should have done, we wrote the paragraph that has brought us so much into notice:

"A little girl from Manly (E.M.—we refrain from giving her full name) sent in a paper marked with the greatest number of words (687) from 'Regulation.' On examining it, however, with dictionaries, we much regretted to find she had used words which she herself must have invented to make up a large score. She is disqualified. We hope this will be a warning to our young competitors. A word here and there wrong we can account for as slips, but when given in large numbers to make a big total we can only think they are done with deliberate intention."

The paper went to press and in due time came out. The first thing apprising us that anything was wrong was — not as might have been expected — a quiet explanatory letter from the child's father, pointing out the various unusual sources from which the words were obtained, but a lawyer's letter demanding abject published apology and payment of fees already incurred.

Thinking we must have been in error, we submitted a list of 300 of the words to Professor Scott of the Sydney University, who examined it and returned it with the following note (read in Court):—

"Dear Miss Turner, — I have looked through the list of about 300 'words' as to which you asked my opinion. I found only 23 among them at most which can possibly be described as *English words*, taking the term in the widest sense, and including some well-known proper names. Of the rest, some are words belonging to foreign or ancient languages (French, German, Italian or Latin), but the greater number have no meaning in any language known to me.

Faithfully yours,
W. Scott."

The Rev. Zachary Barry, LL.D., and several other highly educated men gave the same opinion, and we felt ourselves thereupon justified in refusing to apologise.

Several lawyer's letters followed, sent to us as Editors and Proprietors of the paper and holding us responsible. Suddenly there was a change, and the correspondence sent to Gordon and Gotch, vendors of the paper. Why, we are still in doubt, as they and everyone must know we were morally responsible, and costs must therefore be paid by us.

We thought from the first it was a most absurd and trivial thing to occupy the time of a court with, but since, as his Honor kindly put it in the summing up, "we could not be convinced that we were wrong, and seemed to have made up our minds on the subject," and since the defendant still insisted on a humble apology, the case for five long months dragged its slow length along.

All through the correspondence with the plaintiff we were always ready and had offered, if it were proved that the words existed, to state the fact but he would not be satisfied with anything short of an apology couched in terms that our advisers declined to allow us to adopt. We then offered to abide by the decision of two gentlemen of standing, and to do whatever they thought right, but this also produced no satisfactory result.

The Plaintiff's case was that part of the words could be found in Webster's Unabridged Dictionary. For a very long time we could obtain no copy of this rarely used work, but at last consulted one at the Free Public Library, and found many of the words were to be found there, a large proportion being however entirely obsolete.

The rest of the words we were told might be found in an atlas, by Bryce, Collier and Schmitz, (an atlas, not a dictionary). We were quite unable to obtain this work, nobody seemed to have heard of it, and at last plaintiff's Solicitors, Messrs Spain and Moore, forwarded to us their client's own copy. Even then, after consulting this, there remained and still remain thirty-five which can not be accounted for at all.

During the process of the case Mr McKinney was asked to explain these thirty-five words, which he himself had marked as doubtful.

He replied that his daughter had mis-spelt them, but intended them for other words.

Were we supposed to be able to decide to a nicety whether the words were inventions, or merely words meant for other words? Life, — Editorial life at any rate — is too short to be wasted in such abstruse deliberation.

That we had no "malicious intention" against the little girl would, we should imagine, appear from the facts that, in the first place we did not know her in the slightest degree; in the second, that the month before she had been awarded a first prize for a similar competition; and, in the third that in the same prize page in which we so terribly injured her, we gave her an honourable mention for another competition.

That we were wrong in attributing a motive to anyone we see now most clearly, although last August we were not so well versed in the many technicalities of the law as we now are.

That we were entirely wrong, we do not see, and could not were fifty verdicts with costs brought against us.

APPENDIX III

These are several of the poems written by Herbert Curlewis. He often wrote verse in Greek, or translated it from Greek and Latin.

This one he submitted to the *Parthenon* soon after he had met E. T. when he was a boy of 20.

July 1889

Rondeau

Could you but know — those clear cold eyes
Where never gleam of pity lies
    Lift to my own so quietly
        Those eyes whose wrath were worse to me
        Than aught that cruelty could devise.

Would anger pity or surprise
Or scorn from their clear depths arise?
    I wonder what my fate would be
        Could you but know.

Could you but know — in tender wise
Entreat my boldness nor despise
    Him who would gladly die for thee
        Will you not know? Will you not see?
        Ah, would you love, (my heart denies)
            Could you but know?

H.R.C.

In the September publication of the *Parthenon*, Ethel Turner acknowledges this poem by saying 'Among the verses a few stanzas by H. R. Curlewis show more than usually good form':

July 1890

There is None Like Her, None

Long time ago God made the world then made He
    The lights of Heaven. His task to perfect make
Fairest of all His works He sent my lady
    And kindly views the world for her sweet sake.

God said 'the snow-drop is the sign of her
    That is more pure and small than others be
And well wot I to earth nought lovelier
    Than this my angels send for men to see'.

Dare I that am her bondsman hope for grace
   Since she so wondrous and so perfect is
Save that for pity she may turn her face
   Smiling upon me and say softly this

Seeing thou lovest me so and art so true
   And ever strivest so to do me praise
Take me — of thy great love 'tis gurden due
   And deal thou gently with me all thy days.

H.R.C.

This poem accompanied the letter that he sent Ethel on Christmas Day:

Dec. 1891
Dear lady mine, the coming years
   To me but happiness can bring
   For with your love no evil thing
May come to me till when life nears
   The quiet of its long evening.

But sweet, will you be still content?
   I dare not think it will be so.
   When my unworthiness you know
Have you no fear you may repent
   The promise made then long ago?

And yet, My Ethel, it may be
   That by your love more noble made,
   I shall not vainly love essayed
To keep God's Sacred gift to me,
   Perchance no need to feel afraid.

Yes God, whose sweetest saint you are,
   Will keep you safe whate'er befall
   And would his gift to me recall
If there were danger I should mar
   The life He cares for most of all.

All useless, sweet — there is no way
   To speak the thoughts that overflow
   Thoughts I shall never make you know,
And this alone I find to say
   Sweetheart, I love, I love you so.

H.R.C.

APPENDIX IV

This is a copy of the letter (slightly abbreviated) received by Ethel on 21st December 1894 from Mr William Steele, Ward Lock's representative in Melbourne.

Dear Miss Turner,

Yours of 26th is to hand. I am afraid the critics are right re Judy's death, still those last chapters will gain for you many friends.

Copies of our readers reports have reached me concerning *Growing Up* — it is considered not so good as the first book, the delightful and rollicking humour is missed and the pathos is inferior. It is thought you have a genius for writing about children, and the characters are genuine creatures, but as they grow older you lose something of your hold. I think you should know of these opinions, because, provided they are thoroughly reliable they may serve to guide your decision as regards future writing, and I know when I was in Sydney, you seemed rather uncertain how to shape your course in literary work, at any rate, that is the impression that I rightly or wrongly gained at the time. If upon quiet careful reflection, you think these criticisms should weigh with you, I would strongly advise you to consider the desirability of endeavouring to improve *Growing Up* in its way through the press, especially with regards to strengthening the humorous elements. Mr Bowden wishes you to kindly watch anything slangy, as it is considered this will mar the success of your books. It is certainly a drawback in the Old Country, although looked lightly upon here. As far as Australia is concerned we can safely say that your entrance into literary life is a success, your first book has received the most flattering attention, and the second book will be looked forward to with considerable expectation. Every pains should therefore be taken to bring this second book up to an equal if not higher standard than the first, so that the hold you have obtained may be increased. Any relaxing should be carefully guarded against, as it would mar your chances for a generally successful career. Have you another copy of *Growing Up*? Now I recall the finish of the tale, I think there are some passages connected with Nell's grief, about Meg's illness, which would bear softening down. By this post I send you a copy of *Women Writers*, the last chapter of which is Louisa May Alcott, and I think some of her experiences may afford you food for reflection and assist you to decide for yourself, as to your chances of success in literature, outside what are known as young people's books.

Kindly consider this more of a friendly than a business letter and with kind regards, believe me to remain,

Yours Very Truly,
William Steele.

APPENDIX V

This letter written by Sarah Jane Cope to her youngest daughter Rose gives a heart-warming picture of Henry Turner.

Bukyangi
Killara
19th February, 1912

Dear beloved Wody,

I am delighted with the hanky, and think it is beautifully done, *but* — oh dear your poor eyes, and your tired-out back — don't, *please* don't ever again stitch your soul into things you need not. Truly dear, much as I admire it, it hurts me dreffly when I picture you working for me and you have your hands so very full. Tell my small namesake I think she has done her work wonderfully well, and I shall keep it amongst my treasures. The first moment I can get I will paint a new face for Betty — just now I am without help of any kind — male or female — I had to discharge Eileen last week for impudence, she had quite got the upper hand, I had made too much of her. She was terribly dirty, and when I spoke to her she said 'If she was not able to run this house without my interference it was time to give up'. I said yes it was time, and she could take a week's notice and *give* up — she bounced finely — said I need not imagine mine was the only place in the world, etc. etc. — and when it actually came to the point of going and she saw I meant it, she howled and cried herself ill — 'Oh I don't want to leave you', 'Oh I can't go away', 'Nobody ever was good to me since my mother died except you', 'Oh don't send me away, don't send me away'. Truly it made me quite ill to see her so completely broken up, but she had been getting more and more insolent every week — more dirty and lazy — I couldn't stand it. Last week Lil was ill — influenza again, and before she got right Eric got another dreadful throat, high temperature, etc. Doctor still attending him — Lil about knocked up — no servant — so Eileen has gone to her on a month's trial imploring me if she does her best during that month to take her back — Lil won't keep anyone with a big baby that needs extra feeding and able to crawl about the house, but I won't have the girl back. Since Friday I've been working like a nigger cleaning holes and corners and it will take me some time yet to get straight, so I hardly see myself letting Eileen come in when all is clean and mess things up again — my kitchen is a perfect picture.

Darling Wo I must try to think of things to tell you of your Father — above all he was a *good man*, true, honourable, just in all his dealings, cheery, genial, loving-hearted — always joking and as full of pranks as a schoolboy, indeed he was always much younger than any of his children (I don't include you) and dear always I love to remember how he simply worshipped me — no one could have convinced him I was not the cleverest, best and most beautiful woman on earth — we were rather a mad pair sometimes, altho' he was an invalid. I remember once how he dressed me up in one of the boy's suits and we went out together as

Father and Son — and over the dressing up we went almost into fits of laughter. We had worlds of sorrow and trouble but we never let it crush us and frequently had the maddest, merriest times. Yes dear, it was heartbreakingly sad that he should die so young — you are the only one I can speak to about him from my heart. His other children never appreciated him. Never really knew him, so I never would have talked of him to them, except mere surface talk. He is buried in Coventry cemetery with not a stone to mark his resting place. I was left poor, overwhelmed with trouble and debts from such a cruelly long illness — and with the responsibility of a family of nine on my shoulders. He had a Father living th œe, a wealthy man, and brothers in good positions, you would have thought that they would have supplied a stone, but so far from that they never contributed one single shilling to the cost of his illness or his funeral, and I would have died rather than ask their help. I must tell you one bit of loving pride he had, that was about my foot — he liked to delight in choosing me pretty shoes. I was nearly 20 years younger than he, yet never felt any difference, we were always such thorough chums. I love to remember how proud he was of me.

Once he had been to some races and I was unable to go with him so he brought me home from Nottingham the loveliest Paris bonnet, it had a crown and brim something like a gipsy hat, and a wreath of roses round it, no two alike and no two the same colour and he carried it home so proudly in a box and put it on my head, and then gave me £5 to buy a dress to wear with it — but I bought a new floor covering for the dining room, and he used to say 'Now children I will not have you walk on Mother's new dress in dirty boots'. Before his illness he was so strong and active, he would catch me by my arms and throw me over his shoulders and run round the garden crying out 'Who wants a sack of coals'. It was supposed, that he got a chill on his kidneys from working in a heated factory — he used to lift such enormous weights when they were altering looms or starting new ones, and get excessively heated, and then was careless how he went out into cold and frosty air, then when the kidneys were in an inflamed condition and he was suffering severe pain — friends of his used to advise him to take gin and bitters — and rum — or other such remedies — and it all helped on the mischief — until acute Bright's disease set in and the Doctor said he could not possibly live 3 months, this was about 3 months before your birth — then the disease became chronic and lasted over 6 years. Oh it was dreadful, dreadful — beyond all words dreadful — dear, no living soul knows what my life was. Often when I am alone I re-live the past, and I wonder sometimes that I am still alive — and I was so sorely handicapped by his terribly unprincipled, selfish children.

Darling I must go now, I am *so* tired — I was out of bed at 6 this morn and never ceased work until after 6 tonight.

Goodnight my dear one — oh how your Father loved you — I think he just idolized you . . .

Very Lovingly
your own Mother

I am *so glad* you asked about him.

APPENDIX VI

This article by Dorothea Mackellar about Jean Curlewis was published in *Art in Australia*, eds. Sydney Ure Smith and Leon Gellert, Third Series, no. 32, June-July 1930.

It is not easy to speak in public of a much-loved friend, especially just after her tragic death, but perhaps when one remembers how many people who never had the good fortune to meet Jean Curlewis during her brief life have nevertheless loved her, the thing should not seem impossible. And yet it is hard to decide. She had such deep reserves herself, for all her crystalline articulateness, that if an intimate discussion of her were necessary she would probably prefer it to be conducted by those who were not her closest friends.

I suppose she was about seventeen when we first met: very pretty, with the colouring of a Fortune's Yellow rose in her smooth cheeks, and curling hair. One noticed most of all the beauty of her dark-lashed green-grey eyes, and her swift, dazzling boyish smile. But it was her voice that enchanted me, a sweet, soft voice with unexpected modulations in it, and an odd little deliberateness singularly individual. This deliberateness was not the result of slow thinking, but rather that, much more quickly than most people, she had surveyed several sides of the subject (that perhaps had only just arisen), and she wished to present them all with scrupulous fairness. For she had a grasp, a breadth of vision, amazing in one so young and rare enough at any age. It is not easy to estimate how much Australia lost when Jean Curlewis' long gallant fight came to an end in that hospital room some weeks ago. Her love of life, her sane and humorous outlook, and her quick, warm power of observation were reflected in all she wrote, in the surfing stories that she laughed at and that are such good fun to read, as well as in the vivid articles written in England, whither she went after her marriage.

These qualities found room to show even in the narrow limits of her extremely clear and practical little book, *Verse Writing for Beginners*. With a sense of style such as she possessed, an elementary text-book becomes a delight.

But good as her prose was, from the day the *Bulletin* published her poem, 'Suburban' — (it dealt with the War, as many will remember, and was written when, I suppose, she was nineteen or twenty) — I longed that she should write more poetry.

Suburban is in free verse — that kind of free verse still, unfortunately, rare, which is not merely prose chopped up into irregular lengths, but real poetry swung into shape by the sheer force of the emotions it contains. She once told me that since writing it she had taken a dislike to free verse, and wished that she had given it some other form. To me the form seems absolutely right for that sort of poem, and I thought, and still think, that she spoke in the irritation of reaction, since she was gasping at the moment in a flood of the solemn slovenliness which is neither verse nor free, not to mention poetry.

Nothing could be entirely characteristic of her than her very gracious poem, Youth's Housekeeping, suggested by the happy serenity of an old lady she had lately met:

> *Being, this day of Spring, aged eighteen years,*
> *And, since I am no older, very wise —*

I should quote it at length, were it not that Jean's early death has made its gay wisdom and courage unbearably poignant.

Another delightful and characteristic song of hers begins:

> *I have a painted table and a little yellow chair —*

I have no copy of that. I only read it once, years ago, and some of the words elude me, but as a whole it is unforgettable. The World Lover, quoted elsewhere, was written about thirteen or fourteen years ago — she was eighteen at most. It, too, is very like her, though it lacks the sure touch that distinguishes the later poems.

I do not know if she ever realised that for many of those she met she herself filled the world with freshly apprehended beauty, like the lady of her young and chivalrous imagining, for she was no egotist.

She was the best kind of Australian. A young country needs enthusiasms more than an old one, and more especially does it need them to be clear-sighted, as hers were. Who can say how many lamps she lighted by what she wrote about her own land, and those others that she could appreciate and contrast with it so well? She gave us a great deal, in the short time she had.

APPENDIX VII

1	**1893**	*Seven Little Australians*
2	**1894**	*Family at Misrule*
3	**1894**	*Story of a Baby*
4	**1895**	*The Little Larrikin*
5	**1895**	*Little Duchess* (short stories)
6	**1896**	*Miss Bobbie*
7	**1897**	*Camp at Wandinong* (short stories)
8	**1898**	*Three Little Maids*
9	**1899**	*Gum Leaves*
10	**1899**	*Little Mother Meg*
11	**1900**	*The Wonder Child*
12	**1903**	*Betty and Co.* (short stories)
13	**1904**	*Mother's Little Girl*
14	**1904**	*White Roof Tree* (short stories)
15	**1905**	*The Stolen Voyage* (short stories)
16	**1905**	*In the Mist of the Mountains*
17	**1907**	*That Girl*
18	**1907**	*Happy Hearts*
19	**1909**	*Fugitives from Fortune*
20	**1909**	*Fair Ines*
21	**1909**	*Apple of Happiness*
22	**1910**	*The Raft in the Bush*
23	**1911**	*Ports and Happy Havens*
24	**1911**	*An Ogre Up to Date*
25	**1911**	*Fifteen and Fair* (verses)
26	**1911**	*A Tiny House* (verses)
27	**1912**	*Secret of the Sea*
28	**1913**	*Flower O' the Pine*
29	**1915**	*The Cub*
30	**1915**	*John of Daunt*
31	**1916**	*Captain Cub*
32	**1917**	*St Tom and the Dragon*
33	**1918**	*Brigid and the Cub*
34	**1919**	*Laughing Water*
35	**1920**	*King Anne*
36	**1921**	*Jennifer, J.*
37	**1922**	*Nicola Silver*
38	**1922**	*The Ungardeners*
39	**1923**	*The Sunshine Family*
40	**1924**	*Funny*
41	**1928**	*Judy and Punch*

APPENDIX VIII

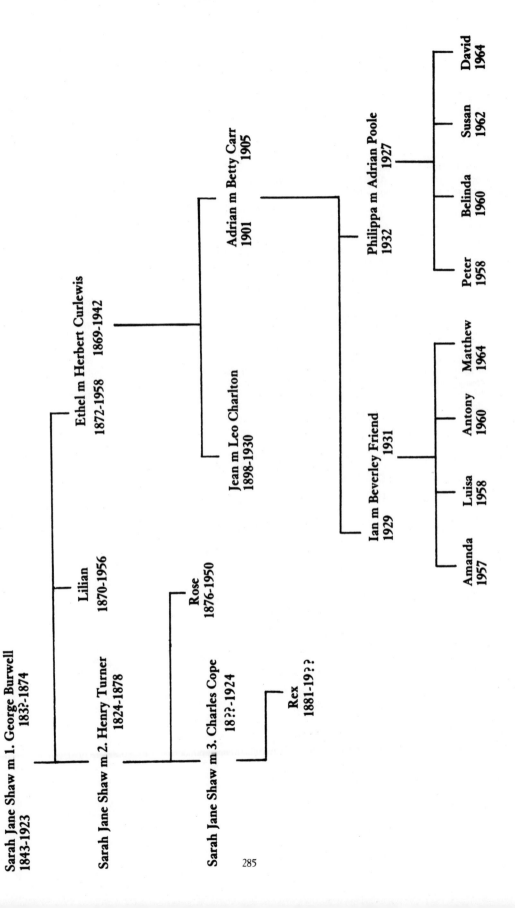

Sarah Jane Shaw m 1. George Burwell
1843-1923   1832-1874

Sarah Jane Shaw m 2. Henry Turner
1824-1878

Sarah Jane Shaw m 3. Charles Cope
18??-1924

Lilian
1870-1956

Ethel m Herbert Curlewis
1872-1958   1869-1942

Rose
1876-1950

Rex
1881-19??

Jean m Leo Charlton
1898-1930

Adrian m Betty Carr
1901   1905

Ian m Beverley Friend
1929   1931

Philippa m Adrian Poole
1932   1927

Amanda
1957

Luisa
1958

Antony
1960

Matthew
1964

Peter
1958

Belinda
1960

Susan
1962

David
1964

285

Index

Abstinence, cause of, 251,252
Adventure of Harry Leland (Smith), 101
Adventures of Harry Richmond (Meredith), 101
Adventures of Huckleberry Finn (Twain), 105
Adventures of Tom Sawyer, The (Twain), 105
'After the Battle', 221-2
Alcott, Louisa, 100, 103, 110, 112, 216, 279
Alice in Wonderland (Carroll), 214, 216
Apple of Happiness, 223, 284
Archibald, Mr, 99, 112, 176, 183
Art in Australia, 282
Arthur, *Dr* Richard, 162, 164, 178, 182, 193, 196, 201, 203, 212, 253
Arthur, Mrs, 184, 196, 202
'As Baby Sees' (H. Curlewis), 177
'As It Fell Out', 90
Ashton, Julian, 36, 213, 261
Ashton, Howard, 190
Astley, Mr, 20, 21, 22, 23, 71, 72, 73, 74
At the Sign of the Lyre (Dobson), 61
At the Roots of Mountains (Morris), 57
'Aunt Elgitha', 14, 82
Australian Broadcasting Commission (A.B.C.), 9, 10, 110
Australian Lassie (L. Turner), 215
Australie, 59

Bancks, J.C., 260, 261
Barracks, Bivouacs and Bugles (Forbes), 72
'Bayonets', 250
Beach Beyond (J. Curlewis), 262
Beaumont Smith, F., 250
Becke, Louis, 124, 237, 149
Bennett, James, 138
Bennett, Mr, 95, 98
Betty and Co., 158, 159, 183, 215, 218, 284
Boer War (1899), 125, 193, 195
Boldrewood, Rolf, 37, 137
'Book of Water Tides, The' (J. Curlewis), 214
Bowden, Mr, 112, 279
'Boys in Brown', 250
Brahan, Mr, 251
Brennan, Christopher, 120
Brennan, Mr, 22
Brigid and the Cub, 254, 284
Bridge Builders (Kipling), 104
Brookes, Mr, 194
Bruce, Miss, 140, 179
Bubbles (Souter), 190
Bulletin, The, 26, 53, 70, 71, 89, 90, 91, 93, 94, 99, 108, 120, 136, 151, 176, 177, 181, 183, 282
Burnett, Frances Hodgson, 112, 134, 181
Burwell, George Watnell, 8, 10, 11, 285
By Reef and Palm (Becke), 124
By the Blue Australian Mountains (L. Turner), 111

Camp at Wandinong, The, 130, 134, 140, 150, 152, 162, 178, 181, 218, 284
Campbell Jones, Mr, 256, 258, 259, 260
Captain Cub, 252, 284
Carmichael, A.C., 252
Carr, Betty, *see* Curlewis, Betty
Carrington, Lady, 22, 32, 38
Carrington, Lord, 19, 22, 28, 31, 38
Carroll, Lewis, 214, 216, 124
Carruthers, *Sir* Joseph, 38, 143, 175
Challis, 194
Charlotte Brontë and Her Circle (Shorter), 162
Charlton, Leo, 257, 263, 264, 285
'Child of the Children, The', 134, 138, 152
Child that was Lost, The, see Mother's Little Girl
Christian, Annie, 13, 14, 19, 22, 39, 64, 78, 112
'Clancy of the Overflow' (Paterson), 105
Clemens, Samuel, *see* Twain, Mark
Closed Door, The (Mackellar), 207
'Coming to the City', 230
Common Problem, The, see The Wonder Child
'Concerning Cables', 201
Cope, Charles, 8-285 *passim*
Cope, Marie (née Steber), 220, 263
Cope, Rex, 11-285 *passim*
Cope, Sarah Jane (née Shaw), 8-285 *passim*
Cope, William, 16, 19, 22, 199
Cosmos, 115
Cowan, Lionel, 36
Cowan, Thea, 140
Creed, Louise, *see* Mack, Louise
Creed, Mr, 42-137 *passim*
Cub, The, 249
Cullen, Lady, 153, 161, 163, 164, 183, 184, 199, 241, 250, 261
Cullen, *Sir* William, **197,** 208, 241, 244, 261, 262
Curlewis, *Sir* Adrian, 7, 10, 145-265 *passim*
Curlewis, Alfred, 156
Curlewis, Betty, (née Carr), **245,** 264, 265
Curlewis, Billy, 113, 120
Curlewis, Claude, 114, 152, 196
Curlewis, Clive, 124
Curlewis, Dolly, 56-213 *passim*
Curlewis, Frederick Charles, **68,** 69, 94, 114, 142, 153, **156,** 183, 262, 263
Curlewis, George, 249
Curlewis, Herbert Raine, 13-285 *passim*
Curlewis, Ian, 285
Curlewis, Jean, 10, 107-285 *passim*
Curlewis, Philippa, *see* Poole, Philippa
Curlewis, Sophia (Marmee), 56-263 *passim*
Curlewis, Rex, 56, 57

Daily Telegraph, 23, 73, 96, 111, 114, 119, 135, 137, 150, 153, 178, 196, 215, 218, 229, 257
Daughter of Ireland, A, 31
David Copperfield (Dickens), 115
David, Professor, 134, 168
Davies, Mr, 103
Dickens, Charles, 75, 115, 121, 154, 191
Docker, Judge, 244
Downfall (Zola), 134
Dream Harbour (Mackellar), 261
Drowning Maze (J. Curlewis), 261
'Early Morning at Browns', 181
Eliot, George, 40, 239
Elsmere, Robert, 42
Evening News, 114
'Evening with the Bushies' (Mack), 191

'Fair Ines', 223
Fairfax, Addie, 59, 74
Fairfax, Mr, 49, 50, 59, 74
Fairfax jnr, John Hyclif, 74
Family at Misrule, The, see also Growing Up, 100, 102, 104, 110, 111, 112, 121, 132, 135, 136, 161, 279, 284
Family at Misrule, The, Sequel to, see *Little Mother Meg*
First Fleet Family, A (Jeffrey and Hecke), 149
'Five Sweet Symphonies not to Mention the Discord', 49
Flower O' the Pine, 243, 284
'Footsteps', 83
'Forsaken Garden' (Swinburne), 42, 44, 51
Friend, Beverley, 285
'Fugitives from Freedom', 223
Funny, 263, 284

Garvin, Mrs (née Walker), 57, 140, 149, 154, 179, 254
Gazette, 12
Gellert, Leon, 266, 282
Gift Impossible, see Mother's Little Girl
Ginger Meggs, 260, 261
Girls Together (Mack), 47
Great Expectations (Dickens), 154
Growing Up, see The Family at Misrule
Guillaux, 244
Gum Leaves, 93, 102, 125, 183, 190, 194, 196, 201

Haines, Cecil, 250
Happy Hearts, 220, 284
Hardy Norseman, A (Lyall), 69
Heney, Mr, 252, 257
Hermes, 22
House on the Beach (Meredith), 135
Howard the Halt (Morris), 63

Hughes, W.M., 252
Hugo, Victor, 44
Hunt, Atlee, 134

Illustrated, 63, 84, 89, 92, 95
In a White Palace (Mack), 236
'In the Coil of Things', 91, 94
In the Days When the World was Wide
   (Lawson), 126
In the Mist of the Mountains, 218, 284
Innocents Abroad, The, (Twain), 105
Institute of Journalists, 252
Iris, 9, 12, 13, 22, 261, 270 271

Jane Eyre (Brontë), 112
Jeffrey, Walter, 95, 97, 98, 104, 112, 124, 129,
   149, 151, 189
Jennifer J., 257, 284
Jerome, Mr, 113
Jersey, Lady, 49, 50, 57
Jersey, Lord, 52, 54
John of Daunt, see also *A Man's House,* 250,
   251, 284
'Johnnie and I Are Out', 191-2
Journalists, Institute of, 252
Judy and Punch, 265, 284

Kearney, Mrs, 189, 194
Keats, J., 49, 129
Keeping Up Appearances, 202, 203
Kelynack, Arthur James, 85
Kernahan, Coulson, 103, 223
Kettlewell, Mr, 72
Kipling, Rudyard, 69, 80, 129
King Anne, 257, 284
Kingsley, Charles, 214

'Laddie', 89
Lady of Shalott, The (Tennyson), 214
Lambert, George, 176, 190
Langan, Mr, 73
Laughing Water, 255, 256
Lawson, Henry, **126,** 181, 182, 189, 190, 196,
   199
Lawson, Mrs Henry, 181, 182, 199
Le Gay Brereton, J., 93
'Leila Watering', 181
Lethbridge, R. Copeland, 16, 17, 20
Light that Failed, The (Kipling), 80
Lights of Sydney, The (L. Turner), 86, 115,
   153
Lindsay, Lionel, 18
Lister, Lister, 36, 190, 241
'Little Duchess, The', 83, 89, 120
Little Larrikin, The, 113, 114, 123, 124, 129,
   130, 132, 135, 138, 161, 163, 284

Little Mother Meg, 181, 184, 193, 194, 202,
   203, 284
Little Women (Alcott), 110, 216
Long, Sydney, 213
Lock, Mr, 163
Lopez, Mr, 32, 34, 35, 39, 52, 58, 63
Lygon, Governor and Lady Mary, 189

Macarthy, Maud, 193, 194
McDonald, Donald, 193, 194
Macdonald, Louisa, 150
MacIntyre, Mr, 109
Mack, Louise, *see* also Creed, Louise, 12-159
   passim, 171, 176, 190, 204, 212, 213, 236,
   249, 271
Mack, Sidney, 16, 35, 42, 50-5 *passim,* 59, 64,
   74, 81, **85,** 90, 101, 109, 129, 142
McKay, Adam, 252
Mackellar, Dorothea, **207,** 244, 257, 270, 282
McKinney v. Gordon and Gotch case, 15, 16,
   21, 23, 28, 29, 30, 273-6
Maclardy, Mr, 23
McMillan, Mr, 183, 252
Maitland, *Sir* Herbert, 22
'Man from Snowy River, The' (Paterson),
   105, 137, 215
'The Man with the Iron Mask', 93
Man's House, A, see *John of Daunt*
'Marmee', *see* Curlewis, Sophia
'Marriage Morn', 155
Maynard, Ethel, **18,** 38, 151, 271
Maynard, May, 38, 151, 153
Meggs, Ginger, *see* also 'Us Fellers', 207, 260,
   261
Meillon, John, 85, 183
Meredith, George, **105,** 120, 124, 129, 132
Mill on the Floss, The (Eliot), 40
Millard, R.J., 36, 43, 52
Miss Bobbie, 23, 31, 33, 40, 91, 113, 115, 116,
   119, 121, 129, 140, 151, 158, 163, 250, 284
Misrule, The Family at, Sequel to, see *Little
   Mother Meg*
'Mist and a Vapour', 153
'Modern Achilles, A', 90
Modern Love (Meredith), 124
Mother's Little Girl, see also *The Child that
   was Lost* and *Gift Impossible,* 215, 216, 284
'Mutable Maiden', 69
'My Country', (Mackellar), 207
My Fair Lady, 138

'New Lenore, A', 158
Not All In Vain (Cambridge), 81
Nicola Silver, 261, 263, 284

O'Brien, Lucy, 50, 51, 52, 56, 79, 109, 113,
   129
Ogre Up to Date, 242
Old World Idylls (Dobson), 54
Omar Khayyam, 120, 124, 172
'On the Manly Rocks', 91
'On the Wharf' (Mack), 191
One of our Conquerors (Meredith), 124
'Orange Blossoms or Weeds' (L. Turner)
Ouida, 81, 92
Our Mutual Friend (Dickens), 121

Parker, *Sir,* Gilbert, 233
Parthenon, 13, 14, 16, 19, 22, 24, 26, 27, 29,
   30, 33, 34, 36, 38, 40, 41, 49, 50, 52, 70, 71,
   72, 74, 76, 78, 270, 273, 277
Parthenon libel action, *see* McKinney v.
   Gordon and Gotch case
'Passing of Arthur' (Tennyson), 235
Paterson, A.B. (The Banjo), 105, 137, 141,
   152, 161, 175, 193, 215
Pickburn, Judge, 53, 54, 55, 77, 83, 98, 100,
   112, 113
Pickwick Papers (Dickens), 75
'Playthings of Fate', 194
Pockley, Rose, *see* Turner, Rose
Poems of the English Roadside (Meredith), 124
Poole, Adrian, 285
Poole, Philippa (nee Curlewis), 7, **248,** 285
Ports and Happy Havens, 229, 230, 231, 232,
   239, 240, 284
Puck (Ouida), 92
'Pygmalion' (Shaw), 138

Queen's Gardens (Ruskin), 43

'Rainbow, The', 216, 217
Reid, *Sir* George W., 23, 275, 276, 234, 235
Retallack, Dr, 253
'Revenge' (Tennyson), 214, 235
Review of Reviews, 49, 66, 72
Rio Grand (Paterson), 215
'Rogue Locomotive, A', 183
'Rondeau' (H. Curlewis), 277
Roosevelt, Mr and Mrs T., 234
Rosetti, D.G., 42, 49
Rubbo, A. Dattilo, 261
'Runaway Engine', *see* 'A Rogue Locomotive'
Ruskin, John, 43
Ruttedge, Dr, 16

St Tom and the Dragon, 252, 253, 284
'Saucepan Sketch, A', 130
'School at Jimbaree', 141
Schreiner, Olive, 151
Schubert Society, 21

Scott, Professor W., 16, 30
'Second Nature', 162
Secret of the Sea, 242
Seivers, Mr, 48
Seven Little Australians, 9, 48, 65, 88, 92, 96,
    97, 99, 100, 110, 112, 115, 116, 119, 124,
    131, 135, 163, 250, 267-8, 284
Shakespeare, William, 172
Shaw, Sarah Jane, *see* Cope, Sarah Jane
Shelley, P.B., 71
Ship that Never Set Sail, The (J. Curlewis) 257
Smith, Saumarez, 37
Smiths Weekly, 259
Society of Artists, 190
'Song of Sydney', 226
Souter, Mr, 183, 190, 258
Spence, Percy, 36, 120
Spooner, H., 83, 84, 89, 95, 104, 193
Squatter's Dream (Boldrewood), 37
Star, 114
Steber, Marie, *see* Cope, Marie
Steele, William, 100, 112, 114, 119, 120, 121,
    122, 124, 129, 131, 132, 135, 153, 163, 202,
    212, 216, 244, 254, 270, 279
Stevenson, R.L., 216
Stowe, Harriet Beecher, 112
'Suburban' (J. Curlewis), 282
Sunday Sun, 252, 255, 256, 257
Sunday Times, 153
'Sundowners, The', 219
Swinburne, Algernon, 37, 38, 42, 44
Sydney Morning Herald, 22, 29, 30, 31, 52,
    111, 114, 116, 135, 137, 153, 178, 249, 251,
    252, 253
Sydney Suburb, A, 161
Swiss Family Robinson (Wyss), 216

Tasmanian Mail, 63, 83, 95, 103, 163
Taylor, Mr, 103
Teens (Mack), 159
Tekel, 74, 90, 98
Tennyson, Alfred, 38, 51, 214
Tennyson, Lord and Lady, 196, 243
Thackeray, W.M., 161
That Girl, 167, 220, 284
Theodora's Husband (Mack), 236
'There is None Like Her, None' (H.
    Curlewis), 277
'Third Great Wave', 98
Thompson, Lilian, *see* Turner, Lilian
Three Little Maids, 11, 152, 158, 162, 163, 164,
    176, 178, 179, 200, 204, 262, 284
Through the Looking Glass (Carroll), 89, 216
'To the City of Raspberry Jam', 121
Tonkin, Mr, 258, 259
Town and Country Journal, 95, 96, 97, 104,
    111, 124, 151, 191
'Toychild', 95, 96
'Trembling Star, A', 177, 181
'Triumph of Time, The' (Swinburne), 38
Troedel, Maclardy, 51, 52
Tucker, Mr, 99, 100, 101, 113, 119, 133, 141,
    142
Turner, Henry, 8, 11, 280-1, 285
Turner, Jeannie Rose (Rose), 11-285 *passim*
Turner, Lilian, 10-285 *passim*
Turner, Tom, 262
Twain, Mark, 105, 135

'Two Doors', 242
'Two Little Bush Flowers', 93
Two Little Wooden Shoes (Ouida), 81

Uncle Tom's Cabin (Stowe), 112
Under Twelve, 123
Ungardeners, The, 261, 284
University Dramatic Society, 34, 70
Ure Smith, Sydney, 266, 282
'Us Fellers', 207, 260, 261

Vanity Fair (Thackeray), 161
Vernon, Barbara, 10
Verse Writing for Beginners (J. Curlewis), 282

Wages of Sin, The (Malet), 93
'Walking to School', 219-20
Water Babies (Kingsley), 214
Weiss, Ada, 32, 33, 35, 36, 52, 53, 60, 71
What Katy Did (Coolidge), 216
While the Billy Boils (Lawson), 18
White Roof Tree, The, 155, 218, 284
'Wig, The', 96, 97, 98, 114
'Wilkes of Waterloo', 95, 96
Windeyer, Judge, 132
Windsor, The, 124, 134, 152
Witch Maid, The (Mackellar), 207
'With Infinite Diligence, With Infinite Love',
    50
Women Writers, 279
Women's Literary Society, 35, 49, 53, 54, 58,
    59, 150
Womens' suffrage, 58, 236
Wonder Child, The, see also *The Common
    Problem*, 183, 194, 195, 196, 199, 284
World is Round, The (Mack), 150, 159
'World Lover, The' (J. Curlewis), 283
World War I, 249

Young Rebel, 43, 57, 62, 71, 72, 76